PELICAN BOOKS

IN SEARCH OF WORK

Charles Leadbeater went to the Vyne Comprehensive School, Basing-stoke, before studying politics, philosophy and economics at Balliol College, Oxford. He worked for the current affairs programme *Weekend World* and is now a staff writer on the *Financial Times*.

John Lloyd was born in 1946, educated at Waid Comprehensive School, East Fife, and Edinburgh University. He has worked for a number of organizations, including London Weekend Television and the *Financial Times*. He won the Journalist of the Year Award in 1985 for his coverage of the miners' strike and in 1986 published *The Miners' Strike: Loss without Limit* (with Martin Adeney). In August 1986 he became Editor of the *New Statesman*.

Charles Leadbeater and John Lloyd

IN SEARCH
OF WORK

Based on a special report, 'Work – the Way Ahead', published by the
Financial Times in 1986

Penguin Books

Penguin Books Ltd, Harmondsworth, Middlesex, England
Viking Penguin Inc., 40 West 23rd Street, New York, New York 10010, USA
Penguin Books Australia Ltd, Ringwood, Victoria, Australia
Penguin Books Canada Ltd, 2801 John Street, Markham, Ontario, Canada L3R 1B4
Penguin Books (NZ) Ltd, 182–190 Wairau Road, Auckland 10, New Zealand

First published 1987

Filmset in Linotron Goudy by Rowland Phototypesetting Ltd
Bury St Edmunds, Suffolk
Made and printed in Great Britain by
Cox & Wyman Ltd, Reading, Berks

CONTENTS

PREFACE

There is a curious paradox about work in the modern world: in more ways than one, people's lives depend on it, yet we have done almost everything in our power to reduce its burden. In a sense, we – the interest groups, parties and Governments of modern societies – have acted as if we want least what we need most. Many otherwise puzzling phenomena have to do with this paradox, and as we look for solutions, we have to remember its origins.

People's lives continue to depend on work. This is not a vague, philosophical statement but a hard fact. Paid employment, crystallized as it usually is in jobs, is at the core of social organization and individual identity. It provides people with the means of existence both by direct income and by being the basis of transfer income. It is the reference point of most entitlements that define people's chances of participation. It describes the pattern that structures people's days, years, lives. Most other activities, including education and leisure-time pursuits and retirement, appear related to the requirement of work. Once this pattern begins to crumble, people wonder what to do with their lives. In this sense, it remains true to say that modern societies are work societies.

But work is dwindling and will continue to do so. Two processes conspire to bring about this effect. There is the deliberate attempt not only to make work easier in physical terms but also to reduce the hours that people spend at their jobs. Few now work much more than half the days of the year and half the waking hours on these days. There is also the cumulative effect of technical change. Technology may create new jobs, but it also replaces human labour. Perhaps both the deliberate reduction and the replacement of work by technical processes have a common factor, that is, the cost of work. But, whatever the reasons, the picture of life has changed. Education, leisure and retirement have gained in importance while work has lost.

It is useful to remember this background as one discusses the three most obvious effects of the paradox of work: significant long-term unemployment, changes in the nature of work and possible changes in the dominant features of people's lives.

Economists like to argue that if only labour markets were functioning properly, there would be no unemployment. In theory, they are obviously right, but then the theory is little more than a definition of labour markets. In reality, at least two major issues cannot be overlooked. One is the cost of removing all obstacles to the functioning of labour markets. These obstacles are, from another point of view, the achievements of a century of social reform. They include reasonable real wages, systems of income transfer and thus non-wage labour cost – in fact, the whole paraphernalia of the welfare state. Dismantling the welfare state would lower effective demand and recreate conditions of conflict that social policy has helped to mitigate. One must wonder whether anyone can regard the cost of such policies as bearable.

But there is another issue. It is that modern economies require less working time from individuals than they did a century or even a quarter-century ago. Current levels of welfare can be sustained, and significant growth brought about, while individuals spend less rather than more time in paid employment. In this sense, and in this sense only, the work society is running out of work. Less dramatically put, the seemingly abundant service of human work – of paid and payable employment, to be sure – is getting scarce.

This takes us straight to the most serious aspect of contemporary unemployment. Scarcity often raises issues of distribution; scarcity of work is no exception. Those who have work cling to it; those who do not have it often try in vain to get it. In the present world the haves are, of course, the overwhelming majority. But this merely serves to emphasize their power. Virtually all known organizations and institutions conspire to draw a boundary between those at work and those out of it. It is particularly difficult for those to get in who have never been in (that is, for the young). But the predicament of immigrants, or of those who for reasons outside their control have dropped through the net once, is not much better. The majority class protects its interest and thus contributes to the emergence of a new underclass.

This is not true in all countries, nor is it the whole truth anywhere. The most important qualification is that the boundary between the new classes is not hard and fast. Increasingly, a grey area is developing, which includes those on limited-term contracts or part-time work, in some countries those who for reasons of seniority are the first to go if there have to be lay-offs. The Japanese notion of a core workforce and a periphery of less stable employment appears to have become general. This is not said with purely critical intent. Not only is such unorthodox employment for many the only way into the world of work, but it also offers at times a highly desirable combination of adaptability for enterprises and flexibility for individuals. Moreover, it may be the beginning of a new distribution of work, though one that appears more precarious than the one to which we have grown accustomed.

For some redistribution of work is necessary. The unemployed are an indictment of all societies and call for the revival of the spirit of citizenship that has informed so much of the history of the past two centuries. This means that increases in productivity cannot in future simply be translated into wage increases for those who have work. Some of these increases will have to be translated into time, thus making it possible for those who were, and are, defined as out to rejoin the fold. In this sense at least, the debate about working time is relevant, though it is used by both sides of industry for ulterior as well as prima facie objectives.

It is appropriate at this point to remember the background notion from which we started and the other problems of the nature of work and the dominant features of people's lives. The desire to reduce the burden of work was not some far-fetched idea. It had to do with an ancient notion that has been expressed in different ways. Men have to do things to live, and they want to do things to express their talents and interests. There is the 'realm of necessity', work, and the 'realm of freedom'. One need not even think of Marx's distinction between the two, where one is concerned with necessities in the narrow sense, whereas the other is a luxury, rather like the mistaken notion of leisure that is still about. Work and activity can be two principles of everything we do. If that is how we see them, the paradox of modern societies may be turned to advantage.

In the world of work this would mean a greater concentration on what is sometimes called the quality of work. Attempts to increase the sphere of personal decisions in work processes, the autonomy of groups, the extent of individual inputs, have been made in many industries, and they have succeeded. Everywhere there are possibilities of increasing people's control over time. 'Flexitime' – flexidays, flexiweeks, flexiyears – is just one example. It is possible to transform work into activity or at any rate to inject a sense of activity into many work processes. Such changes can be combined with the translation of productivity increases into time. The result might well be a classical positive-sum game: greater efficiency, greater satisfaction, more employment.

The principle of activity applies, of course, to people's entire lives. The mistaken notion of leisure to which we have alluded is still widespread. Its essence is that working time is filled with all kinds of needs and rules, duties as well as satisfactions, whereas leisure time is essentially empty, there to be filled by anything, by junk food for the soul, as it were. What an extraordinary waste of lives! Against such fallacies one cannot emphasize too strongly that human life is, or should be, activity throughout. It is about doing things rather than sitting passively to be entertained or perhaps just used. In this process of activity education is not a functional but an autonomous endeavour. Even traditional skills have a firm place in this connection. With the emergence of jobs the unity of life and work that has characterized the ages has been lost, though enormous opportunities of growth have been gained. Perhaps there are ways of putting the two, life and work, together again as a continuous stream of activity.

One further thought is in place. Using the opportunities of the work society that is running out of work, rather than moaning about it, will certainly not solve all problems. Above all, it will continue to be true that there is much to do that is not done because we cannot afford it, and it does not lend itself to voluntary activity. It would seem that this is the place to revive the old notion of service, however objectionable it may seem to some. A general community service, building on the many voluntary beginnings that already exist, could be a part of a more sensible world.

To many, all this will sound idealistic, or at any rate philosophical. They should consider the alternative. The paradox is real: we have reduced what our societies are built on, work. We cannot undo such change and return to an earlier age, nor should we. Thus we must deal with it in a forward-looking manner. This involves a few hard decisions. The majority class will resist any attempt to redistribute employment, as it is doing already. As long as it succeeds, unemployment will remain high and will threaten the fabric of our societies. Moreover, if we do not recognize the opportunities of autonomous activity that we are offered by changes in the world of work, a heteronomous existence will become even more prevalent. People will be the punch-balls of influences that no one controls, unless someone manages to control them for his personal power. Social stability as well as liberty depend on our grasping the nettle. The future of work is the test.

Ralf Dahrendorf

FOREWORD

Has the goal of full employment become unrealistic? Over the last few years the persistence of very high unemployment in the UK and some other industrial countries, principally in Western Europe, has prompted some pessimistic analyses, which suggest that changes in the nature of work, and hence in the demand for labour, will make it impossible to return to the full employment levels that were taken for granted in the early post-war period. Yet there are some countries, such as Japan and Sweden, that, with very different policies, have kept their unemployment relatively low. The USA, where for most of the post-war period unemployment was generally higher than in Europe, has had a remarkable record of job creation in the last few years. Given these varying experiences, it is hard to accept that high unemployment should be taken as an unalterable fact to which Governments, companies, trade unions and individuals simply have to adjust.

What certainly does require adjustment among all these groups is changes in the nature of work, in the way work is organized and in the skills that are required. At the same time institutions, traditions and habits that influence the labour market in general and the wage-setting process in particular have to be reappraised and rethought to meet the changed circumstances.

As an international newspaper, the *Financial Times* reports and comments on these developments as they affect the UK and other countries. Our traditional coverage of 'labour news' has in recent years been expanded to encompass a much broader range of topics affecting the labour market. Because of the importance and complexity of these issues, we decided to commission a major study of the future of work, carried out principally by Charles Leadbeater and John Lloyd but also involving the co-operation of other *FT* writers and outside specialists. This appeared as a special supplement in the *FT* and is now published, in revised form, as a book.

Our hope is that the study will serve two purposes. First, we aim to shed light, through detailed investigation, on the changes that are taking place in the labour market and on the responses to those changes on the part of Governments, companies and trade unions. Especially important in this context is the behaviour of management. Companies have to balance their concern for profitability and competitiveness with their obligations to employees and to the communities in which their plants are located. Interviews with leading companies in Europe, Japan and the USA illustrate how these dilemmas are being tackled.

The second purpose is to contribute to greater clarity of thought about possible cures for high unemployment. While there is wide disagreement among economists and others about the causes of unemployment and the remedies for it – the conflictive theories are described in this book – it should be possible to reach some conclusions, through a study of the facts, on such questions as the impact of technology on jobs and the link between wages and employment. We hope that this book will help to dispel some of the myths and misunderstandings that stand in the way of solving the greatest social evil of our times.

Geoffrey Owen

ACKNOWLEDGEMENTS

Many people helped us to write the special *Financial Times* report, 'Work – the Way Ahead', on which this book is based. We would like to thank Philip Bassett, Samuel Brittan, Peter Bruce (Bonn), David Case, Richard Draper, Ralf Dahrendorf, Alan Friedman (Milan), Lekha Kathrecha, John Kitching, Richard Layard, Marcia Levy, David Marsh (Paris), Jurek Martin (Tokyo), Carey Oppenheim, George Perry, Carla Rapoport (Tokyo), Alice Rawsthorn, Bill Sanderson, David Thomas and Martin Weitzman.

Special thanks go to Ian Hargreaves and Geoffrey Owen at the *Financial Times* for their encouragement, guidance and patience.

We would also like to thank the scores of people in companies, Government departments, trade unions and research organizations who gave us their time and help.

C.L.
J.L.
October 1986

INTRODUCTION

Two intersecting questions dominate concern over the future of work. Will persistent mass unemployment in many of the major economies ever be defeated? This is a question about the capacity of the advanced economies to generate work for all who want it. The second question concerns the nature of work itself. How will the advance of new technology, the growth of the service sector and the development of 'atypical' forms of employment (part-time working, self-employment, etc.) change the character of work?

Not so long ago it was taken for granted that there would be work for all who wanted it. The character of that work was also taken for granted. It would be full-time employment. Now both these certainties are in doubt. Flowing from the two questions above come others with sharper focus.

Will automated machinery do our work for us in future? Will this liberate us or condemn us to leisure? Is big business creating a new kind of feudalism – protective of those inside the walls but tough on those outside? Are we, in the name of flexibility, creating a class of never-never or only occasional workers? Are we bidding goodbye to the traditional working class by creating a new underclass and a new labour aristocracy? Will trade unions survive and, if they do, in what shape? What does the future hold for those who compete for jobs from a weakened position – youth, women, ethnic minorities, those who are discarded in their early fifties, the old?

And what of those inside the walls? Can they be trained and educated to keep pace with change? Will company workers gradually become company owners, and will this make them work harder? Do the black and informal economies of cash in hand or favours in kind offer us new models of work? Should we still aim at full employment as we know it and, if so, by what means should we attempt to reach our goal? What can Governments do to alleviate unemployment? Are small businesses the only route to new jobs? How important is manufacturing industry to regeneration? Or does our economic future lie in services, from finance to fast foods?

These overlapping questions circle around debates about work. Below them nags the doubt that work as we know it has no future. Work, as an economic resource, a source of livelihood and a sense of self-worth, is undergoing tremendous change. When it was plentiful – and in the advanced economies that was for most of the post-war era until the late 1970s – it was little regarded as a good in itself, to be cherished and pursued. Now it has scarcity value and is the battleground for politics.

Although work or, more precisely, full employment may not have been much debated in the twenty-five years following the war, nevertheless it was central to the 'public philosophy' of the times. The maintenance of full employment was a central, obtainable goal of economic policy. Employment was at the centre of the web that made up the social, economic and political order of the post-war period.

The post-war consensus has been undermined for all kinds of reasons, but the disappearance of full employment and uncertainty over the future of work have eaten away at its foundations. Social and economic change – new workers and new work – is changing the terrain of politics. The central institutions of the advanced economies – the state, the law, companies and trade unions – are responding, but slowly and uncertainly.

Should we cling to the old goal of full employment, the old means of achieving it – Government demand management and the coterie of policies known as Keynesianism – and wait for the storm to pass? Can we at least cling to the goal but accept that the means have to change? Do we have to accept that there will be more room for private initiative and less for public, new forms of income policy and more of a role for the market in setting wages?

Or do we have to redefine the goal, develop new policies and new institutions, guided by new values, to cope with the change in the availability and character of work? Do we have to accept that an economy that is fully working – on community projects, on training schemes and in the informal economy – may not be an economy that is fully employed in full-time jobs with companies? That we have to find new ways – for instance, through the social security system – to ensure that work brings a livelihood rather than accepting the wage packet as the sole source of income from work? That the old ethic that claimed that to be 'good' was to work hard needs to be replaced with one that claims that to be 'good' is to relinquish claims to a full-time job throughout a working life?

In short, the public philosophy of the post-war era was based on society's need for traditional work and the ability of the institutions of the economic and social systems to deliver the goods. Does the current crisis over the future of work demand a new public philosophy that will allow individuals to have security, a reasonable income, a sense of self-worth and purpose without giving them work in the traditional sense?

What is clear is that without energetic debate about these issues a new, divisive public philosophy could establish itself piecemeal. We may find ourselves living in a society where mass long-term unemployment, an increasing underclass of peripheral workers and a growing informal grey/black economy become accepted accompaniments of security, status and prosperity for some.

This book looks at the main pressures for change: the rise in unemployment and its refusal to fall; the growing participation of women in the labour market; the influence of new micro-electronic technology on the amount and type of work that is available; and the emergence of atypical forms of employment such as self-employment, part-time work and fixed-contract working. It also examines the ways in which these pressures are remoulding some of the key institutions of work: companies, the state, the trade unions, employment law. How are their roles being refashioned to accommodate and direct change? And the book examines the broader impact of the changes that we are witnessing. Is new technology creating a new class of labour aristocrats while the growth of the 'secondary' labour market creates a new underclass? How will our political systems cope and manage these transformations, and in whose interests?

To help answer these questions, the FT commissioned the polling organization Gallup to conduct a survey of a cross-section of employers in the five major economies – the USA, Japan, West Germany, France and Britain. The survey reveals the common pressures that will affect business decisions about employment; it also reveals the differences between economies, small and large firms, unionized and non-unionized enterprises. Such an international poll is rarely conducted. But it offers a guide to the shape of the future of work rather than precise, accurate prediction. The poll methodology is explained in Appendix 1.

In the course of the book we have drawn on a number of approaches to the future of work. We think none gives a complete answer but all have some contribution to make to an explanation of what has happened and to map out how work may develop.

One approach is that of 'traditional' economists, from Keynesians to the neo-classicals. Although they differ quite markedly in their prescriptions, they share the view that there could be full employment if only economic variables could be arranged in some way to bring into line the demand for, and supply of, labour.

Keynesians, of course, stress the importance of effective demand in explaining why unemployment has risen and how it might be reduced. More classically orientated economists stress price adjustments and, in particular, the adjustment of the real wage. Nevertheless, they share the view that unemployment is primarily an economic problem and demands an economic response.

Recently there have been signs of an emerging consensus among economists over policy prescriptions. The line between those who believe that supply drives the economy and those who believe that demand does is still there, but it is becoming blurred. Keynesians have been forced to accept some of the successes of monetarism in bringing down inflation. Many now acknowledge that money wages (rather than real wages) do play some role in determining employment. Monetarists, on the other hand, have come to accept that even the most robust economies can be pushed into unemployment by too sharp a contraction of demand.

The macro-economists undoubtedly have some role to play in explaining why unemployment has risen and how it might be reduced. Nevertheless, their policy prescriptions are of limited value. Few people now believe that full employment can easily be restored by a simple expansion of demand. On the other hand, in the UK and West Germany stringent policies aimed at structural rigidities in the economy have been in place for several years with no marked improvement in the prospects for the unemployed.

Moreover, macro-economists have very little to say about some of the important changes in the character of work. They prefer to treat new technology as if it were part of a mystical black box. Mainstream economics too has little to say about the causes of change in working patterns. Traditional economics, then, does not have much to contribute to a debate about the changing day-to-day reality of work.

A second general set of approaches could be called the 'structuralist' one; it confers a crucial role on technology's effect on the character of production, and thereby work. In the 1970s one influential strain of this view was promulgated by the American sociologist Daniel Bell. He argued that the advanced economies were becoming post-industrial societies as a result, in the main, of technological change. Bell argued that technological advance in the primary sector of the economy (agriculture and commodities) had displaced labour, which was being taken up by the secondary sector, manufacturing. But in turn this sector has undergone rapid advances in technology, which have raised productivity. Labour is now being displaced from manufacturing and will be taken up in the tertiary, or service, sector of the economy.

Bell argued that as societies become richer, they spend proportionately less on basic goods and more on services, less on potatoes and more on meals in restaurants. Moreover, he argued that as services are labour-intensive, a dollar spent on services will generate more employment than a dollar spent on manufactured goods; as the advanced economies mature, this mix of forces will lead to more and more employment being concentrated in the service sector. This view ties changes in the types of work people do (making goods or providing services) to an explanation of how technological advance alters the structure of the economy.

Some have taken a more pessimistic view of the effects of technological change. They fear that machines will slowly replace workers, to the point where there is nothing left for human hands and brains to do. They suggest that the increasing use of technology, in both factories and offices, will limit the amount of work available and that, as a result, we should pursue new strategies to allocate the amount of work that is available through new arrangements for working time and the encouragement of leisure pursuits, hobbies, and the like.

Some, like Vassily Leontieff in the USA, also urge a new income distribution. Leontieff argues that as machines become more important than labour in the production process, so the returns to capital will outstrip the returns to labour. Simply put, there will be fewer wage-earners around but an awful lot of machines that are making money for their owners. He argues that if we are to avoid increasing income inequalities, we have to ensure that workers displaced by machines have a right to some of the profits that the machines generate.

These views are certainly attractive, but recently they have come in for criticism from those who accord an equally important role to technology. These critics point out that although technological advance means that the same output can be produced with fewer people and less effort, this does not necessarily mean that employment will fall. The productivity gains from new technology should lower the cost of production, which may allow producers to lower the price of their products. As a consequence, demand and employment may rise. Moreover, even if workers are laid off as a result of the introduction of new technology, this does not mean that they will not find work elsewhere. The workers left in manufacturing should be earning higher real wages as a result of the productivity gains brought by new technology. They will want to spend their income on things like services and other products.

In general, all these criticisms are based on the premise that there is no 'lump' of labour. There is no fixed amount of work into which machines are eating. The productivity gains from new technology have to be distributed throughout the economy: some jobs will go; others will be created. The adjustment will take time, but it should occur.

Economists at the Science Policy Research Unit at Sussex University in the UK have developed new theories that accord technological change a more dynamic role in generating economic change and employment. The first line of argument is that Bell's theory of how employment will shift away from manufacturing to services is flawed. In *The New Service Economy* Jonathan Gershuny and Ian Miles suggest that demand for services has not increased, and will not, so dramatically as Bell suggests. If services are labour-intensive, and if wages in the service sector are in line with wages elsewhere in the economy, then the price of services relative to that of manufactured goods will rise. This ostensibly academic point has considerable significance. Compare the price of a meal in a restaurant with the price of a meal you provide for yourself with the help of a microwave. There are limited opportunities for productivity gains in restaurants. Waiters walk as fast now as they did in 1870. As a result, there is little downward pressure on the price of labour-intensive services. However, as the Japanese have shown, tremendous productivity gains can be made in manufacturing. As a result, we have compact discs, which provide high-quality, programmable music at much less than the real cost of a hi-fi bought twenty years ago.

The Gershuny and Miles message is that there is no ineluctable trend from manufacturing to services. Rather, they argue, people have to satisfy certain basic needs like eating, and they will choose between a range of ways of meeting their needs. One way is to eat out – thereby creating demand for services. But with the price of appliances like microwaves coming down, it may become more and more attractive to cook at home. In other words, people will choose to 'self-provision' by using their own labour mixed with domestic capital like fridges and microwaves. This will create employment in manufacturing to make the goods. Taken together, labour in the home, mixed with man-made machines (labour in factories), will displace labour in the service sector. Bell's theory of structural change is turned on its head by a theory that grants technological change an equally important role.

Some go beyond this and argue that faster technological change could generate much higher employment. They claim that unemployment has risen because the great employing industries have run out of steam. The post-war boom in employment was based on Keynesian policies, but it was based also on mass demand for industrial products such as cars, television sets and domestic white goods such as fridges. Demand for these products is now limited largely to replacement demand. As production processes have become more efficient, so labour has been displaced. These 'structuralists', who are associated with the Schumpeterian schools of economics, suggest that what we need is a wave of investment in new technologies that will stimulate new products and new industries comparable with the white-goods industries established after the Second World War. In particular they argue that 'information technology' is vital to economic regeneration. New information-technology services, providing information in the home via telecommunications networks, will generate new jobs in gathering the information, following it up, installing the equipment and so on. These Schumpeterians look forward to a future when the roads will carry lorries bearing goods manufactured in factories but telecommunications networks will also carry new services that exist in embryonic form in services like Prestel in the UK. Moreover, technology may also be important in transforming employment prospects in the traditional industries. Jobs in textiles lost to the Third World because of lower labour costs, for example, may be won back through the introduction of new technology.

Another, entirely different, structuralist view is one that stresses the importance of enterprise and small businesses. The economies of the advanced world may be shifting from manufacturing to services, but there is also some evidence of another shift in structure – from larger to smaller firms. In the last few years large firms have been through a period of restructuring, shedding jobs and subcontracting parts of their business to other companies. There is some evidence that at the same time smaller companies have become motors of growth in the economy. The argument is that it is through the efforts of entrepreneurs in setting up firms that new jobs will be created. It is entrepreneurs who change the pattern of production in the economy and thereby both generate new jobs and change the character of work. Once again this view seeks to explain changes in work by looking at the base of the economy, at the ways in which production is changing.

What these structuralist approaches have in common is the view that changes in the character of production, particularly through the introduction of new technology, explain why work is in crisis and how we might get out of that crisis.

A third approach sees the problem of work as largely a political one, which demands political solutions. Many would agree that it is political in a narrow sense. In the UK trade unionists and Opposition politicians, for instance, blame the Thatcher Government for the rise in unemployment. Conservatives suggest that the cumulative rise in unemployment since the early 1970s has been a result of the misguided policies of previous Labour administrations and that it was the trade unions, in exercising their political clout in 1978–9, that rang down the curtain on the post-war consensus. This is the politics of work in its most familiar setting. However, there are those who argue that the crisis of work will be solved only by a new politics. In the preface to this book Professor Ralf Dahrendorf, for example, argues that we are in danger of creating an underclass that is disenfranchised, in a broad sense, because of its poverty and economic insecurity. Others claim that companies must adopt a new altruism of 'business in the community'. Still others suggest that we need a new work ethic that will relieve us of the need for work, of the guilt that goes with inactivity.

Some, such as the historian Martin Weiner, argue that the crisis of the British economy is traceable to the industrial culture that developed from an odd marriage between the new nineteenth-century industrialists and the old aristocracy. British politicians urge us to be more like our successful competitors. Clichés like the 'hard-working Germans', the 'collective will to succeed of the Japanese', the 'dynamism of the Americans' abound – yet there is an unpleasant ring of truth to them. Is there something about British culture that inhibits economic dynamism?

Others, such as the Swedish political theorist Goran Therborn, claim that the capacity to maintain full employment is vested in societies with a certain political structure – in particular, those countries that have labour movements strong enough to ensure that Governments make, and stick to, commitments to promote and support full employment.

In their different ways all of these views stress the availability of work and the fact that the ways in which we deal with shortages or inequalities are crucially determined by politics and culture. In this book we have drawn on all three approaches to guide us, possibly without doing justice to any of them. Nevertheless, we hope to have given as comprehensive an account as we can of the pressures for change and the capacity of the advanced economies to cope with these pressures.

1. A SENSE OF EXTINCTION

'In the 1930s, those who wanted work had a sense that they only had to wait before their work would be required again. When they talk of those years, they evoke the idle machinery, the eerie silence over shipyard and pithead. Unemployment assailed their sense of worth, assailed their dignity, denied them and those they loved adequate food and comfort. But it didn't rob them of the skills themselves. Now, on the other hand, there is a terminal sense of the extinction of work itself' (Jeremy Seabrook, *Political Quarterly*, January 1981). There is that sense indeed. It comes from the desolate areas of Europe and the USA, the old mining valleys of South Wales, the steel towns of Lorraine and Pennsylvania, the immigrant quarters of the Ruhr, the slums of Naples and Palermo.

There is no question that it is real. Seabrook, a British sociologist who has specialized in bringing the issue to our attention through vividly descriptive writing, quotes an unemployed man in his forties as saying: 'If you've got no work, everything seems to mock you – the television, the adverts, everything. The papers are full of the lives of millionaires; the shops are full of things you can't afford. It makes you feel humiliated . . . It destroys your self-respect.' Who doubts the authenticity of that?

In a survey taken in Lorraine and the north of France in September and October 1985 Elisabeth Bascaud and Bernard Simonin found that of the unemployed families surveyed, 12 per cent had no income in the month preceding the survey and 45 per cent had less than FFr1,500 (£140). In Duisburg, on the Ruhr, Hans Gert Woelke, on the board of the Thyssen steel and engineering empire, is told by a group of local clergy that some of the long-term unemployed in his town get up early and come home late to give their children the impression that they are at work. Unemployment, for most, is not leisure but poverty and misery.

Unemployment will probably not get much worse in the advanced countries in the next few years and, in some, will perhaps improve for demographic reasons at least. The Organization for Economic Co-operation and Development (OECD) does not think that unemployment will change in the main advanced countries over the next couple of years – edging up in the USA, Japan and France, edging down in the UK and West Germany, static in Italy (see table 1).

In June 1986 the Occupation Study Group (OSG), brought into being by a forward-looking industrialist, Sir Austin Bide, president of Glaxo, produced the

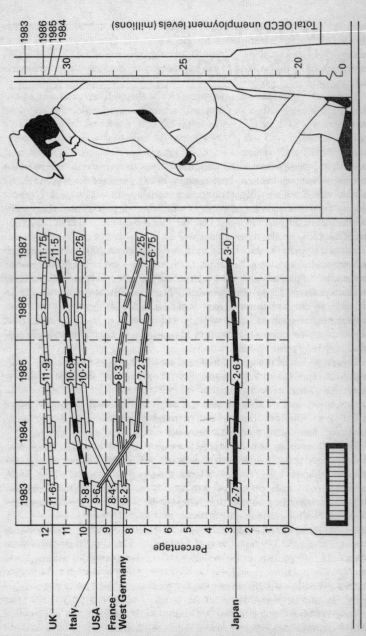

Table 1 Unemployment in the OECD area (% of labour force and totals), 1983–7

best guide to employment trends seen for some time because it asked *companies* to disclose their employment plans for five years ahead rather than relying on macro-level extrapolations. Although it was confined to the UK, and is thus rooted in one of the weakest of the advanced economies, it carries fairly clear indications for all the others.

The study found that the aggregate effect of the company- and sector-level changes it had described was a statistical insignificance, that the employed workforce was likely to decline by some 125,000, from 23.7 million to 23.58 million, between 1985 and 1990 – but that these figures could be out by plus or minus 300,000 and so employment could actually *rise* by 175,000 in that period. In short, it broadly agrees with the OECD: there will be no large changes in the volume of unemployment in the immediate future. The danger is not then (as far as we can tell) that we will get many more unemployed – but that many of those who have been rendered unemployed by the huge upheavals of the past decade will remain in the burgeoning ranks of the long-term unemployed or slip in and out of casual, low-paid, demoralizing jobs for all of their lives.

But the report also shows very large shifts *within* the employed workforce. Self-employment in the UK is likely to increase by some 300,000 and private-sector services (including self-employment) to increase by around 540,000. But production industries will lose some 600,000 workers – many of them reappearing again in the service sector as previously in-house jobs are sub-contracted. Largely because of that shift, part-timers will rise from 21 to 25 per cent of the labour force, and small companies will increase their workforce share by 700,000 jobs.

The growth will come in distribution, finance and business services, leisure and tourism, hotels and restaurants: everything from the Big Mac to the Big Bang. The kinds of people needed will be engineers (especially electronic), scientists, technologists, accountants, data processors, marketing staff, multi-skilled craftsmen and waiters. Not needed will be labourers, single-skilled craftsmen, many kinds of manager and clerical staff.

No need to labour the point: it is happening everywhere, and it is just a matter of how quickly and how smoothly. It is not that manufacturing will become unimportant, just that it will become progressively unmanned. Dr Geoff Robinson, IBM UK's technical director and futurologist, likes to speculate about factories being built just to accommodate machines to which no one will have to go (while conceding the periodic visit from the maintenance worker). He says, 'Until the end of the eighteenth century the economy was agricultural and most employment was on the land: now it's 2 per cent, and it produces much more food. In the nineteenth and in much of the twentieth century it was manufacturing. Now it is, and will be, services and manufacturing will continue to get more and more productive – but the economy will be service-driven.'

Japan, the top manufacturing nation, agrees. The Prime Minister's office has done some crystal-ball gazing and forecasts the same trend, though still builds in improvements in employment in some manufacturing sectors, such as 'electric machines' and 'precision machines' – indications of a confidence that it will still rule these worlds at least. The US Bureau of Labor Statistics, in its look-ahead, saw (by 1990) 360,000 more waiters, 400,000 more fast-food workers, 438,000 nurses, 479,000 sales clerks, 501,000 more janitors and 700,000 more secretaries (despite the fact that their bosses will learn keyboard skills or perhaps because of it). It also saw 247,000 fewer farm operators, 237,000 fewer farm labourers, 176,000 fewer secondary teachers, 52,000 fewer university teachers, 12,000 fewer compositors and typesetters and 8,000 fewer clergy.

Two worrying trends are likely to continue in at least some countries. First, long-term unemployment (twelve months or more), down in the USA and Japan (where it never reached high levels), is still going up in West Germany, Italy and the UK. It has stopped rising in France but still represents some 40 per cent of the total. Says the OECD: 'Lack of work motivation and decay of human capital damage re-employment prospects and lead to a growing segmentation between employed persons with stable jobs and job-seekers who may be becoming progressively less employable.'

The second cause of concern is the jobless young. The numbers are very high in Italy (34 per cent), France (25 per cent) and the UK (22 per cent, though currently declining). Overall, throughout the OECD area, the rate is a high 16.5 per cent. That is unlikely to change much – but it may get worse in France and Italy, better in West Germany and the UK.

All of this is well known. Indeed, massive unemployment figures – the testimony of the unemployed themselves, the forecasts of a continuing crisis – are now so ingrained in the flow of daily events that they have lost their capacity to surprise, certainly to shock. Especially in those states where it has been with us longest – the UK and Italy, Ireland and Belgium – unemployment has been so absorbed by the culture as to have become all but invisible.

This invisibility may have something to do with the present and much remarked upon apathy of the unemployed – and the lack of revolutionary potential they have displayed. Where 1930s unemployment fuelled mass movements of the revolutionary left and the Fascist right, the contemporary response appears more alienated, more individualized – sad but not scary. Seabrook says: 'It certainly isn't the Thirties all over again . . . What the disciplines of destitution and hunger could not achieve may be brought about far more effectively through a destroyed sense of purpose and function masquerading as increased leisure. The only imaginable working-class response to that would be the kind of violence we have seen in the United States and, to a lesser extent, among the young here – "mindless" violence, racial conflict and looting – an anger detached from any conscious political objective . . . It is a measure of the growing political impotence of the working class.'

But will it last? Although it is already clear that unemployment is no mere product of a cyclical downswing, it is *not* clear whether it is with us over a long haul. Governments in all the main states continue to predict its demise when their policies have 'had time to work through'. They continue to lack proof that they will.

The future levels of unemployment depend on so many variables – Government policies on labour markets, public spending, trade, the rate of diffusion of new technologies, the growth in the numbers of women entering the labour market – that forecasting is hazardous. But one variable can be discussed with some degree of reality: demography. We already know, for some four decades ahead, how many people are *potentially* likely to be looking for work.

Oddly, while the science is relatively exact, Governments have been tardy in acting upon it. Mary Mauksch, of the Conference Board in Brussels, points out that work done by the Board in 1980 to show that the rate of growth in the EEC's working population (15–64 year olds) would jump from an additional 2.4 million between 1975 and 1980 to an additional 6.5 million in 1980–85 produced, initially, little or no action by Governments and that 'business in general was not aware of these developments'.

This bulge will, of course, have to work its way through a working, or out-of-working, life, but a change is coming, and in some countries it will come soon and dramatically. In the EEC 1985–90 will see a sharp drop in new labour-market entrants, to 1.6 million – a reduction in the birth rate which is already contributing to unemployment in its own ways by reducing the demand for the army of teachers called into being since the war and greatly reducing the school-building programmes.

West Germany is the extreme case of population decline. Over the next four decades to 2025 Western Europe's most populous state will have shrunk from being the largest of the 'big four' to the smallest – a precipitous drop from 60.9 million people to 53.5 million. Its present economically active population of 29.4 million people is its post-war *peak*: the decline in workers will be even more rapid than the decline in overall population, from 29.4 million to 21.7 million in 2025.

This gives West German policy planners a confusing double-vision: the present, in which unemployment has rocketed sharply, and the short- to medium-term future, in which *under*-employment is likely to be the burning question. The labour-market division of the Federal Labour Ministry predicts: 'In the next few years the scene will be totally changed because of the demographic factors: we will be faced with a declining workforce. The present labour-market slackness is temporary, and in the 1990s we will have quite a new set of worries. By 1990 there will be perhaps 1 million unemployed, but by the *end* of the 1990s we will be trying to get older people to stay on and work longer.'

At Thyssen Herr Woelke deliberately maintains a higher stock of apprentices than the company will need immediately – to build up, as he says, 'our human stock for a future with labour shortage'. In West Germany, at least, the older worker – who, there as elsewhere, has been bribed and bullied out of work as early as possible to make room for potentially troublesome youth – will soon be bribed and bullied to drag himself in to work for longer than his parents did. In 1970 2.3

million West German workers were over 60. That figure more than halved, to under 1 million, by 1980. Now it is on the rise again and will grow to 1.2 million in 1990, to just under 1.4 million in 2000 and to just over 1.4 million in 2025.

The elderly will provide a growing consumer as well as a labour market. Mary Mauksch says that there will be more than 50 million people over 65 by 1990 in the EEC states, compared with 34 million in 1975. Within this group will be 8 million over 80 (5.8 million in 1975). She notes, 'This age group will require special services and medical care, and it's an area open for imaginative use of housing, food and medical resources.'

Many in the other West European states wish they could face West Germany's 'problem' sooner and more sharply than they will. France's population is set to rise, though more and more slowly, from 54.6 million in 1985 to 58.4 million in 2025 – but its active population is likely to peak in 2010 at 26.6 million. The UK will grow from 56.1 million to 56.3 million in 2000 – sliding back gently to 55.9 million in 2025; its active population will peak at 2000 also, at just under 28.1 million, then fall to 26.2 million in 2025. Italy, closest to West Germany in this respect, will have a population peak of 58.6 million in 2000 from a present 57.3 million, which will drop to 57.1 million in 2025. Its active population will top out at 23.34 million in 1990, flatten out to 23.31 million in 2000, then fall relatively rapidly to 21 million in 2025.

Demography, says Mary Mauksch, has a clear and direct effect on unemployment, and the projections mean that 'We can say with some optimism, based on demographic factors alone, that Europe will see an improvement in the unemployment situation in a year or two.'

The USA differs from the European 'pattern'. Its population is projected to grow from a 1985 level of just over 238 million to a 2025 forecast of 311.9 million, and its active population from 116.8 million to 143.1 million. (The Soviet Union maintains an almost exactly proportionate pace: its workforce will rise from 143.3 to 175.3 million – just over a 22 per cent rise in both cases, almost as though the superpowers had agreed a breeding rate.)

But, like Europe, the USA's older workers are expected to be on the increase, though after a dip from the present total of 8.1 million 60-plus workers to 7.4 million forecast for 2000; the totals then rise to 12.2 million in 2025. Like Western Europe too its youth (16–24) population falls off, at least to 2000: from 25.2 million now to 22.3 million then, rising to 25.2 million once more in 2025. The children and young adults of today and the next ten years are in shorter supply because their parents, themselves the products of the immediate post-war bulge or baby boom, are not producing the 2.15 children per family required to keep replacing the population. The boomers, a highly publicized minority of whom radicalized campuses (but little else) in the late 1960s, had it rougher than *their* parents: a *Time* survey (18 May 1986) noted that they were hit, as adults, with inflation and fierce job competition.

Japan's working profile is much more 'European' than those of its rapidly growing neighbours in East and South Asia. Its present population of over 120 million will peak at 133 million in 2010, then decline to 132 million in 2025, but its workforce will peak earlier, at 64.3 million in 2000 and decline much more sharply, to 60.9 million in 2025. Japan, like West Germany, has a specific problem: in its case, the rapid ageing of its presently relatively young population. From being the youngest of the advanced societies, it is expected to be the oldest by 2025 – the year in which the proportion of elderly people is expected to peak in all advanced countries. A rise in the average age of the population of 12 per cent took 175 years in France (1790–1965) and eighty years in West Germany (1890–1970) but will take only forty years in Japan (1950–1990). The ageing of Japan has provoked a worried national debate and has already stimulated a Government, which clearly *does* look at demographic projections, into pushing companies to keep older workers on after the former norm of 55: now, less than 40 per cent of companies (though this includes many of the biggest) insist on retirement at 55, and this is projected to fall further.

The consequences of this fast-motion demographic shift – the change in Japan's age profile from a pyramid with lots of young at the bottom to a cylinder with a bit of middle-aged, then elderly, bulge – are being signalled by many as terribly alarming. Naohiro Yashiro, the (40-year-old) head of the Economic Planning Agency's policy division, says that the high productivity rates, the internal training systems and the seniority wage progression are all threatened, not to mention the more obvious strains that will be imposed on the social security and health services. The disparity in export competitiveness between Japan and the West, he says, 'may ultimately prove to have derived not from special cultural and traditional factors in Japanese society but from the differing demographic structure in Japan, where the burden of caring for the aged is still light compared with that in the West'.

Japan's case is, for the rest of the advanced world, a dramatization of their own dilemmas. In all of them Governments are now grappling with the ageing of their societies and seeking to reach some kind of consensus on a balance between state-funded provision, continuing employment on the part of the elderly and voluntary and family provision for the old.

The issue is particularly live in the UK, where the White Paper on Social Security presented to Parliament in December 1985 lays out in stark bureaucratic prose the problem ahead. On the Government Actuary's calculations, the number of pensioners will increase from 9.3 million in 1985 to 12.3 million in 2025. On an assumed increase in contributors of only 370,000 over the next fifty years, the actuarial calculations present a ratio of contributor to pensioner declining from 2.3:1 now to 1.8:1 in 2025. This means, in turn, that total pension costs will rise from £16.9 billion in 1988 to £35.7 billion in 2025 (1984/5 prices) if they are up-rated in line with prices – or £49.8 billion if up-rated in line with earnings. As if that were not enough, health-service costs would need to rise by 30 per cent over that period, without assuming an improvement in service, simply to keep pace with anticipated needs.

The report, known as the Fowler Report after its author, the Social Services

Secretary Norman Fowler, is controversial in its recommendations for targeting benefits on areas of 'real need' and thus reducing their spread: the facts are not. Every Government will be required to face up to the 'grey hordes' whose needs could overcome welfare systems regarded as triumphs of enlightened provision since the war but the burden of which on the workforce could greatly damage industrial efficiency in economies less robust than the Japanese. A life of easeful (or tedious?) retirement will be less and less on offer to more and more of the West's citizens: a search for useful and self-supporting roles in later life will be – already are – the order of the policy-planners' days. 'Clearly,' says Gérard Calot, director of the Institut National d'Etudes Démographiques, 'the consequences of ageing go well beyond the problems of the financial balances of the pension organizations. In fact, distribution by age shapes the whole of society's dynamism. From an economic as well as a psychological and social point of view, an aged population is a shivering one and is more inclined to preserve than to innovate. However, France's future, as well as Europe's, will be based essentially on the ability of its people to organize a collective life, to promote research, to imagine and develop new techniques. In a world where new economic and political powers will emerge, supported by important resources of raw materials and a large and young population, Europe's privileged position will enter into question. While it is unrealistic to hope to catch up with these countries in the demographic field, it would be catastrophic to surrender, on a permanent basis, to a fertility rate that is noticeably lower than the rate required to replace future generations.'

The advanced countries are not insulated from the much sharper population pressures of developing states even if they seek to be so by maintaining strict immigration controls. Where the population of Europe may (on a low estimate) be no higher in 2025 than the 1975 level of 474 million, Africa, Latin America and South Asia are all expected at least to double their populations and, on a high estimate, to triple or even, in the case of Africa, to quadruple them over the same period. In China and India, where the growth rates are particularly high, strict birth control is being attempted by Governments with, in India's case so far, little success but much protest. Even if these and other programmes succeed, the United Nations (UN) calculates that world population will grow from just over 4 billion in 1975 to a low estimate of 5.8 billion in the year 2000 (a high estimate would be 6.3 billion) and to 7.2 billion in 2025 (high 9.1 billion). Maurice Kirk of Leeds University's social policy department says that Europe's demographic growth is falling well behind: 'The threat to the world's future from new demographic explosions lies in countries that are still insecure and perhaps understandably envious of the wealthier nations.'

It is women who have made much of the difference to advanced countries' labour markets over the past three decades and who will continue to do so for at least another two (longer in some countries). The old trinity of *Kinder – Küche – Kirche* (children – kitchen – church) has been submerged by falling birth rates (especially among the West Germans, who thought of the phrase), better domestic technology and convenience foods, a radical break with traditional attitudes of which religion had been a part – and, most of all, jobs. Women are working before, and soon after, childbearing: the lure of employment is not just cutting down births but also shortening time out taken to rear children and raising the proportion of domestic service after near-disappearance, as middle-class families hire nannies and *au pairs* to support two careers.

There is evidence to suggest the steady growth of women in the labour force in the big advanced economies and that this will continue deep into the twenty-first century before declining once more (this decline is paralleled by a decline in male activity rates: there will be more very young and very old men and women in these later years who will not work). The discovery of a role in work, once made, is not seen as likely to be reversed: Dominique Joss, a senior official at France's Planning Commission (Commissariat du Plan) says, 'Here, as in other countries, there has been a change in women's role and a change in women's values towards work. It's an irreversible movement.'

Much of 'women's work' is part-time. Indeed, that sector of employment has been increasing in many countries at the same time as unemployment rates have been soaring. Between the mid-1970s and the mid-1980s up to 80 per cent of all new service jobs – many part-time – were taken by women. The evidence is that the flexibility offered to employers is at least in part matched by the flexibility that such work offers women with families. Clearly, many women work part-time to supplement another income – though a 1984 survey by the UK Department of Employment found some 28 per cent of part-timers saying they worked for 'basic essentials'.

Mary Mauksch says that the boom in women's employment has been the 'greatest influence on population dynamics and structure': 'Women who work contribute substantially to a family's income, and this alters its purchasing pattern and lifestyle – and helps create employment. It is also a factor behind high unemployment figures, since many women are unskilled and are the first to be made redundant, and a factor of tolerance of high unemployment, since in many cases the woman provides the cushion for the family's reduced income if the man loses his job.'

The growing presence of women at work has been the real force behind the feminist movements in advanced countries – movements that are now losing their sharp ideological edge at the same time as women make real gains in equality in wages and conditions. The British sociologists Michael Young and Peter Wilmott have described the present stage of women's 'emancipation' as being one in which they increasingly share the 'bread-winning' role but still retain the greater responsibility for housework and childrearing. The next step, at best imperfectly realized in a few places, is what they call the 'symmetrical family', where all kinds of work are shared.

Kathleen Newland, formerly a senior researcher in Washington's Worldwatch Institute specializing in women's issues and now a UN official based in Tokyo says: 'Changes in economic and social life around the world during the next quarter-century will be intimately connected to changes in the status and the roles of women. Circumstances are altering the conditions that have for centuries determined women's lot in life. Medical technology makes it possible for women to escape the biological imperative of frequent and often involuntary childbearing. Modern communications are breaching the barriers of tradition.'

In Japan – which Kathleen Newland sees as tardy in coming to terms with the reality of women's employment, even while it is rising – the issue of the breakdown of traditional structures which had lasted longer and appeared stronger than in the West causes more anguished debate. Two of the country's top personnel directors, Futoshi Fujii of Nissan and Takashi Kashiwagi of Hitachi, both give their full verbal commitment to women's equality at the workplace, but Mr Kashiwagi voices doubts that the unions are prepared fully to endorse it (some unions do not even recruit among women, seeing them as birds of passage who will leave the labour market in their early twenties), and Mr Fujii says that there is still controversy about the speed and scope of equal rights. The Government passed an equal-opportunity law in May 1985, which came into force in April 1986: it makes it the duty of the employer to ensure more equal treatment for women in recruitment, promotion and retirement – but, says Tadashi Nakamura, a deputy secretary at the Labour Ministry, it does not insist that seeking to ensure that equal opportunities are open to all means laying down that the *results* must be equal. 'We wish to retain the seniority wages system,' says Mr Nakamura. 'This already means that equal pay for all those who do the same work is not possible. We think that this system is more valuable to preserve than any new one. We also believe that more equality in the labour market between men and women will depend very much on changes in the social norms.'

One source of labour supply in the West European states has now been virtually stoppered: the immigration of workers from other, typically industrializing, countries, often former colonies. The huge movements of population since the war were not the first of their kind. In the early part of the last century the British and the Germans flowed across the Atlantic to the USA, followed, in the second part, by Italians, Spaniards and Eastern Europeans. Between 1800 and 1930 some 40 million Europeans had gone elsewhere for work, mainly to North America. At the same time Irish, Italians, Poles and Jews from all corners of Europe flowed into Britain, France and Germany, generally taking the worst jobs and the most wretched accommodation.

Since the Second World War immigration from the under-developed parts of southern Europe, Asia, Africa and the Caribbean had been high until the 1960s, when France and the UK began to limit their flow. West Germany, which began its 'guest worker' system later than the other two major countries, closed its doors to large-scale immigration (largely from Turkey) in 1973. Since then the pattern has been, in general, one of settlement rather than migration, with workers of foreign origin – whether or not citizens of their host countries – attempting to find stability in their adopted homes.

In all of the countries the workers and their descendants who were brought in to solve (often acute) problems of labour shortage now risk being seen as outsiders in societies where many workers defining themselves as indigenously 'French' or 'British' or 'West German' are themselves without work. Particularly in France, political movements have appeared whose main platform is overtly racist: where the UK's National Front achieved its best results (but no parliamentary representation) in 1979, after five years of a Labour Government, the French Front National brought several MPs into the National Assembly in March 1986, also following a socialist term of office. The continuing unemployment in these countries rules out any prospect of high levels of immigration in the foreseeable future, and the potentially fissile nature of public opinion makes even the continued immigration of dependants a delicate issue.

The German Labour Ministry says flatly: 'None of the Western European societies is likely to open its doors to foreign workers again as they did in the 1950s and 1960s.' West Germany has avoided the worst expressions of racial intolerance, but its careful attempts to integrate its Turks and other workers is accompanied by a much more precise definition of the line between German and non-German citizens than in, say, Britain. (Alfons Mueller, mayor of the chemical town of Wesseling, near Cologne, has the facts at his fingertips: 'We have 3,000 foreigners in the town – 1,500 Turks, 600 Italians, 500 Greeks and 400 Yugoslavs.') It has also, in the past few years, 'exported' some 300,000 foreign workers, including 150,000 Turks, back to their home countries and is discussing new measures to decrease the foreign-worker population. Says the Labour Ministry: 'We don't want more Turks in West Germany: we have 1.4 million and it is enough. We are not about to take on more people with all their problems.'

Of the big advanced states only the UK and the USA appear in the UN's listing of the sixty-plus countries that gain or lose significant numbers of people: the UK has exported some 29,000 people a year for the past few years and is expected to carry on doing so for the next forty.

The USA, of course, is another matter. It is still the biggest recipient of tired, poor and huddled masses in the world: the UN calculates that it takes in some 450,000 people a year and will carry right on doing so until 2025. This is the largest immigration in the world, though not proportionately: the Gulf states, for their size, were huge importers of labour in the first part of the 1980s, and Pakistan, which everyone thinks is exporting its people, had its population swollen by some 320,000 people a year in the first half of the 1980s by refugees from Afghanistan and elsewhere.

But the sheer scale of the US flow and the liberal profusion of its racial groups, all vocally seeking (and often failing to find) places in the sun, makes it still a place apart. Race has long since downgraded class as an object of loyalty and a focus for struggle: black Americans, descendants of one of the biggest forced migrations of labour in the world's history, were preceded and followed by national, religious and ethnic groups who have often kept some part of their 'roots', sometimes transmuted by sentiment into a caricature.

And still they come. Today's labourers for the booming southern and western states come from Central America, usually Mexico. The immigration is overwhelmingly 'illegal' but four successive Bills presented to Congress have failed because of competing pressures from employers, unions, civil libertarians and representatives of the 'illegals' themselves. It is a massive phenomenon, accounting (it is reckoned) for 25 per cent of US population growth: the illegals perform low-paid rural and (increasingly) urban jobs and are hugely vulnerable to bad treatment at the hands of employers because of their inability to go public with protest. The Hispanicization of Southern California and Texas is now proceeding rapidly. There is no agreement on what to do about it.

Work is a forceful determinant of where people live. The work, or variety of work, performed by settled communities dictates its size, growth or decline, wealth and power. Most of us live in cities that first became great agglomerations of people in the eighteenth and nineteenth centuries and continued to grow in the twentieth. Now, in the century's last quartile, are they in terminal decline? Is work moving out?

The process has long been remarked in the USA, in the 'deindustrialization' of large parts of the northern rustbelt: there successive migrations have taken city dwellers first to the suburbs, then to the city's satellite towns, then right out into the country. This process, or something like it, has happened in nearly all major cities in the USA and is happening, a little later, in the UK.

Peter Hall, Professor of Geography at Reading University and the leading authority on urban societies, says that this move is not inevitable. He points to the new US sunbelt and western cities, to the sprawling cities of the developing world, and even – bucking the trend – to some cities in Western Europe. He suggests that the state-cities of West Germany (Bremen, Hanover, Kassel, Düsseldorf, Cologne, Frankfurt, Stuttgart, Nuremberg and Munich) all act as regional centres, retaining high-level service activities and a sense of dynamism. They have also, in many cases, upgraded their public transit systems, though it is doubtful whether this necessarily increases economic activity in itself. Professor Hall deprecates forecasting, noting that the telephone and the motor car could have been seen, in the early part of this century, as the two great dispersers of population but in fact preceded eight decades of huddling together. Yet even while warning against the rashness of prediction, he proposes: 'The future urban pattern could well be a highlighted version of the present one. Major regional service centres, with good transportation infrastructure, will continue to grow but will also disperse. Key workers may choose to live at quite a distance from their jobs, communicating electronically and commuting to their offices on a part-time basis. Others will recolonize the older inner city, rehabilitating and revitalizing it in the process, but the net result, perversely, is likely to be further outward displacement, since the new white-collar colonizers will live at lower densities than the older blue-collar populations they displace. Purely industrial cities, both large and small, are likely to be the main losers in this process, although a few will find new specialized roles as centres of craft industry or of industrial archaeology.'

For the 'great' cities, like New York, Paris, Rome, London, the future remains wholly indeterminate. A further exodus is likely, but much depends on how smoothly they can replace industrial production and goods-handling with information-handling and how far the latter needs to be, or is chosen to be, done in city centre or suburbs. Professor Hall says that he can see arguments both for a continued dispersal and for a counter-trend to that – 'The world's great cities have fooled us before and will doubtless do so again in the future.'

These issues lie behind the generalized population shifts within countries, often, as in the USA, West Germany, France and the UK, from north to south. In the past decade and a half Europe's industrial areas, like Lorraine, Picardie, Pas de Calais, Rhône Alpes, North Rhein–Westphalia, Niedersachsen and Hessen, and most of the north-east of England, the West Midlands, South Wales and Clydeside, have all had a haemorrhage of manufacturing jobs.

It happened to them all, though the UK was first into a process that West Germany's greater industrial strength and France's socialist Government delayed for a couple of years. It has not meant instantaneous and large-scale movements of population: both private and public housing patterns render many of Europe's workers effectively immobile, helping to create skilled labour shortages in the midst of massive unemployment. A leaf from Japan's book: big company workers can and do go everywhere, encouraged by having a company house to move into when they get there. (A cautionary note: many of them are far too cramped for Western expansive taste.)

The number, ages, sex, race and location of tomorrow's workers will help to determine tomorrow's social and economic structures. All of the advanced market economies, except the USA, will see a levelling out and then a decline in their working population within the lifetime of most of their citizens. In West Germany it is already happening. All except the USA have put up the shutters against any more substantial immigration. All will see more women in the workforce. Most will probably have fewer people in their cities, especially the older, often northerly, ones. How many of them will work will depend on how rapidly their societies grasp the future tools of production – which is the subject of another chapter.

2. OLD LEVERS LOSE THEIR POWER

The major industrialized economies, particularly those in Europe, are in a state of structural schizophrenia. Output growth is set to continue at close to trend levels of between 2 and 3 per cent for the next two years. Inflation is down and almost out in Japan and West Germany, low and stable elsewhere. Interest rates are falling in the wake of lower oil prices and sustained fiscal stringency in most major economies. Investment and profits have recovered from the lows of the early 1980s. And there are signs of greater wage flexibility. These economics present a picture of robust good health – but not for the 1.3 million Britons who have been unemployed for more than a year, or the 227,000 who were made redundant in the fourth year of recovery, or the 60 per cent of Italian youth who are jobless. These people may, understandably, believe that the recession has not ended. Unemployment on this scale surely means that the European economies are badly malfunctioning.

A gloomy enough picture, but what would happen if the 'sustainable recovery' evaporated? (It would be foolhardy to assume that the business cycle has been eliminated.) A downswing would add to unemployment – unpleasant but manageable in the 1960s and even in the early 1970s, when OECD unemployment averaged 3 per cent, but now 31 million people are unemployed throughout the area, 19 million of them in Europe. Unemployment rising from this base would push economies and social systems into uncharted territory.

What role has macro-economic policy played in the rise in unemployment since the 1960s? And what kinds of policy could the advanced economies pursue to promote growth and reduce unemployment?

Once upon a time, Western Europe enjoyed something called the post-war consensus. At its core was a broad economic principle: Governments should, and could, intervene in the economy to ensure full employment. In the 1970s monetarist economics, poor economic performance and rising unemployment combined to shatter that consensus. Could a new consensus be built from the rubble of the old to give economic policy a settled place in a strategy designed to bring down unemployment?

A clear line still runs between those who think that Governments can boost demand to create jobs and those who think they cannot. The interesting point today is that the forces of attraction are growing. Keynesians have had to face up to the successes of the past few years – particularly the decline in inflation and the consolidation of public finances. But monetarists also have to face the challenge of unemployment – the political and economic attractions of more active demand management to cut the dole queues. And on at least two major issues there is emerging agreement.

The first is that macro-economic policy can play only a limited role. There is widespread acceptance that, to be credible, policy has to bow to the magnitude of the unemployment problem. Moreover, few Keynesians would now claim that demand management alone can drive the economy forward. There is greater emphasis on improving the supply-side efficiency of the economy.

The second major area of agreement is that both blades of the scissors will have to be used if unemployment is to be reduced. Debates about Government borrowing and spending in the future may be over how much, rather than whether, deficit financing should be used.

Similarly there is growing agreement that keeping pay under control is crucial to bringing down unemployment. 'Wage growth may pick up despite post-war record unemployment because, should high unemployment persist, the unskilled minorities, youth and other weak social groups will bear virtually all the social costs without much effect on the wage bargaining of core experienced workers,' the OECD warns in its Summer 1986 *Employment Outlook*.

Competitive pressure from the unemployed seeking work may well not be enough to restrain pay. In the future more direct, and perhaps novel, ways of containing pay pressure may have to be pursued if the 31 million unemployed throughout the OECD are to have a good chance of returning to secure employment.

This chapter examines the sharpness of the scissor's blades: on the one hand, the effectiveness of expanding demand and, on the other, measures to prevent the labour market from throwing up excessive pay pressure.

The Role of Demand

The old confidence that Governments can solve the problem of unemployment has gone, perhaps for good. We no longer live in a world where well-oiled levers of economic policy can be pulled with certain consequences. A Government commitment to maintain full employment, once the cornerstone of policy in the UK and elsewhere, would now seem incredible.

For most of the post-war era economists and policy-makers revelled in consensus: Governments, it was generally thought, could use higher borrowing to finance extra spending in order to stabilize the economy at full employment in the short term. At the centre of the political settlements following the war was the idea that Governments would, and could, maintain demand at a level that would ensure full employment.

In the 1970s this approach to policy came under consistent attack. The intellectual revolution was led by the American economist and polemicist for the free market, Milton Friedman. Friedman predicted that Governments' attempts to depress unemployment below some natural rate determined by the structure of the economy would lead to growing stresses and strains and eventual failure: 'The post-war commitment to higher employment has to lead to higher unemployment. The way to foster productive employment is to end the counter-productive policies that Government has pursued in the name of full employment.'

Far from being a golden era, the post-war period and active demand management contained the seeds of its own destruction. 'It was not events but ideas that propelled us towards the increasing inflation rate,' said Harvard Professor Martin Feldstein. 'The upward drift in inflation was the result of a fundamental set of beliefs about the economy and macro-economic policy that were shared by economists and policy officials.'

The basic monetarist case against active Government demand management was developed by neo-classical economists Robert Lucas and Thomas Sargeant in the USA. The crux of the neo-classical argument is that prices in the markets for goods and labour are immensely flexible and that economic agents, such as trade-union leaders and marketing managers, are well-informed and forward-looking. To understand the consequences of this view of the world for economic policy, take the following example.

Imagine phoning a shop and being told that a lamp you want to buy costs £40. For some reason you tell the shopkeeper that you will arrive with £50 and intend to spend the remainder to employ an out-of-work electrician. When you walk through the shop door you find, to your surprise, that the lamp's price has shot up to £50. There will be no money left to create work for the unemployed electrician.

This is a rough approximation to the neo-classical view of the world. In the macro-economy the lamp purchaser becomes the Chancellor who announces an expansion of demand. If a Government were to expand demand, workers, sales directors and greengrocers would work out what was going to happen and would try to gain as much as possible. They would put up their prices to match the extra demand, and all the boost to money demand would be soaked up by prices.

The key to the case for activist demand management is the converse proposition: that prices do not adjust fully or immediately to a demand boost. If prices were sticky, therefore, the extra spending would lead to more output and jobs. The Government would have the equivalent of the £10 that you intended for the electrician. In the neo-classical case the same quantity of goods would be produced and the same number people would be employed: it is just that everything would be traded at higher prices.

The neo-classical explanation of unemployment mirrors this. If a Government cuts demand, economic agents have a choice. If they want to maintain employment and output, they have to adjust their prices downwards. The same quantities of goods and labour will be traded but at a lower price level. Should workers and firms refuse to adjust their prices to the tighter demand, unemployment will result. But this is a consequence of their choice: their bankruptcy and unemployment will be voluntary.

Of course, there may be obstacles in the way of this adjustment. The main UK protagonist of the neo-classical approach, Patrick Minford, has consistently attacked the role of trade unions and social security services in preventing full price flexibility. 'Now may be the last major opportunity that Governments have of pushing the tide out,' he warned in 1979.

By the late 1970s many Conservative politicians seemed persuaded that if demand were restrained, this would disturb the economy only temporarily. The UK Treasury Budget document of 1980, for instance, warned: 'The process of reducing inflation almost inevitably entails some losses of output initially, though it promises better growth of output in the longer term. The size and duration of these initial effects, however, will depend in large measure on how quickly behaviour, particularly pay bargaining, takes account of new monetary conditions.' In the same year a UK monetarist, D. E. W. Laidler, put the case more directly: 'It should be acknowledged explicitly that the adoption of gradual monetary restraint does rest on the belief that high employment is neither the only, nor always the most important, target for macro-policy.'

But the erosion of confidence in the foundations of post-war economic policy was not just an intellectual movement. Most major economies performed poorly in the 1970s. Slow growth and surging inflation seemed to bear out Friedman's warnings. This combination of poor macro-economic performance and intellectual revolution changed perceptions of the role that Government demand management could and should play in economic policy. The rise in inflation, from 2.2 per cent in the four major OECD countries in 1967 to 10.2 per cent a decade later, focused attention on the part that deficits played in money creation. In the late 1970s macro-economic policy in most OECD countries was directed away from its traditional role of supporting output and employment and towards combating inflation.

The widespread introduction of stricter monetary controls carried implications for fiscal policy. Government spending in excess of tax revenues can be financed only by borrowing or by money creation. To avoid the risk that deficits could add upward pressure to money growth (and thereby inflation), they had to be brought under control. As a recent OECD study shows, after the second oil shock fiscal policy in the main European economies and Japan became the handmaiden of monetary control rather than playing an independent role supporting demand and output. Economists were concerned about the depressing effects of higher long-term interest rates and taxation, reflecting a general concern over the way in which public, non-marketed activities could sap and limit private-sector dynamism. So since 1979 the focus of Government policy in Europe has shifted from short-run fine-tuning to medium-term stability, from demand management to the way in which Government borrowing and spending affects the supply-side efficiency of the economy. This change in the overall thrust of policy in most OECD countries has had a dramatic impact on output and employment in the short run.

The best measure of the stance of fiscal policy is not the raw, nominal deficit but the so-called 'real structural deficit'. This takes into account the effects of inflation on the value of the debt and the way in which the deficit automatically rises in a downturn because of higher transfer payments and lower tax revenues. As table 2 shows, in the OECD as a whole there has been a tightening of the fiscal stance of about 0.4 per cent of OECD Gross Domestic Product (GDP). In most of the big seven OECD countries, however, fiscal policy has been much tighter. Since 1978 there has been a tightening of policy in Japan (by 3.2 per cent of GDP), West Germany (3.7 per cent), France (1.9 per cent), the UK (3.9 per cent) and Canada (1.4 per cent). The medium-term outlook for all these countries, on current Government strategies, is continuing restraint.

But the trend towards fiscal restraint has not been universal. Some smaller European countries and Australia have pursued more active demand management. The major exception has been the USA, which in 1982 moved into a significant structural deficit. In 1981 the USA's structural budget was in surplus, equivalent to 1.4 per cent of GDP in 1981. But in the following three years US fiscal policy eased substantially, by 2.8 per cent of GDP. By 1984 it was running a structural deficit equivalent to 1.4 per cent.

The new approach to budgetary policy, widespread in Europe since the late 1970s, has had significant success in reducing inflation. In the four major European economies inflation fell from 12.8 per cent at the start of the decade to 6.2 per cent four years later. In the OECD as a whole inflation fell by 7.6 per cent to stand at just over 5 per cent in 1984. 'Average OECD inflation has been declining for five years, the longest period of disinflation in the post-war period,' says the OECD's Chief Economist, David Henderson. 'This is an achievement

Table 2   Budget balances, 1970–84

	General government budget balances (% of GDP/GNP)						
	USA	Japan	W. Germany	France	UK	Italy	Canada
1970	−1.1	1.9	0.2	0.9	3.0	−5.0	0.9
1978	0.2	−5.5	−2.5	−1.9	−4.2	−3.1	−1.8
1980	−1.2	−4.5	−3.1	0.2	−3.5	−2.5	−2.0
1982	−3.8	−3.4	−3.5	2.6	−2.1	−5.3	−5.8
1984	−3.1	−2.3	−1.4	−3.5	−2.8	−5.3	−5.7
	Inflation-adjusted structural budget balances						
	USA	Japan	W. Germany	France	UK	Italy	Canada
1970	−1.2	0.7	−2.0	0.0	5.1	−5.3	−0.9
1978	0.5	−5.1	−2.9	−2.1	−2.1	−2.7	−4.0
1980	1.1	−3.3	−3.2	0.7	4.0	3.3	−2.6
1982	−0.4	−2.7	−1.6	−0.7	4.5	−2.2	−1.8
1984	−1.4	−1.3	0.8	−0.2	1.8	−2.6	−2.6

to be noted and helps to explain why we think the recovery seems likely to continue.'

But the redirection of budgetary policy has also run into major obstacles. First, neo-classical and monetarist economists predicted that tighter demand would lead to only a temporary rise in unemployment while wages adjusted. That adjustment has taken much longer than expected, and the associated employment losses have been greater and more permanent. Second, the monetary and fiscal restrictions that most Governments introduced had a deflationary impact on OECD economies. The move to fiscal and monetary tightness, especially evident in 1980–81, was associated with recession, stagnant investment and the rise in unemployment. Third, increased unemployment-related transfers, such as social security payments and welfare benefits and lower tax receipts, put upward pressure on deficits, frustrating attempted reductions. Fourth, the actual budget cuts achieved, though they may have had a large impact on demand in the short run, were not large enough to engineer a significant fall in interest rates before the fall in oil prices in 1986. In a nutshell, then, the initial restraint intended to bring down the deficit had a deflationary impact in the short run that was much more severe than anticipated.

A few of the longer-run gains that a policy of budgetary restraint promised, through lower interest rates and taxation, are yet to appear. In the four major European economies the tax burden rose by 3.5 per cent of GDP between 1979 and 1983, to stand at 45.1 per cent. Long- and short-term real interest rates are also higher in these economies than they were in the last four years of the 1970s. Rates in Japan and the USA have followed a similar path. Indeed, two OECD analysts, Jean Chouraqui and Robert Price, concluded a survey of medium-term budget strategies with this warning: 'Attempts to cut deficits, in conjunction with restrictive monetary targets, contain the danger that lower demand and sustained high interest rates will deter investment and will risk locking the OECD economies into a slow-growth trap.'

Growth in the OECD economies is in line with past rates of growth. The problem is that actual output is still below the level needed to sustain full employment. If this gap is to be closed, in the short run, a period of growth above trend is required. The questions for demand-management policy are these: can an expansionary policy achieve this boost to growth, or are there sound economic reasons for continuing restraint? Are Governments responsible for the steep rise in OECD unemployment since the first oil shock?

The case for the prosecution, assembled by trade unionists, Opposition parties and disenfranchised economists is clear. Economic policy has been directed away from full employment towards defeating inflation. To this end Governments have squeezed demand out of the economy; output has fallen in a sharp recession; and people have been thrown out of work.

The case for the defence is that the problem lies not with Governments but with labour markets – with trade unions, unnecessary regulations, geographical immobility. As the 1984 UK White Paper on Employment made clear, 'The weak link in our economy is the labour market. The one thing clearly not responsible for unemployment is lack of demand.'

The truth lies somewhere between these two extreme views. Demand management undoubtedly does matter. A sustained, deep cut in demand can push even the most robust economy into rising unemployment. But the faster and more fully labour markets respond to a fall in demand, the more likely it is that unemployment will be transitory.

A number of international studies have attempted to capture the role that fiscal and monetary policy has played, along with supply-side factors connected with the level of the real wage. Most of these studies find that depressed demand has assumed a dominant role since the second oil shock in the late 1970s. But supply-side rigidities, particularly in the mid-1970s, were equally relevant to the cumulative rise over the whole period. 'Wages played an important role mainly in the mid-1970s, but their relative importance for most countries diminished during the period 1978–82,' says Professor Michael Bruno of Jerusalem's Hebrew University. In this last period most of the incremental rise in unemployment can be attributed to shifts in aggregate demand.' Professor Bruno is no Keynesian; his model accords the real wage an important role in determining employment, but in this last period demand was three times more important than pay in forcing up unemployment.

Bruno's conclusions are confirmed by another piece of new research, covering eighteen OECD economies, produced by the Centre for Labour Economics. 'Our estimates confirm that both demand and the level of real wages affect employment. The decline in demand, relative to potential, seems to have been an important cause of the rise in unemployment, especially in the EEC. But it is clear that supply-side factors played an important role. It seems, over the period, that it's six of one and half a dozen of the other,' the report concludes.

The most detailed analysis of the rise in UK male unemployment (which rose from 2 per cent in the 1950s to 17 per cent in 1985), completed by Professor Richard Layard and Professor Stephen Nickell, finds that between the mid-1950s and early 1970s greater union power, more generous social security benefits and higher employment taxes were the most important factors behind the rise in unemployment (see table 3). Government demand management played a negligible role. In the 1970s the rise in real import prices (particularly the first oil shock) and union power were the strongest push variables. However, Government budgetary policy became the third most important factor, having been the least significant in the previous period. In the final period, between the end of the 1970s and 1983, demand was overwhelmingly the strongest force. Between 1980 and 1983 the male unemployment rate almost doubled, to 15.8 per cent. Layard and Nickell calculate that 84 per cent of this increase was due to a contraction in demand. Of this contraction 88 per cent was due to budgetary policy, either directly or through the appreciation of the exchange rate that it encouraged, thereby damaging competitiveness. The remainder was due to the downturn in world trade. The analysis also suggests that demand fell more than five times the amount that was required to keep inflation stable. According to the papers from a 1986 conference, 'The International Rise in Unemployment', these findings are confirmed by research in West Germany, France and Italy (published in *Economica* in May 1986).

The link between demand contraction and higher unemployment is not universal, however. In particular, unemployment in Japan rose from 2.2 per cent to 2.5 per cent between 1980 and 1984, though over that period the Government's budgetary stance contracted by 2 per cent of GDP. 'The key to Japan's low unemployment is the way in which firms and the labour supply adjust to downturns,' says labour economist Kiochi Hamada from the University of Tokyo. When product demand is slacker, firms may cut back on output but not on employment by anything like the same amount. Moreover, there is a particularly swift reduction of the available labour supply as many women stop looking for work.

It is clear that while budgetary contraction has been one of the main forces pushing up unemployment in the 1980s, its impact has been determined partly by how quickly labour markets have adjusted to the change. In some countries the extent and speed of adjustment is associated with co-operation between unions, employers and the Government at a national level (Austria); in others institutional arrangements between individual firms and their employees count for more (Japan); in yet others flexibility in the open market plays more of a role (the USA). Whatever the cause, it is clear that a combination of budgetary contraction and a labour market that is slow to adjust represents the worst of both worlds.

So what scope is there for Governments to introduce policies that will boost employment? The *FT* jobs poll shows that the most important factors that will influence companies' future employment decisions lie largely outside the range of

Table 3 Changes in British unemployment rate (male), 1956–83 (%)

Explained by	1955/66–1967/74		1967/74–1975/79		1975/79–1980/83	
Employers' taxes	0.25	(4)	0.38	(4)	0.44	(4)
Benefit-replacement ratio	0.54	(3)	−0.09	(6)	−0.1	(6)
Union power	1.18	(1)	1.17	(2)	0.80	(2)
Real import prices	0.58	(2)	1.47	(1)	−0.93	(5)
Mismatch of working vacancies	0.16	(5)	0.20	(5)	0.49	(3)
Demand	0.12	(6)	0.54	(3)	6.56	(1)
Income policy	–		−0.36	(7)	0.49	(3)
Total	1.67		3.31		7.75	
Actual change	1.82		3.01		7.00	

Note: Figures in brackets give rank order.

direct Government policy. Overall, the factors that will have most influence on firms' employment decisions will be profitability (mentioned by 74 per cent), the state of domestic demand (69 per cent) and domestic competition (62 per cent). Labour costs and technological innovation were mentioned by 58 per cent. Changes to employment legislation (mentioned by 37 per cent of firms), export performance (36 per cent) and import penetration (28 per cent) were the least important factors.

But in each country particular factors play a strong role. Employment in British firms will be particularly affected by export performance and import penetration. Overseas demand ranks as the fourth most important factor influencing employment in Britain, whereas it ranks ninth in the sample as a whole. Import penetration is of well below average importance elsewhere but of average importance in the UK. Changes to employment legislation would have little influence on employment; these rank thirteenth in importance, with 17 per cent. The industrial-relations climate will have the least influence on employment, with only 16 per cent of firms reporting this as a factor.

In West Germany the character of labour supply is much more important than in other countries. The availability of skilled labour will affect 79 per cent of firms and ranks second most important in West Germany compared with eleventh in Britain and the USA. Labour costs are a factor for 77 per cent of West German employers, compared with 58 per cent overall and 33 per cent in Britain. French employers give new technology a very important role in influencing employment. Three-quarters mentioned new technology as a factor, compared with 38 per cent in Britain and 31 per cent in Japan. Industrial relations is the most important factor influencing future employment in Japan, with 65 per cent of employers reporting this as a factor influencing their future employment plans. Industrial relations is the eleventh most important factor in France and West Germany and fourteenth in Britain.

Employment in the USA will be particularly affected by the availability of capital. Three-quarters of US employers say this will affect employment, compared with a cross-country average of 47 per cent and a low of 6 per cent in Japan.

However, the FT jobs poll shows that companies would respond to a range of Government measures to create new jobs. Only 13 per cent of firms say that nothing would induce them to expand employment. A tax concession to encourage companies to hire new workers is the most popular measure overall, with 40 per cent of firms saying that this would lead them to take on workers. This is particularly important in France, where 54 per cent of employers would take on more workers, twice the number that would respond to a demand expansion. Only 34 per cent of British employers say they would participate in such a scheme. Demand expansion is the second most important measure, but it is particularly important in the UK, where 48 per cent of firms say this would induce them to expand employment. A quarter of firms say that relaxation of laws on part-time working would expand employment (46 per cent in France), while only 7 per cent say that abolition of minimum-wage legislation would expand employment. Incomes policy would be particularly effective in West Germany, with 48 per cent saying this would expand employment compared with an average of 20 per cent across all countries. Fifty-nine per cent of British employers say they would support an incomes policy, but only 9 per cent say they think it would boost employment.

The days when generalized reflation was accepted as an answer to unemployment are gone. Those who argue for an expansion of demand face very different political and economic obstacles from those that challenged their counterparts fifteen years ago. Paradoxically, pessimism over the unemployment problem has been reinforced by the current recovery in output. Despite respectable rates of growth over the last few years, unemployment is high in most European countries and still rising in some. Surely, to press the growth pedal any harder would risk overheating the engine?

In the past Keynesian policy has been aimed at fine-tuning the economy, not at removing mass unemployment. The internationalization of capital markets and imbalances in the world economy now constrain a country's freedom of manoeuvre. Political parties and economists who advocated expansionary policies have started to adapt to the new political economy of the 1980s. As a first step in the UK, for instance, both Opposition parties have backed away from commitment to restore full employment within the course of a single Parliament. The emphasis has switched towards credibility and responsibility in the pursuit of job creation. 'The electorate just did not believe that we could do what we set out in the election of 1983,' says a UK Labour Party senior economic adviser. 'The aim of restoring full employment within a Parliament just was not credible to the voters.' And the Social Democrat–Liberal Alliance envisages a policy that would cut unemployment by 750,000 after three years, financed by extra borrowing of £3.5 billion. This would still leave the UK with more than 2 million unemployed.

It is, above all, the public's fear of resurgent inflation that a 'reflationist' has to address. If a Government chose to expand demand, inflation could creep up for any one of three reasons, or all of them.

First, part of the expansion might be financed by an expansion of the money supply. Many Keynesians accept the need to keep a check on domestic monetary conditions, reinforced by targeting the exchange rate. 'Most Keynesians would agree on the need for a broad nominal target, like money GDP, as a guide to policy,' says Gavyn Davies, chief UK economist at Goldman Sachs and economic adviser to the last British Labour Prime Minister. 'The need for attention to monetary growth is widely accepted. It's the detail that is disputed.' 'New' Keynesians would now admit that a medium-term financial plan, which set out future Government policy, would help to establish a resolve not to accommodate inflation.

A second source of inflation in a period of expansion would be the exchange rate. In a typical European country anything up to 40 per cent of extra demand created by the Government could go on imports. A growing deficit on the current account of the balance of payments would force down the exchange rate. Foreign goods would become more expensive, and this would initially push up prices in the shops. Higher prices in the high street would be reflected in subsequent wage bargaining.

A key element of any reflationary package, then, must be a mechanism that insured against the inflationary consequences of a falling exchange rate. Its task would be complicated by the speed with which increasingly internationalized foreign-exchange markets react to changes in Government policy.

The idea of exchange controls has not entirely disappeared. In 1985 the UK Labour Party unveiled a proposed tax on investments abroad to encourage institutions to repatriate their funds. But in a lecture to the UK's Employment Institute in the same year the American economist Professor Rudiger Dornbusch advocated what has now become a widely favoured remedy. 'The way in which monetary and fiscal policy are combined would be as important as the aggregate expansion of demand. The key feature must be to rule out an exchange-rate collapse,' says Dornbusch. 'Monetary policy must be exchange-rate-oriented.'

Dornbusch argues that if the UK Government, for instance, loosened fiscal policy to stimulate demand by cutting taxes, simultaneously it would have to tighten monetary policy. This would push up interest rates, increase the relative return on sterling assets and attract international capital flows. This inflow of capital would help to maintain the value of the pound.

Exchange-rate management, however, would require careful handling. A higher exchange rate would be good for inflation because it would make imports cheaper than domestic goods. This would lead to greater import penetration and would threaten employment in those sectors of the economy that were open to international competition.

This is exactly what has happened in the USA. The dollar's strength has been the major force behind the fall in US inflation. But the cost has been greater import penetration. In 1985 the US current-account deficit was 2.8 per cent of Gross National Product (GNP) ($118 billion). This benefited exporters in other countries, particularly Japan, which had a 1985 trade surplus of 3.7 per cent of GNP ($50 billion), and West Germany ($413 billion, 2.1 per cent of GNP). The destabilizing economic and political effects of exchange-rate management have grown enormously in the USA, even though it is a relatively closed economy. In European economies the pressure would build up much more rapidly.

A third source of inflationary pressure would be bottlenecks in the labour market. As expansion got under way, shortages of skilled workers might develop and, in response, employers would bid up wages to attract skilled labour. In the long term this kind of bottleneck could be overcome only through training. But in the short term, Keynesians now argue, reflation should be targeted at high-unemployment groups and regions, where the labour market is very slack, and away from areas where the labour market is already tight. 'In an expansion money should not be spent across the board so that employers are trying to take on as many computer programmers as machinists,' says Professor Richard Layard. 'It is machinists who are unemployed, and if firms can be encouraged to employ the less skilled and the unemployed, there will be less upward pressure on wages.' Layard advocates a new scheme to provide the long-term unemployed with jobs guaranteed for a year. The scheme would be reinforced by a restructuring of employers' social security contributions to encourage the recruitment of un-skilled workers and a regional employment subsidy for disadvantaged areas. Of course, this kind of approach is not assured success, so most proposals for reflation are also backed by some form of incomes policy to contain the rate of wage increases and thereby inflation.

New ideas for reforming wage bargaining through tax-based incomes policies, profit-sharing or new forms of arbitration have been proposed, along with more traditional remedies such as a form of social contract between Government and unions. Despite these new ideas, the key problem remains: how do you make any policy stick?

Keynesian-inclined policy-makers are under pressure to find an alternative to the free-market approach of many current Governments and the periodic incomes policies of the past. None of the new ideas has won unanimous approval, even among those who think incomes policy has an important role to play. Even with a workable incomes policy there would still be constraints that could limit the effectiveness of a demand expansion. And even if most of the extra spending were not dissipated in higher prices or more imports, there would still be the possibility that it could be 'crowded out' by higher interest rates. With greater Government borrowing and a tight monetary policy to defend the exchange rate, interest rates would almost certainly go up. This would increase firms' borrowing costs and would possibly dampen investment enough to impede recovery. 'The details of fiscal policy have to take this risk into account by making provision for compensating investment incentives,' says Rudiger Dornbusch. 'The US is a case in point: tight money and easy fiscal policy have not stood in the way of an investment boom because the expansion involved a sizeable incentive to investment.

A final constraint on expansion arises not from economic theory but from the international setting of policy. Highly integrated goods and capital markets make a policy of 'reflation in one country' highly risky. If a single European country decided to reflate, it would bear all the risks of higher inflation and interest rates, but a large part of the extra demand would go to foreign goods and jobs. So a single country has little incentive to risk reflation alone. But winning an agreement for concerted economic expansion would be political torture. Even on the most optimistic outlook, a demand expansion would still leave a major unemployment problem.

A more active approach to demand management may play an important role in future attempts to reduce unemployment. But there is no doubt that it could not return us to full employment.

The Role of Wages

Industrialists warn of unit labour costs rising ahead of those of international competitors; Government economists in the UK have focused on the level of the 'real wage'; Keynesians argue for measures to restrain the growth of money wages. Each accords a crucial role to the wage in determining the level of unemployment in an economy, yet each proposes a different analysis of the wage–unemployment relationship, all based on divergent views of how the economy works.

In recent years, as Governments have rejected active demand management as a tool by which to stabilize employment, policy-makers and politicians have turned their attention to wages as the villain of the piece in the labour market. 'Whenever a market does not clear, economists look for an influence that is hindering price adjustments. The prime market that is not clearing at the macro-level is the labour market, and wage rigidity becomes the natural suspect,' says Daniel Mitchell, Professor of Industrial Relations at the University of California. Yet, as the essays in *Wage Rigidity and Unemployment*, edited by Wilfred Beckerman, make clear, there is no unified theory of what causes wage rigidity or even of which wage should be the focus of policy.

There is a range of candidates. For instance, if money wages in one country are higher than those of competitors and rising at a faster rate, then this will lead to a loss of competitiveness. If there is no offsetting adjustment of the exchange rate, foreign demand will fall and unemployment will rise. This kind of wage problem particularly afflicts open economies like the UK, where persistent wage pressure has been blamed for poor international performance. For example, in the period 1971–83 hourly earnings in UK manufacturing were below the average of the seven major economies in only three years. In the UK the average rate of annual increase across the period was 14 per cent, whereas in the USA it was 7.7 per cent.

That this international effect is an important wage–unemployment link is not in dispute. What is contested is the effect that the wage has on unemployment, regardless of its impact on competitiveness. At the core of the debate is the claim that unemployment is the product of a real wage that is too high to make it profitable for firms to produce. Even if there were more demand, firms would still not make enough profit to make it worth their while to expand output, so unemployed workers have to price themselves into jobs by offering to work at wages that will allow firms to make higher profits.

This kind of argument has won support from economists at the European Commission, the OECD and national Treasuries, but its most articulate proponents are Michael Bruno and Jeffrey Sachs. In *The Economics of Worldwide Stagflation*, which draws together work from the late 1970s and early 1980s, Bruno and Sachs outline a supply-side explanation of unemployment, backed by an impressive array of international data. They concentrate on the relationship between labour costs and the value of the output a worker produces: the share of a firm's revenue taken by wages rather than profits. One of the main sources of unemployment, they argue, is the 'wage gap' between actual labour costs and hypothetical costs that would be necessary to produce full employment.

In the early 1970s workers' pay persistently rose faster than the value of the output that they produced. According to Sachs, even prior to the oil shocks the major economies faced declining profitability and growth. After the first oil shock, labour costs did not decelerate to make way for the rise in raw-material prices, so the squeeze on profitability continued. Between 1969 and 1975 labour's share of value added in the manufacturing sector rose by 9.2 per cent to 80.2 per cent in the UK, by 8.3 per cent to 74.1 per cent in France and by 7.9 per cent to 60.5 per cent in West Germany. The major exception to this trend was the USA, where labour's share rose by only 0.6 per cent to stand at 71.6 per cent in mid-decade. In the final phase, though, labour costs did decelerate into the 1980s, as did productivity growth, in consequence of the low investment induced by declining profitability. Not only did this lead to lower employment in the short run but it also put the economies into a tail spin. As Sachs says: 'Demand management could no longer restore non-inflationary full employment, since firms were not willing to hire the full-employment workforce at prevailing factor prices. Second, the high factor prices reduced the profitability of capital, and thereby played an important role in the slowdown of capital accumulation and productivity growth in the 1970s and 1980s. Many of the major economies entered a low-profit, low-growth trap in which wage levels contributed to slow productivity growth, which in turn reinforced the excess of wages-market clearing levels.'

Bruno's and Sachs's work has had a powerful impact on policy-makers. Although it is immensely sophisticated, it has an intuitive appeal because it focuses on something very simple: the way in which wage pressure can erode the profit incentive. However, in the last few years Sachs's 'wage-gap' approach has met increasing scepticism.

As Professor John Sargent points out in a Bank of England paper on the real-wage debate, wage pressure on profit margins can be offset by lower costs for other inputs. He calculates that in the 1960s the real product wage rose by 3.4 per cent per annum, but the costs of capital were consistently reduced. This eased pressure on profits but also provoked higher investment and productivity in line with wage increases. Sargent argues that the rise in labour's share of the proceeds in the 1970s may have been due as much to a rise in the costs of capital as to independent wage pressure.

A second problem is the choice of a 'full-employment' starting period. Evidence for both the USA and the UK shows that even at times of full employment the wage share has risen. According to leading Brookings Institution economist George Perry, 'The rising labour share of the 1970s looks quite like a continuation of a trend established in the full-employment years of the 1950s and 1960s.' Moreover, it is not clear that the wage gap alone accounts for the rise in unemployment even in the 1970s (as Bruno and Sachs recognize). For instance, between 1961 and 1979 labour's share of manufacturing value added rose by 10.2 per cent in Japan and by 9.8 per cent in the UK. Yet, as a report from the Centre for European Policy Studies' macro-economics group notes, wage pressure is far less of a problem in Japan than in the UK.

But, according to some economists, there is a much more fundamental problem with the wage-gap approach. 'There is a growing feeling that the statement "Real wages are too high" is poorly defined. It is not clear what it means independent of what is happening to demand,' says Martin Weitzman of the Massachusetts Institute of Technology (MIT). The key point that has forced this reassessment is that the *real* wage is not set in the labour market. Firms and workers bargain over the money wage, but both are motivated by the target of the increase that they can afford in real terms.

Profitability is squeezed only when firms cannot accommodate higher wages with higher prices. So if wage pressure is to cut profitability, there has to be some cap on firms' ability to raise their prices. In some sectors competitive pressures ensure a limit to price rises: a price rise above the prevailing level will drive a firm out of business. But in most markets in the UK, for instance, prices are not set by strict market forces. 'Over the greater part of private-sector production the system is one of administered prices. In some way or other, firms reach a point of view about the scale of profit that is "satisfactory" and thereafter seek a price whose relation to normal costs yields this profit,' says Sir Bryan Hopkin, an academic adviser to the Bank of England.

So what stops firms with some degree of discretion over their prices from simply passing on higher wages to the consumer? If firms did this across the economy, there would be a constant 'battle of mark-ups' between workers and firms. Firms would respond to higher-than-expected wages by putting up prices. This would fuel inflation, which in turn would provoke workers to bargain for higher wages. 'What eventually should put a stop to this contest is the Government stepping in to "referee" it,' says Professor Richard Layard. 'This would dampen demand, forcing firms to cut back on output and employment. Higher unemployment should force wage-bargainers back into line.'

Indeed, unemployment would rise even if Governments did not act to cut demand but merely kept money demand on some stable path. If price inflation rose in response to wage pressure, then more of the extra demand would be dissipated in higher prices and less would be left over for output and jobs. 'The real-wage outcome is really a secondary matter,' says Oxford economist Stephen Nickell. 'The key thing is that money-wage pressure will lead to higher prices and lower real demand.' This reassessment of the wage problem has important consequences for policy. Pressure from trade unions may be one source of the problem, but it will be compounded if there is a large number of near-monopoly firms in the economy. Lack of competitive pressure on these firms means they will have some leeway to pass on wage pressure in price rises.

Some economists detect the signs of an emerging consensus about the wage issue after years of bitter argument. There may be a movement away from seeing unemployment as either classical (that is, due to a real wage that is too high) or Keynesian (that is, due to a lack of demand) and towards a single position that encapsulates both demand and the wage. 'The real issue is whether an economy has got the right money wage/money demand mix,' says Robert Solow, Professor of Economics at MIT. 'Money wages may be too high, given the level of money demand in the economy. But it is also possible that money demand may be too low, given money-wage levels. It is really a single equation, and you can choose which side to put emphasis on, but both have to be there.'

So relief can be sought by either route. But by far the most effective way to cut unemployment is to act on both together, says Stephen Nickell. His calculations on the UK Treasury model show that a demand boost accompanied by 2 per cent lower wage pressure would be three and a half times more effective in cutting unemployment than a reduction in wage pressure alone. A demand expansion without falling wage pressure would risk fuelling inflation but would still be a less effective remedy for unemployment. 'The important point arising from the Treasury calculations,' says Nickell, 'is that to reduce unemployment without increasing inflation we need a reduction in the pressure for nominal wage rises allied to a Government-induced increase in real demand. The fundamental question is: how is a reduction in wage pressure to be engineered?'

When unemployment is high, the supply of labour exceeds demand. What stops the price of labour from falling, like the price of tomatoes, to ensure that supply and demand are in harmony? 'The reason why wages are not fully adjusting to restore hopes of a fall in unemployment is the key question we are trying to answer at the moment,' says a senior economist of the UK Department of Employment. Mrs Thatcher's former economic adviser, Professor Alan Walters, also admits that the obstinacy of wage setting in the face of high unemployment is a 'mystery'.

The source of this confusion is straightforward classical economic theory, which says that unemployment should be self-correcting. Wages, or the pace of wage growth, should fall to price workers into jobs. According to this view of the world, wage adjustment should be an effective, almost automatic, remedy for unemployment. Simply, unemployed workers should find it preferable to be employed than remain on the dole. They should be interested in any job that pays some margin above the social security benefits they receive. Employers should have an incentive to accept these low-wage offers because they should make a higher profit. But wage-cutting should also dampen wage pressure from the employed, who should respond to the pressure of competition by moderating their wage claims, thereby protecting their jobs.

A review of UK economic work by London School of Economics labour economist Andrew Oswald confirms that there is a link between unemployment and wage inflation. Oswald reports that most studies find that a doubling of unemployment eventually produces a 10 per cent fall in the real wage. And in a multi-country study OECD economist David Coe found that a 1 per cent increase in unemployment slowed wage inflation by less than 0.65 per cent in most of the major OECD economies. Coe's index of how much real wages respond to unemployment shows that Japanese real wages have a rigidity rating of 0.3, compared with 3 in France and 6 in the United Kingdom.

But, despite their findings, Oswald and Coe sound a warning to those who think that the general level of unemployment has a straightforward and direct effect on wage pressure. According to Oswald, 'It is now widely accepted that old-fashioned competitive theories of the labour market are inadequate. The stereotype of the economist who thinks of the market for labour as much like the market for tomatoes should be gone for ever.' In similar vein Coe warns that the link between the level of unemployment, competitive labour-market pressure and wage inflation may be breaking down. 'The sharp rise in unemployment between 1980 and 1984, to rates far higher than most estimates of the natural rate (NAIRU), was accompanied by an impressive deceleration in inflation,' he says. 'Yet although unemployment rates are generally projected to level off or increase somewhat more over the period 1985–88, inflation is expected to remain relatively stable.'

Both these comments address the same worry: that, despite a lengthy period of high unemployment, wage inflation has not slowed enough to price workers into jobs. Why has pay not responded enough to restore near full employment? And why is it that ever-increasing amounts of unemployment seem to be needed just to keep inflation stable? The stubbornness of wage inflation has prompted a search for new explanations of obstructions to competitive downward pressure on wages.

One possibility is that the wave of reforms introduced by the Thatcher Government in the UK, and others in Europe, to free up the labour market may not have gone far enough. Despite radical reforms to the legal position of UK trade unions, the 'trade-union mark-up', which is a measure of the extra pay that a worker receives just for being a member of a union, stands at a record level. According to calculations produced by Professor David Metcalfe of the London School of Economics, the mark-up rose from 8 per cent in 1979 to 12 per cent in 1983.

Allied reforms to minimum-pay legislation, individual employment protection and employers' social security contributions may free up the bottom end of the labour market. 'These reforms may well have some impact, but it's clear that the problem of wage pressure comes from the well-paid rather than the lower-paid,' says Professor Stephen Nickell. (Between 1980 and 1984 workers in the bottom 10 per cent of the earnings distribution took a real wage cut, whereas those in the top 10 per cent enjoyed a real wage rise of 13.6 per cent.)

The rolling programme of trade-union and labour-market reform may rightly be regarded as one of the most significant achievements of the Thatcher Government. But it is clear that there are sources of pay pressure that structural reform has failed to cap.

A second possibility is that the general level of unemployment may be a poor guide to the extent of competitive pressure in the labour market. The rise in unemployment throughout most of Europe, and particularly in the UK, is due largely to a rise in the share taken by long-term unemployment. Long-term unemployment has risen throughout the OECD area, but the high-unemployment European economies have been particularly hard-hit. 'The majority of people now, as earlier, are never unemployed, while those who are unemployed nowadays really get it in the neck,' says Professor Richard Layard.

The growth of long-term unemployment raises serious questions about social and distributive justice, but, as the OECD's *Employment Outlook* (1985) points out, it becomes a kind of economic trap: 'Many of the long-term unemployed are in the most depressed areas, where the chances of finding work are very low indeed. The mere fact of being out of work for a long period of time may itself be a negative signal to employers. Finally, skills and work motivation may deteriorate through disuse.'

So, though the long-term unemployed are counted in the active labour force, many have become so discouraged that they no longer really compete for jobs, which means they exert little downward pressure on wages. This has led some economists to suggest that a demand expansion targeted at the long-term unemployed in depressed regions could be a macro-economic free lunch. 'Getting the long-term unemployed into work would hardly diminish the counter-inflationary impact of the current level of unemployment,' says Gavyn Davies, chief UK economist at Goldman Sachs. 'Indeed, if training and job experience made the long-term unemployed more of a competitive force in the labour market, they could conceivably lead to higher employment and a lower real wage.'

Programmes to re-integrate the long-term unemployed into the labour market thus have a social and economic rationale. But they do little to stem the pay pressure that is coming from well-paid, skilled workers who have secure jobs with successful firms. New economic analysis and industrial relations research shows that it is these workers and firms that are the source of pay pressure. But why should these firms calculate that they will reap greater profits from keeping their existing employees – and, moreover, paying this workforce above the market clearing rate – rather than from taking on new labour at lower wages?

The explanation is, broadly, that pay is not determined solely by the interaction of supply and demand in the general, national, 'external' labour market. There is increasing evidence that internal considerations, such as the need to retain and motivate skilled labour, weigh very heavily with some firms. 'The need to retain skilled workers in a competitive market, and our profitability, are the major factors influencing what we pay skilled people,' says John Kerslake, head of personnel for Barclays Bank. 'The reality is that there is more than one England, and unemployment does not affect pay bargaining very much, especially in the South-East.'

In strictly economic terms, it may be in a firm's profit-seeking interests to pay above the market rate to reap productivity gains over a period of years. The net benefits of this approach may outweigh the rewards of taking on low-wage labour with all the attendant redundancy and turnover costs. Firms may well strike implicit contracts with their key employees by offering them secure, well-paid employment, insulated from the competitive forces of the labour market, in return for productivity gains. 'If you rented a warehouse on a long lease, the rent would not vary according to the periodic business position of the lessor. Why should it be different with labour that firms want to keep for a long period?' asks Daniel Mitchell, Professor of Industrial Relations at the University of California.

Unions have a strong incentive to go along with a company personnel policy that offers stable, well-paid employment for its members. Unions, however, do not comprise a grey mass of identical workers who automatically have common interests. For instance, the widespread practice of distributing redundancies on a 'last in, first out' basis means that unless the entire firm is faced with closure, senior workers may feel little threat of losing their jobs. While the most vulnerable workers may see some merit in taking a pay cut to protect their jobs, they could well be outvoted by senior workers who do not need to offer a lower wage to secure their employment.

In some European countries the rise in unemployment may simply have redirected the wage-inflation problem rather than solving it. As one senior OECD official puts it, 'The continuing problem of wage rigidity may best be explained by the conflict of interest between employed workers and managers, who are on the "inside", sitting at the pay-bargaining table, and the unemployed "outsiders". They have no place at the table, and that may be particularly true of the long-term unemployed. It is a plausible story.'

Indeed, the *FT* jobs poll confirms the analysis that 'external' pressures, such as the level of unemployment, are less important in determining pay than 'internal' pressures, such as profitability and productivity. Despite record numbers of people out of work, unemployment is the least important factor affecting pay. Only 15 per cent of firms said that the level of unemployment would influence pay settlements within their firms in the next few years. Only 10 per cent of British employers report it as a factor. The most important influences are: profitability (77 per cent), payments to be compensated by future productivity gains (55 per cent – though considered most important in France and West Germany), inflation (54 per cent) and the availability of skilled labour (50 per cent). The last factor is one of the most important influences in West Germany, where it will affect 77 per cent of firms.

British employers were also asked why pay in the UK is running ahead of competitors' pay settlements. A majority blamed weakness in management (52 per cent); 41 per cent said that it was a result of the need to attract skilled labour; and 31 per cent said that it was because of a rise in profits.

The poll also confirms that companies do not regard trade unions as a major source of pay pressure. Only one-fifth of employers say that union strength would affect pay within their firms, though 47 per cent of the firms surveyed are unionized. Paradoxically, although Japanese employers are most worried by the industrial-relations climate, only 5 per cent think that unions will affect pay within their firms, compared with 15 per cent in France and 16 per cent in Britain.

Given the unions' restricted influence in British pay negotiations, it is not surprising that 82 per cent of British employers think that another round of trade-union legislation would be unlikely to help in maintaining or increasing employment. Among strongly unionized firms 64 per cent think that labour costs are a factor that will influence employment, compared with an average across all firms of 58 per cent.

The alarming upshot of these arguments is that the recession of the early 1980s may have inverted the logic of classical economics. The lack of wage flexibility in high-unemployment economies is mystifying because the logic of economic self-interest is supposed to drive workers to offer lower wages and firms to accept them. The 'insider–outsider' approach suggests that outsiders could not force themselves into the bargaining process even if they wanted to. And even if the unemployed outsiders could find a place at the pay-bargaining table, employers might calculate that it was not in their interests to accept lower wage offers.

Thus, despite high unemployment, the pay-bargaining system continues to throw up wage pressure. This in turn limits any Government's ability to stimulate the economy through higher demand. In economic jargon, high wage pressure is an externality, like pollution. It is produced by wage-bargainers, but all the costs are borne by another group – the unemployed. As two Oxford University economists, Derek Morris and Peter Sinclair, note in, a review of international unemployment: 'Until recently it was thought that unemployment would be temporary, arising from adverse shocks and the transitional costs of bringing down inflation. But there are reasons for believing that unemployment breeds unemployment.'

'One is also, simply because one knows no solution, inclined to turn a blind eye to the wages problem in a full employment economy,' wrote Keynes in 1945. The lesson from the UK and other European economies since 1982 is that wages can still be a problem in a high-unemployment economy. Confidence that demand could do the trick and bring down unemployment has gone. But so has the belief that unemployment, and measures to free up the labour market, will provoke sufficient wage flexibility to restore full employment.

Of course, the rise in unemployment has produced wage moderation. 'The period 1982–4 was the longest period of unit-labour-cost stability recorded since 1958–9,' the OECD noted in its *Economic Outlook* in 1986. And there have been institutional changes to bargaining in many countries. In 1984 in the USA union wage settlements were the lowest for seventeen years. Up to a quarter of union workers negotiating new contracts in 1984 accepted wage cuts or freezes. 'Changes in bargaining patterns have been less marked in Japan and West Germany, but money-wage increases are now at about half the level they were at in the 1960s,' says the OECD.

In countries where wage indexation is an important factor in wage determination – Denmark, Italy, the Netherlands – there have been widespread changes in coverage. But, despite this moderation, there are problems. According to the OECD, in Norway, Switzerland and the United Kingdom real labour costs grew more rapidly between 1982 and 1984 than in the previous two years. And it seems that ever-increasing amounts of unemployment are required to keep inflation stable (see table 4). Between 1963 and 1973 unit labour costs in manufacturing in the major seven OECD economies grew at 3.2 per cent per year. During this period unemployment in these economies was 3.1 per cent. But in the following decade, despite higher and rising unemployment averaging 5.9 per cent over the period, unit labour costs grew by 7.6 per cent per year.

Unemployment is an extremely costly way of controlling pay inflation, so in the past few years economists and policy-makers have searched for new ways of restraining wage growth. As a starting point, one could look at how labour markets function in relatively successful employment economies. In *The Economics of Worldwide Stagflation*, for example, Michael Bruno and Jeffrey Sachs draw up an index of labour-market efficiency with two dimensions.

The first is the degree of 'corporatism' in wage setting: simply, whether unions, employers and the Government reach agreement over the permissible level of wage increases and enforce it. Bruno and Sachs argue that this depends on well-established channels of consultation, an underlying social consensus and centralized bargaining. This gives union leaders and employers' federations the clout to bring recalcitrant members back into line. The two economists find that the more corporatist economies were able to slow inflation much more effectively during the 1970s and early 1980s. In other words, they required less unemployment to bring price rises under control. Their findings are confirmed by a more recent study completed at the London School of Economics. 'We found that unions are not necessarily bad for employment. It depends how they are

Table 4   Unit labour costs in manufacturing (% average changes p.a.) and unemployment (% of labour force) 1963–83

	Labour costs	Unemployment	Labour costs	Unemployment
USA	2.4	4.80	7.0	7.55
Japan	3.9	1.25	2.8	2.1
West Germany	4.0	0.80	4.4	4.6
France	3.1	1.30	10.8	6.1
UK	4.8	1.95	14.3	6.6
Italy	5.3	5.3	16.4	7.55
Canada	2.4	5.1	9.9	8.3
Total	3.2	3.05	7.6	5.9

Source: OECD.

organized in bargaining,' says Professor Charlie Bean. 'Labour markets can work efficiently with unions if they have a high degree of corporatism.'

The other dimension of the Bruno and Sachs index of labour-market efficiency is 'money-wage responsiveness'. They find that in the USA and Canada it takes a relatively long time for price increases to be reflected in subsequent wage bargains. 'In most countries prices are evenly and completely reflected in wages within eighteen months,' says OECD economist David Coe. 'In the USA it takes four years for price rises to be transmitted fully to wages.' In the USA, then, there is a relatively gentle wage–price spiral, produced by an amalgam of weak unions, long-term wage contracts and competitive labour markets. 'Macro-economic misery, measured by higher inflation and slower GNP growth, is importantly related to structural labour-market features. High corporatism and low nominal wage responsiveness helped countries to avoid a serious profit squeeze and the worst of stagflation in the past decade,' say Bruno and Sachs.

The choices facing Governments with a pay problem are stark. One is to pursue a policy to encourage the competitive characteristics of the US labour market. But freeing up labour markets is no easy task. Another is to pursue some kind of centralized incomes policy along the lines of the highly corporatist economies. But in the UK, for instance, incomes policies are associated with the political turmoil of the 1970s. This casts doubt on their economic effectiveness. A third option is to look to new ideas like profit-sharing or tax-based incomes policies to reform pay bargaining. But their novelty entails the risk of uncertainty.

It is clear that in the UK and other countries something needs to be done to curtail pay directly. The question is: what?

An obvious option would be to introduce some systematic mechanism to restrain wages growth. The most familiar mechanism in the UK is some form of incomes policy. The FT jobs poll shows that only West German employers believe strongly that an incomes policy would help to expand employment. In West Germany 48 per cent of firms say they think an incomes policy would help to boost employment, compared with an average of 12 per cent elsewhere. British employers also show strong support for a new incomes policy: 59 per cent say that they would support a new agreement between the Government and unions, though only 9 per cent say that they think this would generate more jobs.

There have been fifteen periods of voluntary, statutory or 'compulsory' incomes policy since the Second World War. Few have survived changes of Government, and many have become economically ineffective because of the political problems of maintaining them. Most policies have been central to economic policy, so when they have broken down (for instance, in the 1970s) the ramifications have spread beyond the arena of wage bargaining to rock the credibility of the Government. Moreover, the structure of bargaining does not make the implementation of a centrally agreed strategy easy. The trend toward decentralized, plant-based wage negotiations is continuing, according to industrial-relations analysts. Unlike the central trade-union bodies in Austria and Sweden, the British Trades Union Congress (TUC) has no very direct role to play in wage negotiations and relatively little power over its affiliates. 'The principal reason why the British bargaining system has been so disastrously effective in amplifying inflation acquired from the world economy has been its fragmentation,' says William Brown, Professor of Industrial Relations at Cambridge University. There is on offer a menu of new ideas that claim to meet these goals and that, the authors assert, could be usefully applied throughout the OECD and not just in high-unemployment countries.

Interest in profit-sharing has been stimulated by the low unemployment in Japan, where profit-related bonuses are an important part of pay for large numbers of employees. The UK Chancellor has embarked on a consultation process with the prospect of tax breaks to encourage firms to introduce profit-sharing. The economics popularized by MIT economist Martin Weitzman are relatively simple. If pay is fixed and demand for a firm's output goes down, then the most direct way to cut labour costs is to reduce employment. If pay were related to profitability through a profit-share bonus, it is pay that would vary and not employment. So profit-sharing is good for maintaining employment. What is less clear is whether it would generate extra employment.

Weitzman says that profit-sharing firms will become 'labour-seeking vacuum cleaners, sucking in labour'. In a wage system the firm has a stark choice. The employer knows that if it hired an extra worker, it would have to pay the going wage – say, £100. But that extra worker might generate only £90 in revenue. The firm would have no incentive to hire because the extra costs would outweigh the extra revenue. But in a profit-share system the firm's incentives would be dramatically altered. If pay were set as a share of revenue, then no matter how much extra revenue was created, there would always be something left over for the firm: the extra costs of hiring a worker would always be below the extra revenue generated.

If the top 500 firms in the economy instituted profit-share schemes they would all drop prices to sell more output and employ more people. The entire economy would turn into a labour-seeking vacuum cleaner. 'The traditional wage system offers a fixed money compensation for a majority who have work,' says Weitzman, 'but no guarantee of full employment and a raw deal for those without work. A profit-share system offers full employment to all at variable pay.'

Nevertheless, there are problems with the profit-sharing approach. Initially at least, those already employed would stand to lose because the pay of everyone in a firm would go down as more people were employed. The scheme would expect workers to bear the risk of lower pay to allow the firm to take on extra workers. Tax concessions could smooth the way and cushion employees from excessive variability, but there must be a danger that they could become embedded and that the scheme would turn into a straightforward tax subsidy on employment. A related problem is that firms and unions could agree on a profit-sharing formula that won tax concessions but was, in fact, a disguised wage.

The most fundamental problem, however, is to do with the sharing of risks.

Employees would be required to forgo a fixed, relatively secure wage for the sake of expanding employment. Because of the increased risks, workers might legitimately demand a greater say in the running of a business. Far from being a simple micro-economic tool, to be effective profit-sharing might require a transformation of business organization and culture.

The FT jobs poll shows that few firms introduce profit-sharing to expand employment. Yet firms with profit-sharing arrangements do have a better than average employment record. Overall, 44 per cent of firms offer their employees some kind of profit-sharing, in the form of an occasional bonus, preferential treatment in buying shares or as part of a pay packet that goes up and down with profits. Broadly defined, profit-sharing is most common in France (56 per cent of firms) and the UK (53 per cent) and least common in West Germany (27 per cent). Only 14 per cent of firms expect to expand or introduce profit-sharing, though 43 per cent of British firms said they would be interested in profit-sharing if the Government offered them £5 per worker per week as a tax concession. However, only 6 per cent of firms running profit-sharing schemes said that they did so to expand employment and 26 per cent claimed that their aim was to make labour costs more flexible. Firms mainly use profit-sharing to increase the motivation of their workers (mentioned by 77 per cent) and to improve productivity (53 per cent).

Though profit-sharing is generally not aimed at increasing employment through making labour costs more flexible, the poll does reveal a clear link between profit-sharing and job growth. Overall, the poll shows there will be net job growth in 20 per cent of firms. But there will be net job growth of 30 per cent among profit-sharing firms, whereas firms without profit-sharing will have below-average growth.

An alternative is tax-based incomes policy (TIP). The best-known and most widely respected TIP is the brainchild of Professor Richard Layard, who proposes simply that a tax on wage settlements above a certain norm would alter the incentives of both employers and unions. 'It would be up to the firm and those who it bargained with to fix whatever pay packages they wanted,' says Layard. 'There would be no constraints, just one more tax to be considered in making a business decision.'

So, for instance, if a firm paid a worker £1 above the norm, it might also have to pay the tax authorities an extra £1. This would discourage firms from being easy-going about pay, but the unions would also realize that a £1 increase to their members would entail a £2 increase to the employer, which would put jobs at risk. All round, the tax should lead to slower wage and price rises and higher employment.

There are obvious problems with such a scheme, however. First, though Layard claims the scheme would allow free bargaining, it would penalize the most efficient and innovative firms, which might well regard pay rises above the norm as justified because of productivity gains. Second, the drawing up of the details of the plan could also be hideously complicated. (A TIP proposed in the

USA during the Carter administration was lost during endless redrafting in Congress.)

One of the main attractions of the plan is that it would roll on like any other tax: it would run itself. But this lack of politics could also be a drawback. The scheme would rely on the establishment of a national norm. For some critics the mechanics would be relatively unimportant; what determined the strength of the policy would be the way in which the norm was established. 'However clever the modes of enforcement, no incomes policy is likely to work unless there is a fairly widespread understanding of the rationale for the policy and a fairly widespread acceptance of it,' says Professor Ronald Dore. He proposes an institutional framework to set the norm, within which the views of Government, employers, unions, the low paid, the unemployed, consumers and pensioners would be heard. Rather than assuming that unions and others would follow their sectional interests, Dore argues that the purpose of the 'great pay debate' would be to engender genuine national consensus. In the UK both the Labour Party (with a National Economic Assessment) and the Alliance (with a national pay forum) have proposed ideas along these lines.

Critics claim that this is just the old corporatism with better public relations. The kind of national consensus that characterizes Japan and Sweden, say, emerges not from a two-day meeting at a hotel but from the deep roots of social history.

Advocates of two-tier pay argue that the problem of unemployment is relatively simple. Firms find it unprofitable to employ more workers at going rates of pay, so they should introduce a second, lower, tier of pay for all new workers. The pay of those already employed would not go down, as it would initially under profit-sharing, so they would not object. (General Motors have introduced this type of arrangement at some plants in the USA.)

Some labour-market economists would say that the labour market in the UK is developing toward a clear two-tier system. 'The outcome of current Government policy is likely to be two clear segments of the labour market, much more distinct than in the past,' says Oxford University industrial-relations specialist Ken Mayhew. 'On the one hand, there is likely to be a core of workers with relatively secure jobs, reasonable career prospects and satisfactory pay. And, on the other, there may well emerge a group of secondary workers with low security, few prospects and poor pay.'

The development of a rigidly two-tier market raises all kinds of questions of social justice. But it still leaves a major economic problem unsolved. Pay pressure is coming from high-earnings groups, the core of the workforce. There would be little or nothing to stem this pressure.

Since the late 1970s the forces behind high levels of unemployment have changed. The rise in unemployment can be explained largely by a contraction in effective demand, engineered by Governments, though this contraction has also been a response to the underlying economic problems of the decade. Since then too continued fiscal restraint outside the USA has contributed to keeping unemployment at a high level. But by far the most worrying development of recent years is the way in which labour markets have responded to mass unemployment. European labour markets may be segmenting, so that a large core of workers are now able to work and earn as 'normal', while those knocked out by the recession of the early 1980s are finding it very difficult to get a firm foothold in the labour market. Those in steady, full-time jobs with good earnings are now feeling the flush of security and prosperity. For the foreseeable future, unemployment is unlikely to touch them; they will have little incentive to bear significant costs in order to bring it down. Those who most need new policies to reduce unemployment – the long-term unemployed, youth, peripheral workers – are, by and large, disorganized, depressed, disadvantaged and disenfranchised.

Large parts of the advanced economies that came through the recession may now be leaner, fitter and more efficient, with a stable future ahead of them. But others have been left behind. The most disturbing conclusion is that through this division in the labour market unemployment may be breeding itself. This does not mean that we should give up or that macro-economics has no useful role to play. On the contrary: ten years ago it seemed that double-digit price inflation was endemic to the advanced economies; it is still possible that in ten years' time mass unemployment will be a thing of the past.

3. FOUR VIEWS OF
UNEMPLOYMENT

Many well-established economic rules of thumb have been thrown into doubt in the 1980s. Those economists who believe that the Government's manipulation of demand is the crucial determinant of the level of employment are still coming to terms with the criticisms rallied against the conduct of economic policy in the 1970s. Yet those who argue that the level of employment is crucially determined by the price of labour are struggling to explain why, in economies such as the UK, pay is not responding as predicted to high levels of unemployment. These reassessments have led economists to look for new explanations of unemployment and new policy prescriptions.

In this chapter we present the views on unemployment of four leading economists. Mr Samuel Brittan, the *Financial Times*'s economic commentator, argues that persistent pay pressure is the result of a division between 'insiders' who are part of the pay-bargaining process and 'outsiders' (mainly the unemployed) who exert little influence on pay determination. As a consequence, pay is not responding to the general state of the labour market: workers who want to price themselves into jobs may not be able to do so because they cannot adequately influence pay setting. Mr Brittan argues for reforms to pay bargaining allied with new measures to raise the incomes of the unemployed in order to prevent this division from becoming a permanent social rift.

Professor Martin Weitzman, of the Massachusetts Institute of Technology, argues that unemployment is the product of the interaction between money wages and money demand. He says that macro-economic management needs to be combined with measures to promote the systematic reform of the labour market through the introduction of profit-sharing. Professor Weitzman argues that profit-sharing in which a significant proportion of employees' pay is tied to the fluctuation of profitability per employee is much more likely to reduce both unemployment and inflation than a fixed-wage system.

Professor Richard Layard, of the London School of Economics, puts the case for special measures to reduce long-term unemployment. The long-term unemployed are exerting no competitive downward pressure on wages, so if they were put into jobs, there would be little risk of a rise in pay pressure and inflation, he says. However, Professor Layard also proposes a tax-based incomes policy as a tool to contain pay pressure and allow demand to be raised without fuelling inflation.

Finally, Professor George Perry, from the Brookings Institution, Washington, DC, argues that European economies should redirect their policies toward higher growth and lower unemployment. The importance of removing inflationary pressures should not be underestimated, he says; nevertheless, policy-makers are unlikely to find a better opportunity, or a more pressing need, for demand-led expansion.

A Fresh Look at Pay and Work *by Samuel Brittan*

One of the many ambiguities of the unemployment debate is the issue of on whose behalf the prevalent concern is being exercised. Is it on behalf of the people who cannot find work because of the loss to their dignity and gradual demoralization, as well as their having to live on the dole rather than on a normal wage? Or is it a more selfish concern on the part of the 86 to 87 per cent of the working population who have jobs? Is there resentment at having to pay not only unemployment and social security benefits but also for all the expenses of government for which the unemployed are unable to make a tax contribution?

Precise analytical distinctions may not be very apparent in the vague and guilt-ridden public anxieties of the moment. But they have to be pressed all the same if we are not to be landed with 'cures' that may be worse than the disease itself.

The need emerges in relation to the doctrines of the neo-classical school of economists who often express ideas that political Thatcherites entertain but dare not utter. Their diagnosis amounts to saying that some, most or all of the unemployed are in that state because it does not pay them to take a job. The remedy is supposed to include reducing benefit levels or making benefits more strictly conditional on proven efforts to find a job.

The thesis that I want to advance is that the neo-classical school is at least partly right about diagnosis but wrong about remedies. No 'ought' proposition is implied by any statement of cause and effect, and one is free to accept part of the neo-classical diagnosis without in any way endorsing proposals to harass the unemployed or make life more difficult for them. Indeed, this will be one's position if one's concern is for the unemployed themselves rather than for the loss to the other 86 or 87 per cent or for the political embarrassment of the unemployment statistics.

But, before going any further, something must be said about the controversies between the Keynesian school, which blames unemployment on lack of demand, and the view of the British Chancellor, Nigel Lawson, and of some of the economists in international organizations, that unemployment results from workers being priced out of jobs.

In principle either or both factors can be at work. If there is a collapse in 'demand' – i.e. in total spending, or nominal GDP – one would expect a slump and a loss of jobs. The most dramatic example is the Great Depression of the 1930s, when the US national income fell by over one-third. Lesser but still severe instances occurred in the USA in the 1982 recession and in Britain in 1980–81, when there was a very sharp reduction in the *rate of growth* of nominal GDP. Again, after the 1986 Budget it became clear that nominal GDP growth was falling below the Treasury's own projections. It is important to correct such deficiencies before they get out of hand and to try to see that unavoidable periods of under-shooting are roughly balanced by periods of over-shooting and vice versa. The Chancellor has many times assured us that the Government's Medium-Term Financial Strategy is an assurance as much against deficient as against excessive demand, and this undertaking must be pressed on ministers. It. is not a sufficient excuse to say that a particular setback is part of a world slow-down.

Britain is part of the world and part of such inner directorates as the Group of Five and the Group of Seven, in which finance ministers of the main Western countries try to harmonize their policies. Contrary to some American statements, it is not necessary to override the domestic judgements of the West Germans and Japanese, for instance, on their own policies for nominal demand. All that is required is that they should have a policy and that abrupt stops and starts should be avoided.

In the longer term other countries can adjust, by means of modest terms-of-trade changes, to whatever rate of growth prevails in West Germany and Japan, which are too easily made scapegoats for domestic weaknesses in the English-speaking countries. In the shorter term Britain can do quite a lot to ride out worldwide fluctuations in demand and output by varying the mix between fiscal, monetary and exchange-rate policy. There was nothing inherently wrong with the successful American effort to emerge from the 1982 recession by means of a mixture of fiscal stimulus and fairly tight money. The trouble was that the fiscal boost was not a temporary measure, as it should have been, but the beginning of a growing secular budget deficit that continued to trouble both the USA and her trading partners for years afterwards.

But, as Professor James Meade never tires of emphasizing, maintaining an adequate growth of nominal demand is only half – and the less important half – of employment policy. Even if the Chancellor could keep demand on a pre-determined path, year in, year out, there could still be very heavy unemployment if too much of the demand growth were diverted into rising pay and prices and not enough into output and jobs. Despite occasional under- and over-shoots, the average rate of nominal demand growth since the trough of the 1980–81 recession would have been ample to convert the rise in unemployment into a decline if pay per head had not been rising by 7 to 8 per cent per annum most of the time, almost irrespective of the wider economic environment (see table 5). Pay increases are, indeed, likely to drop by a couple of percentage points as a result of the 1986 fall in the Retail Price Index triggered off outside the British economy by a fall in oil and commodity prices. But they will have to fall far farther than seems likely if enough new jobs are to be generated to make major inroads into unemployment and if inflation is to be consolidated at 3 per cent.

Table 5 Output–inflation split (% increase on previous year), 1981–90

	1981–82	1982–83	1983–84	1984–85*	1985–86*	1986–87†	1987–88†	1988–89†	1989–90†
Nominal GDP	10	9¼	7¾	8¼	8¼	6¾	6½	6	5½
GP deflator	10	7	4½	4¼	6	3¾	3¾	3½	3
Real GDP	0	2¼	3¼	4	2¼	3	2¾	2½	2½

Notes: * Adjusted for mineworkers' strike.   † Treasury projection.

Incidentally, I now think that those who revived the pricing-out-of-jobs theory (myself included) made a mistake in talking about 'real wages'. It is much better to ascribe unemployment to inappropriate rates of pay or labour costs without specifying whether these are real or nominal. The one good point that the opponents of the pricing-out theory make is that pay is settled in money terms and that real wages, in the relevant sense, depend on the profit margin superimposed. On the other hand, to insist on the rise of *money* incomes – as many Keynesians do – as the obstacle to high employment without runaway inflation is to suggest an unlikely sort of illusion: that wage bargainers are more interested in paper symbols than in what wage packets are worth. In a money economy pay awards are normally in money terms, which does not mean that people are indifferent to their real value or will fail to react if their expectations are disappointed. Occam's Razor suggests that we focus on the movement of pay or labour costs *per se* without prejudging too many issues by inserting the adjectives 'money' or 'real'.

Numerous econometric studies are available: I am going to cite one, which seems to give broadly sensible results – 'Wage Inflexibility in Britain' by A. Curruth and A. Oswald. The results are the following.

First, the responsiveness ('elasticity') of real wages to unemployment increases with the unemployment rate, but it is still low (0.11) even at current rates. Second, internal pressures on a firm's pay – for example, from a profits or liquidity crisis – can break through wage rigidity and even bring about nominal wage cuts, but extreme pressures are required. Third, the recession and shake-out of 1980–82 were a big enough shock to lead to small cuts in *real* wages – via nominal pay rises slightly behind the 'cost of living'. There was a similar occurrence during the pay policies of the mid-1970s. But as soon as output and profits began to recover, real pay started rising again, even though unemployment was still increasing.

Why did pay per head continue to rise by 7 per cent when inflation fluctuated around 4 or 5 per cent or less and registered adult unemployment was well over 3 million, or nearly 14 per cent, and continuing to rise after the big upsurge of 1980–81 by 0.5 per cent per annum?

The traditional answer has been union monopoly power or some euphemism that means the same thing. It is not a sufficient rebuttal to say that workers priced out of work by union power can find jobs in the non-unionized sector, which now accounts for about 50 per cent of employees in employment. The public services, which provide a quarter of all employment, are almost 100 per cent unionized. Manufacturing, which accounts for another quarter or fifth and in which the big job losses have occurred, is still highly unionized. Men, whose employment prospects have suffered in relation to women's, are also more heavily unionized. If men priced out of work in the union sector were to price themselves into work outside that sector, many would have to crowd into relatively limited and unfamiliar occupations, where wages might have to fall to subsistence-level or lower.

If I ascribe somewhat less blame to union pressure for our stagflation problems than I used to, it is not because of any of the formal arguments but because of the very strong impression that it is employers rather than unions who have been making the running in pay awards in recent years. We have to tread carefully here. The much publicized weakening of union power since the advent of the Thatcher Government in 1979 has been connected not only with new legislation but also with a bigger rise in unemployment than anything seen even in the inter-war period. We have yet to see how subdued union power would remain if unemployment improved or if there were a Labour Government. Moreover, some actions that are apparently employer-determined – such as the pursuit of a highly paid but small labour force – may reflect residual fear of unions or the decision to pre-empt their reappearance. The most ironical possibility of all is that employers offer high wage increases to 'weaken unions', thereby simulating the monopolistic wage settlements that are among the objectionable features of union power in the first place.

There is, of course, an obvious, if superficial, reason why pay has remained so impervious to both low inflation and high and rising unemployment. The simple clue is the behaviour of profits. Even excluding North Sea oil, they rose by an average of 18 per cent per annum between 1980 and 1985 and by 11 per cent after allowing for inflation. The total cumulative real rise over those five years was well over 80 per cent and should reach 100 per cent some time in 1987. Non-North Sea oil profits (excluding stock appreciation) reached 13.3 per cent of GDP in 1985. This is not far off the 14.5 per cent achieved in the 1960s. By contrast, profits were down to 9 per cent of GDP in 1980 – a proportion very similar to the low point of 1975. Profits have recovered from their deep depression and are now as high as a proportion of national income, and almost as high as a return on capital, as during the Golden Age of the 1950s and 1960s.

With profits rising twice as fast as pay, it would have been quite surprising to see downward pressure on pay settlements. Despite warnings about falling international competitiveness, employers en masse found for a long time that 7 per cent pay increases were consistent with rising profits and rising output. These facts suggest that ministerial exhortations to pay less ran up against the fact that employers were well able to afford the pay increases they offered.

Company heads are clearly maximizing their own personal utility by their pay behaviour, and included in their utility is not only corporate profitability and executive remuneration but also such gains as a quiet life, the ability to upgrade the labour force without having to introduce embarrassing pay differentials for workers whose aptitudes and attitudes differ and to build up a loyal labour force with firm-specific skills. Ministerial exhortation is, in effect, pressing these company chiefs to concentrate not on maximizing their own personal utility but, more simplemindedly, on maximizing profits at a time when profits have done quite well in any case. It is a reasonable presumption that, if companies are paying more than the market rate for workers, they could increase profits still further by paying lower wages and taking on more workers. But there is no suggestion that the gain would be very great, especially if their competitors were doing the same thing. A company that has already seen a real 80 per cent increase in profits might have a prospect of gaining another 10 or 20 per cent if it pursued more ruthlessly competitive pay policies; these increases would not be without strife nor risks. Ministers are, in fact, asking companies to be more selfish than they actually are – for the sake of the general good. This paradox – that altruists should behave as if they were selfish to give effect to their altruism – is inherent in the political economy of Adam Smith but has hardly ever been properly expounded.

The advice would be fully valid, though paradoxical, if there were consensus on who ought to own the profits that would be increased by the recommended behaviour. If the mass of workers take a pay cut for the sake of the unemployed, there would indeed be a shift in the distribution of the national income to the unemployed, but there would be an additional shift from the bottom and middle ranks of the already employed to the upper ranks that have disproportionately large holdings in corporate ownership, whether directly as shareholders or indirectly through pension funds.

This does not mean that ministers should cease striving for pay settlements that are lower on average and reflect more closely the varying balances of supply and demand in different parts of the labour market. Indeed, I shall suggest below that exhortation needs to be supported by more definite incentives and deterrents. The point here is that a policy for market-related pay needs to be backed by a policy for capital ownership.

Governments of every political colour face many obstacles in both halves of the needed strategy: the spreading of capital ownership and pay settlements that promote employment. Beliefs and attitudes are important in accounting for economic behaviour. Traditional opposition to large differentials between young and mature workers or between high- and low-unemployment regions are real barriers to the reduction of unemployment, as is the popular hostility to 'under-cutting' and the belief that the high-wage employer is a good one and the low-wage employer a bad one, irrespective of employment effects. These beliefs are not simply high-minded mistakes. They reflect the self-interest of the majority of workers already employed vis-à-vis both employers and fellow workers without a job.

We are moving towards a dual economy of insiders with well-paid, secure jobs and outsiders who drift between ill-paid labour and the dole. The insiders will not lightly surrender their privileges. Nevertheless, if some of the outsiders could take jobs at pay that is superior to what they can gain on the dole or in the casual economy but inferior to the pay of the established insiders, they would gain and the insiders need not lose. (This would be called, in the jargon, a Pareto improvement.)

The British insistence on the 'rate for the job' makes a two-tier wage system difficult to establish formally. But the trend towards cheaper contract labour is an informal move in that direction. Professor Meade's proposed 'labour–capital partnerships' are intended to combine the benefits of employee ownership and participation with a job-creating effect by allowing new workers to be hired on terms initially inferior to existing partners. The Weitzman scheme for profit-related pay, which has attracted the Chancellor, in the last analysis works at the level of the individual firm by inducing insiders to sacrifice pay for the sake of outsiders who are hired. This is true whatever else the ultimate economy-wide consequences of a massive adoption of this type of profit-sharing.

Weitzman's critics are right to emphasize that existing workers will seek to influence hire-and-fire decisions to prevent this from happening. But rather than either throw up our hands in despair or fight a losing battle for managerial dictatorship, it should surely be possible for new recruits *not* to receive the profit-related element in their pay until they have gone through an agreed procedure lasting perhaps a few years. Indeed, the Government's Green Paper on Profit-related Pay specifically permits such two-tier structures for tax-incentive purposes. The best hope for tackling stagflation lies in a change in the labour market that would make a *substantial* proportion of pay profit-related, as Weitzman explains in this volume. Unfortunately, the Green Paper's proposed modest incentives would work far too slowly, and many companies would probably get stuck with a profit-related element that was far too small in relation to basic pay.

As the Government's discussions with employers have shown, something more drastic than a modest incentive for an optional scheme is required if complacent employers are to be impelled into courses of action that take into account those outsiders, without a job or on the fringes of the labour market, who are the real victims of current pay bargaining. Here lies the attraction of Gavyn Davies's scheme for combining profit-related pay with the old idea of a tax on pay increases. The core idea is to impose a severe – say, 100 per cent – tax on pay increases above a 2 per cent norm, to be paid by employers with more than 100 workers. The one and only 'gateway' by which a firm could escape would be if it registered a profit-sharing scheme and pay rose in proportion to profits.

The profit-sharing gateway is no mere cosmetic. Both traditional incomes policies and, to a lesser extent, the Layard tax (see pp. 76–8) penalize profitable and expanding firms. Such firms could, under the Davies scheme, pay what they needed to attract employees, provided their pay increases represented increased profits per employee. A weak objection is that the pay surcharge would be passed on in prices. But is complete passing on of a 100 per cent impost likely when there is firm control of monetary demand?

I doubt whether a 100 per cent tax on pay increases, if introduced next year, would still be there in the year 2000. But if the plan lasted even a few years, it would, as Davies says, virtually guarantee a major shift to profit-related pay, which would become the main force for pay flexibility. My own prediction is that an inferior version of the Davies plan will be produced later, in response to a run on sterling, which the financial establishment always takes more seriously than mere unemployment. But how much better it would be to start now, when 'there is little need to ratchet inflation downwards, but only to force pay deals to catch up with the reality of reduced inflation,' as Davies puts it.

Mechanistic schemes of the kind outlined may be essential emergency treatment. They are no substitute, however, for deeper probing of the situation that has made them necessary. For the actual evolution of pay remains puzzling. The persistence of high settlements is unlikely to be due just to misguided moralism. If it were, there would by now be more cracks in the wage façade. Some employers would have risked opposition to taking on larger, low-paid staffs, or overseas-owned firms would have taken the plunge, or the unemployed would have priced themselves into jobs by setting up co-operatives or making use of the many sources of funds now available for new small businesses. At the end of the day one should try to take seriously the view of many employers that they *have* to pay current wage increases to retain a properly motivated labour force. If asked why they do not recruit any of the unemployed, the answer is rarely clear-cut, but it amounts to saying that the unemployed either do not have the right skills or attitudes or live in the wrong parts of the country.

There is much circumstantial evidence pointing in this direction. Vacancies are now well above the recession low and much higher than in some years in the 1970s, when male unemployment was less than a third of its present level. Reported skill shortages also correspond with those experienced ten years ago, when unemployment was much lower. The entire additional rise in unemployment since 1981 has been among those without a job for over a year. The number of short-term jobless has actually fallen slightly. There has also been a broader spread of pre-tax *earnings*, with the top 10 per cent of wage earners rising in relation to the norm and the bottom 10 per cent falling. Meanwhile the share of wages in the national income has more than lost the sharp rise of the mid-1970s. Labour productivity has returned to the growth rates of the 1960s, while 'total factor productivity', which includes the contribution of capital, has fallen. But despite the drop in union membership and restrictive legislation, the estimated mark-up of union wages over non-union ones remains several percentage points higher than in the 1970s.

This all adds up to a highly segmented labour market, with a large minority of workers demoralized by long-term unemployment or otherwise lacking in the skills, attitudes or geographical locations that are attractive to business. These distinctions help to rationalize the attitude of employers who side with their existing, 'inside', labour forces, which prefer high pay to taking on 'outsiders'. We are left with a large hard core of the unemployed, who can be broken up schematically into those whose earning power ('marginal product' in economic jargon) is so low that it does not pay them to move from social security to a job, and those who cannot afford to move to the prosperous parts of the country because of housing costs.

The existence of the first category is often denied by academic studies, which show that few of the unemployed are, in the statistics, better off on the dole. Statistics are usually stated in terms of 'replacement ratios' (that is, net income on social security divided by income in employment). According to the Institute of Fiscal Studies, less than 4 per cent of all households and 8 per cent of households with two children have replacement ratios of 90 per cent or more. The average ratios are over 60 per cent and nearly 70 per cent for families with two children. But these comparisons are inconclusive. Even if net income on social security is only 60 to 70 per cent of net income at work, it does not take much – by way of earnings on the side, or do-it-yourself activities, or lost leisure and dislike of regimental working hours – to eliminate the gain from taking a formal job.

The second category of workers deterred from seeking new jobs by the cost of new housing is less controversial. Average male earnings in the first half of 1986 were running at just above £210 per week. After tax, National Insurance and child benefit a man with two children would have taken home a net £165 per week. On such earnings a typical wage-earner looking for a house in the south-east of England would have had to finance the purchase of a house costing, on average, over £44,500. The typical mortgage on such a house was £29,400. Mortgage payments on a loan of this size would have come to a little over £56 per week net after tax relief. If a wage-earner needed a 90 per cent mortgage he would have to pay over £75 per week – or getting on for half his net earnings.

Mortgage interest relief seems to ease the problem but ultimately aggravates it by driving up land, housing and interest costs. In addition, the cowardice of the Cabinet, in rejecting even the gradual decontrol of new lettings, makes the renting option extremely difficult. The most promising way round the housing problem at present seems the 'house-price-linked mortgage'. Under such mortgages the buyer pays much less annually in return for sharing with the lenders the capital appreciation on the property. In contrast to earlier low-start mortgage schemes, under which borrowers were deterred by the rising payments profile, house-linked mortgages have proved popular. The bottleneck at present is that the institutions that ultimately provide the finance are hesitant, not because of the risk – the mortgages are insured – but because they are not easy to classify according to conventional categories.

The least that corporate executives who beat their breasts about unemployment could do is to lean on their pension-fund managers to favour house-price-linked mortgages. Yet it would be naïve to suppose that simple reforms would solve all the problems. Property and land have always been expensive in capital cities, from Imperial Rome onwards. High real-estate values are providing signals that low-value-per-acre activities are uneconomic in the nation's economic centres. A sufficient cut in the dole, or a more stringent enforcement of the work-search condition would undoubtedly force many people to find – or create for themselves – more low-paid jobs, of which the extreme example is selling matches at street corners. Thus the pressures would increase on citizens who already face much less attractive conditions than their fellows. Whomever else such policies helped, it would not be the unemployed.

But, having rejected policies for starving the unemployed back to work, it would still be desirable for people on the dole to be able to earn something extra in a legal way without losing their social security entitlements, both to top up their own incomes and to contribute to the tax base. Entitlement to social security for non-retired adults is largely conditional on specific misfortunes, such as unemployment. This system has difficulties in coping with people who are occasional, casual or part-time workers or who have very low earnings.

It is possible to move away from status-related benefits in two opposite ways, either of which may be an improvement. The first is to move to income-related benefits. The model for this is the Family Income Supplement (FIS), to be transformed into the Family Credit, which, it is hoped, will have a much higher take-up. A further step along this route would be to make the benefit available to all households, with or without children, whose incomes fall below the basic minimum. Above that minimum the payment would taper off.

The second alternative would be a social dividend for all households, irrespective of earnings and with no taper. The model for this also exists already in child benefits, which are universal, not means-tested and not clawed back. The social dividend would be paid as of right. It would enable people who are content to live at a conventional subsistence scale to do so – on the grounds that a rich society can afford to have some people 'opting out'. Any work done to supplement this minimum would attract tax at the normal rate; thus there would be no unemployment or poverty trap. The big disadvantage of a social dividend is that it would be extremely expensive. If it were fixed at current supplementary benefit level, it might mean a basic-rate income tax of 50 or 60 per cent (and a still higher tax take if indirect taxes were included). The advantage of selectivity and means testing is that they concentrate help where it is most needed and can therefore be more generous while being less expensive. Their disadvantages include the inevitable probing into household affairs, the problem of uptake and the inevitability of high implicit marginal tax rates as benefit is taken off. This is the source of the unemployment and poverty traps. The advocates of integrating tax and social security into a negative income tax do not always realize that this is in itself only a desirable administrative simplification. The designers of the integrated system will still have to choose between alternative principles in drawing up the scales of net payments.

Although the social dividend is utopian at present, it need not remain so. But if there is anything in the dream (or nightmare) of a world with a few microchips or robots to do all our work, then by definition the earnings of capital will one day be sufficient to provide incomes for all, even if labour earnings are low. The social dividend could be paid through the social security system as a negative income tax. Alternatively, a similar result could be achieved by much more widespread citizen ownership of an equity stake in the nation's capital assets, achieved through the redistribution of shareholdings. A drawback of the share ownership route is that, as some citizens will dissipate their capital, it will be less effective in relieving poverty, and it will probably require a fresh redistribution of holdings as wealth is passed on from one generation to the next.

Nevertheless, citizen shares are more clearly property rights and less liable to every gust of the political wind than are social security payments. The link with return from capital is much clearer, and if it were successfully achieved, there would be no further grounds for being opposed to profits or worrying about an increase in their share of the national income. Moreover, a start could be made on a small scale (for example, by the free distribution of privatization shares). A tiny beginning has been made in the case of gas, since a small number of free shares has been made available to workers in the industry. The citizen-ownership principle requires that they be distributed to all adults – or at least allocated on some universal principle (for instance, to the retired or to young people coming of age).

Eventually, citizen ownership would require the 'watering' of existing equity holdings. From the beginning, ordinary citizens would have the advantage of a modest investment income, hitherto confined to a small minority. Eventually, these holdings could be enough to give all households a choice between living on rentier income or topping up that income with earnings from work. The benefits of a 'modest competence' were enjoyed by the members of the propertied classes of the eighteenth and nineteenth centuries, such as those who figured in Jane Austen's novels. The only thing wrong is that they were available to so few. A modest competence available to all could be regarded as the culmination of popular capitalism and libertarian socialism alike.

These matters are not a digression from the issue of unemployment but central to the problem. Classical economists who rightly argue for market rewards usually fail to face the problems of those whose work has a low market value. Popular capital ownership might enable us to bypass the whole problem of 'scroungers' by allowing those who want to do so to embrace that status without opprobrium.

Profit-sharing and the Two Sides to Unemployment
by Martin Weitzman

The biggest issue in the future of employment is making sure that employment *has* a future. Right now many 'European-style' economies seem unable to reconcile reasonably full employment with reasonable price stability. Expansionary policies dissipate themselves, to an excessive degree, in too large wage and price increases rather than in expanded employment and output.

One school of thought blames the adverse situation on a high 'natural rate of unemployment'. For reasons no one has been able to make terribly clear, the 'non-accelerating inflation rate of unemployment' has apparently deteriorated. In practice this explanation amounts to saying that the unemployment rate is high because the unemployment rate is high.

Another non-starter is the *au courant* explanation that European-style unemployment is of the classical rather than the Keynesian variety and is caused by 'too high' *real* wages. The problem with this line is that real wages no more 'cause'

employment levels than the other way round. Both are simultaneously determined within the economic system. Given money wages and aggregate demand,
companies *choose* employment levels and prices. Hence, the *real* wage (money
wage divided by the price level) is no less determined by the decisions of firms
than is employment.

What, then, is causing unemployment? There is only one answer. But, like a
coin, the answer has two sides. Side one is that unemployment is caused by
insufficient aggregate demand (relative to money wages). Side two is that
unemployment is caused by too high money wages (relative to aggregate
demand). Sometimes it is useful to stress one side of the coin, sometimes the
other, but it is always the same coin.

In either case, the key to non-inflationary full employment is an economic
expansion that holds down the marginal cost to a firm of acquiring more labour.
Pure macro-economic policy alone – the purposeful manipulation of financial
aggregates – is no longer sufficient to guarantee full employment without
inflation because labour costs begin to rise well before the economy starts to
strain at full capacity. Where, then, do we go from here?

Economic policy should focus more directly on the labour market itself to build
in automatic flexibility and to reform structural rigidities so that we do not have
to rely so exclusively on macro-economic sledge-hammer 'cures' to maintain
non-inflationary full employment. What is required is bold institutional change
in incentive structures to make it in the employers' interest automatically to
maintain high levels of output and to keep prices low. There are many
possibilities here – including two-tiered wage systems, tax-based incomes policies, employee ownership, profit-sharing and several others. I am in favour of
maintaining a positive attitude towards all these measures. But, as an economist,
I must say that profit-sharing is the most solidly based of the alternatives and, I
believe, holds by far the most promise.

A profit-sharing system, under which some part of a worker's pay is tied to the
firm's profitability per employee, puts in place exactly the right incentive to resist
unemployment and inflation. If workers were to allow their pay to be more
flexible by sharing profits with their company, that would improve macro-
economic performance by directly attacking the economy's central structural
rigidity. The superiority of a profit-sharing system is that it has enough built-in
flexibility to maintain full employment even when the economy is out of
balance. If workers' compensation were shifted to a lower component of base
wages and a higher component of profit-sharing, then the average cost (or pay) of
an employee could stay the same, while the employer's marginal cost of hiring
another worker would be lower. Because of the automatic profit-sharing cushion,
employers are slower to lay off workers during a recession and quicker to hire
more of them when conditions are good. And, as a very important side benefit,
profit-sharing workers have a direct incentive to co-operate in increasing the
productivity and profitability of their firm because part of their salary depends on
it. A profit-sharing system is not anti-labour and does not rely for its beneficial

effects on lower workers' pay. The key thing is not to get real pay down – it could even go up within reason – but to lower the base wage or marginal cost component while raising the profit-sharing component accordingly.

In a profit-sharing economy firms acting in their own self-interest will tend automatically to create a tight labour market, high output and low prices. This will not happen overnight. But if the incremental, hardly noticed decision at the margin has more of a bias under profit-sharing to lean towards letting go of fewer workers during bad times and taking on more of them during good times, then gradually the system will steer itself towards an ever-tighter labour market. And standard macro-economic policy is much more effective in an environment of widespread profit-sharing because it is essentially the base wage, not total pay, that, in conjunction with the usual macro-economic policy variables, determines the critical characteristics of the system, such as unemployment and the price level.

Any economy is full of uncertainty. There are no absolute guarantees in this world, and if the uncertainty does not come out in one place, it will show up in another. It is much better, much healthier, if everyone shares just a little bit of that uncertainty right at the beginning rather than letting it all fall on an unfortunate minority of unemployed workers who are drafted to serve as unpaid soldiers in the war against inflation. It is much better if people agree that only 80 per cent of their pay is going to be tied directly to the funny-looking green pieces of paper – which are themselves an illusion, although a very useful one – and 20 per cent will be tied to company profits per employee. Then the economy can be much more easily controlled to sustain full employment *and* stable prices.

So I see a future of employment that is very much contingent upon labour and management taking on new roles and attitudes. European-style economies can break out of the stagflation trap, but only if workers care more about increasing productivity while managers care more about increasing employment. The key change is to alter the incentive structure by tying a significant fraction of each worker's pay (about 20 per cent) to profitability per employee. It is best to be under no illusions about the political realities involved here. Strong doses of moral suasion and significant tax concessions will be required to convince workers to participate in a profit-sharing system with no restrictions on new hires.

When all is said and done, no matter how well designed are the incentives, such change will require genuine consensus, cutting across left–right political lines, that the broad social gains of permanent full employment without inflation are worth more than the narrow private losses that will inevitably be incurred here and there. Yet the benefits are so enormous, the potential for increased national income so great, that my recommendation would be to move decisively in the direction of profit-sharing. If these ideas are wrong, little will have been lost by trying them out. And if the ideas are correct, a serious move towards widespread profit-sharing would help greatly to make involuntary unemployment an obsolete concept. That is the 'future of employment' I would like to see.

No Excuse for Timid Inertia *by Richard Layard*

Unemployment in Britain is now as high as it was in the early 1930s. Yet for years wage inflation has obstinately refused to fall. This is the central dilemma of our time. It means that, to reduce unemployment, we cannot simply stimulate demand. We must at the same time improve our ability to supply the extra output without more inflation. This means reducing the 'non-accelerating inflation rate of unemployment' (NAIRU). So we must first understand why this has risen.

Some take the view that our labour market has just become more and more rigid through employment protection laws, union power and unemployment benefits. But rigidities have not exactly increased since Mrs Thatcher came to power. Yet unemployment has trebled since then. So unemployment cannot have risen because the labour market has become more rigid. The truth is that we already had a rigid labour market in 1979 and then subjected it to a massive demand shock. The share of taxes in GNP rose by over four points (between then and now) and the exchange rate became greatly overvalued. The economy was not able to absorb these shocks, and unemployment soared.

To understand why it has not bounced back, we have to look at the form that the extra unemployment took. The number of people who are unemployed equals the number of people who become unemployed each month (the inflow) times the number of months for which on average they remain unemployed (the duration). In 1986 roughly 375,000 people became unemployed each month and they remained unemployed on average for nine months – hence total unemployment was 3.25 million. The figures for 1979 and 1986 are shown in table 6. So roughly the whole increase in unemployment has been in the form of longer duration. No extra people have become unemployed. This helps to explain why unemployment has not become a bigger political issue: the same number are unfortunate, but they are just more so. It also helps to explain why wage inflation is not falling despite the huge level of unemployment. For, as Stephen Nickell and I have found in a series of studies of UK unemployment published by the London School of Economics's Centre for Labour Economics, the long-term unemployed exert no downward pressure on wages.

A rival view is that inflation has stopped falling simply because unemployment has stopped rising. On this view (favoured by Blanchard and Summers of MIT) there is no NAIRU, and only *changes* in unemployment affect inflation. Blanchard and Summers believe that when unemployment rises, this dampens wage pressure. But once unemployment settles down at its new higher level, the

Table 6 Unemployment figures, 1979 and 1986

	1979	1986
Inflow per month	375,000	375,000
Duration	3.3 months	8.8 months
Unemployed	1,250,000	3,300,000

unions lose interest in those who have lost their jobs and press on wages as much as they ever did before.

It is important to sort out which of these accounts is right. For, if there is no NAIRU, we can, in principle, get unemployment down to whatever level we want and have stable inflation from then on. (Inflation will rise in the meantime while we reduce unemployment.) Nickell and I question this account, for one simple reason. The union-based story fails to explain why there are now as many vacancies (properly measured) as there were in the late 1970s, yet unemployment has trebled. According to the union-based story, once employment has been lost, unions do nothing to encourage the creation of new vacancies, so vacancies should stay permanently down. According to our story, vacancies can rise again after a downturn, without a fall in unemployment, precisely because the long-term unemployed have given up looking for work and employers do not want to hire them.

If this is so, it will be very difficult to reduce unemployment without a wage explosion unless a major part of the extra demand for labour is directed at the long-term unemployed. This is why the report of the all-party House of Commons Employment Committee is so important. They recommend that within three years there should be a guaranteed offer of a one-year job for all the long-term unemployed (those out of work for over a year). Their programme would provide something like 750,000 extra jobs. Many people naturally jib at such special measures as a way of getting the economy moving. But unprecedented situations (with over 40 per cent long-term unemployed) call for unprecedented solutions.

Are there any other labour-market measures that would help us to expand employment without running into wage pressure? Two stand out. First, we should cut the tax on labour (employers' National Insurance contributions) for those types of labour that are in excess supply. This means the semi- and unskilled, who represent nearly half the unemployed and whose employment rate is four times that of non-manual workers. We know that these people are in genuine excess supply and not just lazy because only 2 per cent of firms say they are short of such people, compared with over 10 per cent who are short of skilled labour. So if we increased demand for the low-skilled, we should not create any serious wage pressure. To do so we should cut National Insurance contributions drastically for lower-paid workers.

But all this will not reduce unemployment enough. To get unemployment down to roughly the level of the late 1970s we shall have to have an incomes policy. The French experience since 1982 has shown how successful incomes policy can be (inflation fell from 15 per cent to 3 per cent). However, since there is a NAIRU, one needs a permanent incomes policy to induce a permanent fall in the NAIRU. The only plausible incomes policy that could be permanent is one based on tax penalties. The merits of profit-sharing as an alternative remain much more intangible and unclear.

So much for supply-side measures to improve the working of the labour market. There is also the danger that shortages of capital might generate inflationary pressure bearing directly on prices.

Meantime our private non-residential investment is forecast by the OECD to grow by only 2.5 per cent in 1987. This means that we should not attempt a consumption-led recovery generated by cuts in personal taxes. Instead we should supplement labour-market measures by a time-limited investment tax credit offering accelerated depreciation to all investment undertaken in the next few years. It is a fallacy that cheap capital is bad for employment. New capital is good for employment.

When unemployment is as high as it is now, we must for a few years contemplate growth rates of the order of 4.5 per cent per annum, such as we had from 1933 to 1937. This will require a temporary expansion of the budget deficit of the order of £8 billion. When our debt/income ratio is otherwise set to fall, this is quite acceptable. US experience has shown the power of a fiscal deficit to create jobs, just as European experience has shown the power of a fiscal contraction to destroy them. When we are surrounded by so much human misery and have available responsible programmes for non-inflationary growth there is no excuse for timid inertia.

If not Now, When? *by George L. Perry*

Major countries in Europe are suffering from a bad case of social myopia. They seem to have mislaid the idea that the prosperity of all is a concern of government. Overall, unemployment in Europe has been rising for a decade. Furthermore, labour markets are becoming increasingly polarized as long-term and youth unemployment become steadily greater and more entrenched. During the first five years of this decade youth unemployment rates rose by 50 per cent in the UK and 67 per cent in France; they more than doubled in West Germany. Governments continue to rationalize high unemployment as somehow inevitable and specifically rule out as unacceptable steps to stimulate demand as a way to reduce it.

One argument in support of this stance is that the unemployment is structural, reflecting problems from the supply side. It is alleged that the work experience and skills of the unemployed would not match the requirements of new jobs that a demand expansion would bring and that growth in industrial capacity has not kept pace with growth in the labour force, so that capital would become a bottleneck to expansion before unemployment could be reduced very much. It is safe to say that today's unemployment rates could not quickly be brought down to the rates of the late 1970s because of such structural problems. But that is to miss the crucial point that the building of both physical and human capital are endogenous to the performance of the economy. Starting with today's high unemployment, demand would create its own supply. Fixed investment, relevant work experience and an adaptation of jobs to workers would all flow from a demand-led reduction in unemployment.

The idea that European unemployment is 'classical', resulting from excessive real wages – or, equivalently, an excessive labour share – has been another argument offered against demand stimulus. This idea, which implies that firms would be unwilling to expand their sales at existing prices, never had robust support from theory or the data, but even if it had some role to play in explaining the unemployment of the late 1970s, labour shares have declined since then, making it implausible as an explanation of today's much higher unemployment rates.

The most paralysing line of thought comes from the idea that policy cannot change without losing its credibility as an inflation fighter. According to this idea, a steady anti-inflation policy is expected not only to stop inflation but also to restore high employment. However, the record supports only the first expectation, and that only partly. Real activity does not gravitate towards higher levels without a proper setting of the policy dials. In the USA highly restrictive monetary policies reduced inflation and created a deep recession. Unemployment started to decline only after the fiscal–monetary combination turned expansionary during 1982. Most of Europe introduced deflationary demand policies even before the USA did, and inflation there dropped sharply as well. But (unlike in the United States) these policies have not been geared towards expansion, and unemployment has continued to rise.

In recent years the economies of Europe and Japan have piggy-backed on the strong US fiscal policy that provided them with rising export demand. But that is over. Now that US fiscal policy is turning the other way and the dollar has declined sharply, the need for more expansionary policies in Europe is growing more urgent. European economies will have to expand domestic demand just to maintain their growth rates of recent years. To grow faster in order to reduce unemployment, they will have to stimulate domestic demand even more.

Between 1982 and 1985 the US current-account deficit grew by $120 billion. This was offset by shifts toward surplus of about $40 billion each in Japan, Europe and non-oil less developed countries (LDCs). In coming years US policy will aim to eliminate, or at least sharply to reduce, the US current-account deficit. The offset will have to come from falling trade surpluses in Europe and Japan. And to keep those declining trade surpluses from raising unemployment further, domestic policies will have to become more expansionary.

An examination of the US budget leads to the same conclusion. After rising by 3 per cent of Gross National Product (GNP) in the past few years, the US structural deficit is scheduled to move towards surplus by a similar amount over the next three years. The first big step came in the autumn of 1986, when the structural deficit for fiscal 1987 was expected to decline by $50 billion to $70 billion. To avoid a sharp contraction in worldwide fiscal stimulus, Europe will have to move to more expansionary budget policies. Lower real interest rates worldwide would provide another offset to the tightening US budget and are sorely needed to help LDCs service their debts. To be at all safe, the world economy needs both fiscal stimulus outside the USA and lower interest rates all around.

None of this denies that the odds of a gradual rise in inflation will be lower if demand management remains restrictive and unemployment stays high (or even rises) than if stronger expansions now reduce unemployment. The prolonged period of rising unemployment in Europe has reduced inflation and subdued the politically powerful unions that contributed to the wage–price spiral of the 1970s. But this attack on wage demands through high unemployment reached severely diminishing returns some time ago.

The credibility of the fight against inflation has surely been well-established, and the plateau of wage increases on which some countries now find themselves must be regarded as quite insensitive to maintained policies that produce sluggish growth and rising unemployment. Perhaps a dip into depression would discipline wage-setting again. More optimistically, the present plateau of wage increases is also well-established and is unlikely to be much affected by faster growth.

To the extent that Europe does face some inflation–unemployment trade-off, there is no reason to believe that demands originating from sources other than policy change – if that is what policy-makers are waiting for – would have any especially favourable effects. Whatever special benefits there are to credibility come from the experienced outcomes in markets and on order books, not from the setting of the policy dials that produced those outcomes.

It was peculiar that Europe's policy-makers should reject the pursuit of stronger demands that would have followed from more expansionary budgets or lower interest rates, while welcoming the boost to demand that came from currency declines vis-à-vis the dollar in 1982–5. If anything, stronger demand from a weakening currency automatically brought with it special inflationary pressures. The only way to make sense of favouring demand from depreciation but not from policy stimulus is that, if anything goes wrong, Governments and central bankers could point out that at least they had not misbehaved.

There may never be a time when more prosperity does not entail the risk of more inflation. But the present is certainly a time when, for Europe, those risks are modest and the costs of not taking them are considerable. With an enormous pool of unemployed, pressures from tight markets are minimal or non-existent; with currencies now appreciating and oil prices sinking, the downward pressure from foreign prices will help to moderate the overall price level.

A long post-war cycle in economic performance and policy concerns has come full circle. During the first twenty-five post-war years Governments emphasized stimulating investment and real growth and minimizing wasteful unemployment. The extremely low unemployment rates achieved in that era brought with them deep-seated inflation. As the oil-price explosions of the 1970s added to the home-grown inflation, the policy emphasis in most countries shifted to restraint and tolerance of high unemployment as a necessary cost of bringing inflation under control.

Appropriate as that change in emphasis was, it is now time to redirect demand management in Europe towards more expansion and lower unemployment. The lesson of the post-war period is neither that demand management caused inflation nor that real activity and unemployment will adjust to optimal levels whatever the setting of the demand dials. Rather it is that demand can be too strong as well as too weak and that the inflation risk must be taken seriously because it is so hard to eliminate once it is deeply entrenched.

Today the demand balance is too weak, and it will become significantly weaker as the US budget deficit is reduced. The battle against excessive union demands may re-emerge some day, and policy should continue trying to diagnose and remedy structural problems. But none of this is a reason for not stimulating domestic demand in Europe today. If not now, when?

4. THE MARCH OF THE MACHINE

'During the short time I recently passed in Nottinghamshire not twelve hours elapsed without some fresh act of violence . . . I was informed that forty Frames had been broken the preceding evening . . . these machines superseded the necessity of employing a number of workmen, who were left in consequence to starve. The rejected workmen in the blindness of their ignorance instead of rejoicing at these improvements in art so beneficial to mankind conceived themselves to be sacrificed to improvements in mechanism.' With these words Lord Byron, in his maiden speech to the House of Lords in February 1812, sought to explain the renewal of Luddite protest that was shaking the English social order. And in doing so he explained the crucial paradox of technological advance.

The introduction of new technology leads to improvements in productivity that are the dynamo for a rising standard of living. Simply, the same amount of output, whether it be knitting or compact discs, can be produced with fewer inputs: as a society we get the same output of goods and service for less effort. But one of the keys to productivity growth is that people are often replaced by machines. Thirty years ago it took several thousands of switchboard operators to handle 1 million long-distance telephone calls. Now, with electronic switchboards, it takes just a few dozen.

Technological change disrupts the established pattern of economic life and, in the process, people suffer. In Byron's time it was textile workers who were replaced by frames; today it is paint-sprayers and secretaries who are displaced by robots and word-processors. Workers displaced by technology today may not starve, as they did in Byron's time, but will the economy be able to provide them with new jobs?

In the 1950s and 1960s technological advance was hardly an economic issue. Low unemployment, accommodatory macro-economic policy and a steady rate of technical change seemed locked together in a virtuous circle of growth. In the 1980s the situation has dramatically reversed. Workers displaced by new technology will join an already large pool of unemployment in the OECD. Constraints on macro-economic policy, whether real or imaginary, are likely to remain in place. On top of this a revolutionary set of micro-electronics technologies, spanning the range from the word-processor to computer-integrated manufacturing, with great labour-saving potential, are seeping through industry.

'Our products are now getting into the heart of other sectors of industry, raising productivity, cutting labour costs but also stimulating innovation and new products,' says IBM UK's technical director, Dr Geoff Robinson.

The greatest economy-wide effects of information technology (IT) on employment, skill requirements and product markets are yet to come. But it is accepted by both academics and industry specialists that IT will transform established products and processes and will create new firms and industries. 'Just as the 1930s are now seen as an important period in which the industrialized world adjusted from the coal-based technologies of the nineteenth century to the new technologies based on oil and electricity, so the 1980s are increasingly viewed as a period in which the world economies are adjusting to the new technologies of the end of the century,' says Margaret Sharpe, editor of *Europe and the New Technologies*.

The widespread impact of micro-electronics is confirmed by the *FT* jobs poll, which found that since 1980 61 per cent of firms have introduced new technology that has affected their employment outlook. (The range was from a high of 72 per cent in the UK and 64 per cent in West Germany to a low of 50 per cent in France.) In the years to 1990, 45 per cent of firms plan to introduce new technology. Sixty-eight per cent of Japanese employers said that they were planning to introduce micro-electronics into their plants, 59 per cent in Britain and just 16 per cent in the USA. New technology will be less important in shaping new patterns of work than moves to increase the efficiency of existing equipment, however. Fifty-one per cent of employers said that they had plans to use existing capital more efficiently and that this will have more of an impact on employment levels than the introduction of new technology.

The poll shows that new technology will affect not just manufacturing companies; firms in the service sector are as likely to introduce it. Forty-eight per cent of manufacturing firms plan to introduce new technology and 47 per cent of service firms. Services will play the leading role in the USA and West Germany, manufacturing in France and Japan, while in Britain both sectors make an average contribution to growth in the use of new technology.

Our findings reveal a clear correlation between new technology and job losses. Net job growth in firms using high technology will be 16 per cent, below the average net growth of all companies of 20 per cent. (For an explanation of the term 'net job growth' see Appendix 1.) While 45 per cent of the sample as a whole plan to introduce new technology, 64 per cent of firms expecting to employ fewer people in the future have plans for new technology. In Britain 77 per cent of firms projecting job losses have introduced new technology in the past five years. Table 7 shows an estimate, prepared for the UK National Economic Development Office, of the impact that information technology will have on different sectors of the economy.

Some jobs will disappear, but new ones will be created. The key questions are these: will enough jobs be created to make up for the jobs lost, and will the workers who lose their jobs be qualified for the vacancies that come up? Three

Table 7 Information-technology applications by economic sector

SYSTEM TYPE	SECTOR						
	Agriculture, etc.	Extractive	Construction plus utilities	Manufacturing	Goods*	Information*	People*
Integrated text and data-processing	●	●	●	●●	●●	●●●	●●●
Transaction clearing	●	●	●	●	●●●	●●●	●
Online inquiry systems	●	●	●	●●	●●●	●●	●●●
Management information systems	●	●●●	●●	●●●	●●●	●●	●●
Professional problem-solving	●●	●●●	●●	●●	●	●●	●
Professional databases	●	●●	●●	●●	●	●	●●
Electronic mail and teleconferencing	●	●●	●	●●	●●	●●	●●
Material planning, stock control, scheduling systems	●●	●●	●●	●●●	●●●	●	●
CAD and draughting	●	●●	●●●	●●●	●	●	●
Computer-aided manufacturing		●	●●	●●●			
Computer-aided fault-diagnostic systems	●●	●●●	●●●	●●●	●●	●	
Remote-sensing devices	●●	●●●	●●●	●	●●	●	

Notes: *Services. ● Level of application of information technology in specific sectors over the period to the year 2010.

Source: 'New Information Technology Products and Services', NEDO, February 1986.

basic approaches to these questions are on offer to guide us through the disruption of the predicted technological revolution.

For mainstream economists the principal issue is how the productivity gains made in a particular firm or industry may be distributed through the rest of the economy. Although technical change may initially displace labour, there should be all kinds of offsetting compensation that work primarily through the way in which the price of output and labour changes.

New technology should raise productivity and lower the unit costs of production. If these productivity gains are translated into a lower price for the output, then demand for the product should go up. As a result, firms may not shed labour because demand will rise to offset the rise in labour productivity. According to West German industrial-relations specialist Wolfgang Streek, this is exactly what has happened at the highly automated Volkswagen Wolfsburg plant. 'Robots hypothetically replaced one thousand workers, a fifth of the workforce. But employment at Wolfsburg has hardly fallen because sales of the Golf expanded after automation; labour was redeployed but not displaced,' says Streek in a report for the International Institute of Management.

Another motive firms will have for introducing new technology is to improve the quality of their product. This quality improvement may attract new demand, which in turn may sustain employment. A striking example of this comes from banking. 'Many banks have used the new technology of automatic teller machines to redeploy labour, moving people out of routine tasks and into selling and customer advice, extending the range and improving their services,' says Richard Barras of London's Technical Change Centre. However, if extra demand is not generated, a firm's output will remain fairly stable: it will be able to make the same number of goods with fewer workers. In this case the beneficiaries of the productivity gains will be the company's workers and stockholders, who should see their wages and profits rise.

But even here there is hope for displaced workers. The extra spending power of the retained workers will feed back into the rest of the economy. They will want to spend their higher incomes on new products and services, which the displaced workers could provide. They may have to lower their wages to find work, but as long as they do, they will not be unemployed for long.

A further route for redeploying displaced workers comes via investment. If in the future more people will be building more machines, then more people will be required to make them. There should be some shift from the manufacturing of consumer goods to the manufacturing of capital goods. There is consensus that this will offer only a limited form of compensation. The electronics, computer and telecommunications sectors, which are building the machines that will staff the offices and factories of the future, have the highest labour-productivity growth rates.

There are two major problems with the ostensibly plausible approach of mainstream economics. The first is that technology does not just change competition between firms in a single economy such as the UK's; it can also alter international competitive advantage. For example, textile firms in developed countries have beaten off imports from the Third World by introducing microelectronics. The garment makers of the OECD who will enjoy this new security are unlikely to spend their money employing Indian textile workers who have lost their jobs. More important, Japan's lead in pioneering new production technology may be a source of continuing strain in the international economy. So there are geographical limits to the reach of these compensation mechanisms.

But a second problem is that even within a single economy they can take an agonizingly long time to work through. It will take time for new firms to be set up; workers may have to move and be retrained to ensure that they have the skills for the new jobs. 'If compensation effects do exist, there is every likelihood that any employment created will not match the labour force released in either skills or characteristics. One cannot say that the magnitude and timing of the compensation effects will always be such as to yield equilibrium in the labour market,' according to an OECD report, *Microelectronics, Robotics and Jobs*. The report estimates that 60 per cent of the jobs lost directly through new technology will re-emerge elsewhere in the economy through compensation effects. But it warns that only a major retraining effort will keep open the possibility of full employment.

The second approach to dealing with the disturbing impact of new technology is most eloquently outlined by the American economist Vassily Leontieff. 'Human labour, from time immemorial, has played the role of principal factor of production. There are reasons to believe that human labour may not retain this status in the future,' warns Leontieff.

According to Leontieff, the challenge for modern economies is to harness the productive power of new technology without plunging into social disruption. Wage adjustment might allow some displaced workers to find new jobs in services, but the pace of labour-saving technological change in the future will exert a continual downward pressure on wage rates, which will inevitably lead to social disintegration. Higher investment to create more secure new-technology jobs would be self-defeating, as this would involve installing more labour-saving machinery. Luddite barriers to technical change, aimed at creating more labour-intensive jobs, would mean forgoing the benefits of higher productivity.

Leontieff urges new approaches designed to combine technical advance with social harmony. One is to translate the productivity gains into a shorter working time. The fall in the average working week in US manufacturing since 1879, from sixty-seven hours to forty-two, has withdrawn many millions of working hours from the labour market. But since the Second World War the working week has remained virtually static. As technical change has proceeded, reducing labour demand, the labour supply has not contracted as it did in the past. The result has been a steadily rising underlying rate of technological unemployment, says Leontieff. Governments should adopt measures designed to reduce the working week in order to ensure that productivity gains are translated not into fewer people working the same hours but into the same number of people working shorter hours.

The FT jobs poll reveals that overall 58 per cent of firms plan to take some measures to shorten the amount of time that their employees spend at work. The range is from a high of 78 per cent in Japan and 76 per cent in West Germany to a low of 25 per cent in the USA. A shorter working week is the most popular measure and will be pursued by 24 per cent of firms overall, 41 per cent in West Germany and 35 per cent in Britain. However, the poll does not show that firms that introduce new technology are more likely than average to reduce working time.

Unfortunately, dealing with unemployment by this means is not a simple matter of arithmetic. Would real wages fall in line with shortened working time? If they did, many workers would resist the change. Would production capacity and investment fall in response to the reduced labour supply? How would the Government's tax revenues be affected? Simulations on various European economic models show that a shorter working week will boost employment, but most also show that output, private consumption and exports will fall while inflation rises.

Leontieff highlights a second major social problem that technical change will throw up: income distribution. 'The kind of incomes policy I have in mind goes beyond minimum-wage legislation or collective bargaining,' says Leontieff. 'It means supplementing the labour income of blue- and white-collar workers by transfers from other income shares (like profits).' The change that Leontieff envisages has also recently been advocated by the British economist James Meade. And it has been achieved in the past through the mechanization of agriculture.

On a prosperous Iowa farm fifty years ago a farming family would have worked long hours with horses and possibly a tractor. Their income would have amounted to the wages of a seventy- or eighty-hour week. Today that farm will be highly mechanized, and the family will do less work. But their real income will be higher than it was fifty years ago because they will be enjoying a return on their investment in capital. 'If in the future the returns to capital grow more quickly than the returns to labour in the form of wages, this will only create more inequality if capital ownership is concentrated. If capital ownership were more disbursed, this would ease the problem,' says Meade in a recent paper. If machines replace more and more people, these workers will lose their income unless they own part of the machines and get some of the profits from their use.

The third approach to the problems associated with new technology is entirely different from the other two. Most economists accept technological change as a given: the crucial economic question is how to adjust to it. All economists agree that investment and technical change are essential to economic growth. All also agree that investment fluctuates much more than consumption and that the volatility of investment is close to the heart of business cycles. Only economists following in the tradition of Joseph Schumpeter put technological change at the centre of their analysis. They argue that innovation and technical change are not smooth processes but come in waves. They are concentrated initially in certain sectors and spread slowly and unevenly through the rest of the economy. But when a new technology such as micro-electronics starts to diffuse through the economy, growth takes off. Entrepreneurs see new opportunities for profit; investment grows; firms are born; and new products come on to the market. Eventually, however, so many firms swarm around the market that profit margins are cut; investment, technical change and growth stagnate. The economy is left waiting for the next 'gale of creative destruction' to move it forward to new growth.

According to this view, unemployment is being experienced not because too much new technology is being installed but because there is not enough. The opposition of trade unions, the reluctance of management, the lack of relevant skills in the workforce and the inadequacy of industrial policy are inhibiting the introduction of micro-electronics and the boom in investment, output and employment that this will bring. In a paper for the OECD Colin Freeman and a colleague, Luc Soete, calculate the kind of output and investment that would be needed to ensure that employment remained at its 1981 level, given trends in 'best-practice productivity'. Investment would have to be well in excess of its average level in the period 1973–81 in France, West Germany, Japan and especially the UK, where investment would have to be six times its historical average. Soete and Freeman argue that this is because more and more capital is being used to produce one unit of output. So, if the available labour force is to be employed fully in the future, more and more capital will be required to support it. The need for machinery and equipment, however, could outstrip the amount of investment available. So people could be unemployed because of a capital shortage: there will not be enough machines for them to work with.

The way out of this impending capital shortage crisis, they argue, is micro-electronics. While the new technologies are labour-saving, they are also capital-saving. An ICL computer bought in 1968 might have cost around £3 million and would have taken perhaps four days to complete a punch-card program. A modern ICL computer could do the same job in an afternoon and would cost around £300,000. 'The dramatically increased capital productivity of micro-electronics alleviates to some extent the fears of capital shortage. New electronic technology allows output to be produced with less capital than before,' says Luc Soete.

This trend is exemplified by the electronics sector itself, the producer and a major user of the new technology. Of the sixteen UK industrial sectors that Soete and Freeman studied, electronics was the only one to show gains in both capital and labour productivity: all the others showed gains only in labour productivity. 'Widely diffused micro-electronics could drive down costs, raise productivity of both labour and capital and lead to new products, new firms, new industries and employment growth,' says Freeman.

The main barrier is that we are not ready for it yet. In the post-war era the growth of industries providing consumer durables like washing machines, televisions and fridges was linked to wide-scale social changes in the way that people lived and worked. According to Sussex University analysts, a similar social transformation would be required before there could be a market for new information-technology products like teleshopping. Work would have to be transformed as well. It would not be enough to continue to introduce new technology piecemeal, a robot here, a word-processor there. To reap the full benefits of new technology entirely new systems of production, such as computer-integrated manufacturing, would have to be developed, new skills taught, new management structures erected.

None of these approaches offers a full or easy answer to the question of how we should gather in the benefits of new technology and limit the costs. It is likely that we will need some aspects of each to take us through what the chairman of General Motors calls 'the technological ride of our lives'.

Manufacturing and Technology

Technology alone rarely transforms work, but when new technology is combined with new ways of organizing production, change really takes off. The factories of the industrialized world are on the verge of just such a transformation. Microelectronics is seeping into many industries and areas, from computer-aided design to robotized production lines. But the big leap will come when entire production systems are integrated through computers. We are a long way from the widespread use of computer-integrated manufacturing. There is still considerable scope for piecemeal automation of distinct parts of production. But the trend towards integration is clear. And it is *integrated* automation, rather than automation alone, that will transform factory work.

The car industry underwent such a change in the first three decades of the century as a result of Henry Ford's combination of flowline production, rigidly separated, routine shop-floor work and a pyramidal, highly differentiated management structure. This change in production techniques had effects that extended far beyond Ford's factories. The whole industry moved from building custom cars to high-volume mass production, and the Americans enjoyed a competitive advantage that allowed them to eat into foreign markets.

The emphasis on a rigid division of labour, designed to produce standard products at high volume in order to reap economies of scale, persisted. 'For a long time the only significant changes were an increase in the scale of operations and the mechanization of more and more steps in the production process,' says Sussex University car-industry analyst Dan Jones. But now, under the pressure of Japanese competition, Western industry is looking to new models of production utilizing new technology, new management structures and new working practices. The technological components are clear. A 1985 report for NEDO outlines the basic inputs to computer-integrated manufacturing.

Computer-aided design could be used to draw up products to be made by flexible manufacturing systems (FMSs). Information could be fed directly from the design computers to robots working together under the control of a central computer. This same computer could control automatic warehouses and automated carriers designed to transport parts through the production process. Office computer systems would allow management to keep a close check on the production process but would also link it with the outside world. Terminals in retailers would instantaneously transmit orders to the factory to prompt manufacturing decisions. The whole production process, from design to delivery, would be integrated via computers. Brighton Polytechnic's Innovation Research Group analyst, John Bessant, notes: 'When treated in isolation, lists of new-technology products tend to suggest ways of doing what we are already doing somewhat better: robots to replace paint sprayers, for example. But what will be more significant than applying information technology to distinct phases of the existing production process is the possibility of integrating production to form an entirely new system. The grand areas of design, production, financial and managerial co-ordination, marketing and distribution could be integrated more and more closely.'

This type of new production system exists in embryo. The clothes firm Benetton links its franchised retail outlets with the firm's Italian headquarters through a computer system. As sales are recorded, this triggers movements in the company's robotized warehouse, and the management sends out orders to suppliers. A computer-aided design system at Boeing generates not just a drawing but a computer program that is fed directly to robots to guide them in making the parts. Various stages of production at Fiat, from design through production to sales, are integrated in a similar way.

Nevertheless, there is still a long way to go before computer-integrated manufacturing becomes the norm. The basic components of the system are still not widely diffused. Although the robot population is growing at the rate of 40 per cent a year, there were 16,500 robots in Japan in 1983 but only 10,363 in the four main economies of Western Europe, according to a 1986 European Commission report. Even in the car industry robots are yet to be applied to all stages of production. Volkswagen is leading the automation of the finishing stages of production, and others expect to follow. But Ford, for instance, expects this stage of automation to take much longer than previous episodes. Early experiments with FMSs have also been plagued with difficulties. There are only about 300 in the major economies, split equally between Europe, the USA and Japan.

The FT jobs poll shows that companies introducing new technology are not likely to introduce wide-ranging changes in production techniques. The poll found that there is no strong link between new technology and other changes in the organization of work, such as the adoption of 'just-in-time' production techniques or the use of multi-skilled workers. Overall, 45 per cent of firms plan to introduce new technology, but only 34 per cent plan to employ more multi-skilled workers, and only 20 per cent plan to use 'just-in-time' production techniques. In Britain, for instance, 59 per cent of employers have plans to introduce micro-electronics, while only 16 per cent aim to introduce 'just-in-time' production. However, 40 per cent of West German firms plan to introduce 'just-in-time' production, twice the all-country average.

The trend toward more flexible, integrated manufacturing systems is likely to continue. The question is: how far and how fast?

In the UK around 70 per cent of components produced by the engineering industry are made in batches of less than fifty. This is too small for a dedicated automation system to make economic sense: these lines require high investment and high volumes to generate a pay-back. Changing machine tools to make different batches of product is time-consuming and costly. Small- and medium-batch production is inefficient for a number of reasons and could benefit from automation, according to a report by the Innovation Research Group of Brighton Polytechnic. 'Machine utilization is low; as a result there is a tendency to use many machines to keep production going. Because of this, manning levels are high. An enormous amount of money is tied up in work in progress queuing to be put on machines. This requires high inventory levels and generates long lead times.'

An FMS that integrates storage, handling, machine feeding and machine tools through a central computer control offers a solution to many of these problems. One of the key features of an FMS is that the machines are reprogramable. A change of product that in the past could have been achieved only through changing the machine tool can now be achieved through tapping a new program into the computer. So the flexibility of an FMS means it is well suited to smaller batch production of differentiated products. A survey of forty firms using FMSs found that, following their introduction, the lead times for changes to the product mix were cut by an average of 74 per cent; work in progress and inventories were reduced by 68 per cent; machine utilization went up by 63 per cent; and turnover on average rose by over 300 per cent. Firms also reported higher labour productivity, higher product quality, better control of shop-floor production and improved speed and quality of management information.

However, many of the benefits have flowed not from the technology but from the reorganization of production that the technology has brought in its train. An FMS requires more flexible forms of working, better management of inventory and stocks, more attention to quality and improved management systems to control production. The planning process that prepares for the installation of an FMS highlights inefficiencies in existing custom and practice. One estimate suggests that almost half the benefits of FMSs come from the re-ordering of production rather than the technology per se.

So there are good reasons for expecting FMSs or smaller flexible manufacturing cells to spread. They could bring economies of scale to the small- and medium-batch production that dominates much of the engineering industry. But, despite this apparent economic logic, serious obstacles stand in the way of rapid diffusion. A wide range of machines are available, but many are incompatible. This puts a premium on personnel who can plan the integration of diverse technologies and write complex software packages. These people come at considerable cost. Kearney and Trecker, the major American FMS supplier, estimates that it cost 130 very expensive man years to develop its current generation of software.

The machines themselves are very expensive too. The average cost of the FMSs covered by the Innovation Research Group report was £2.4 million. And much of the technology still needs refining. Developments to allow FMSs to be applied to non-metal-working industries like plastics, footwear and clothing are in the pipeline but could take some time to emerge. Other developments in laser-inspection technology, control and communication systems, tool management and handling and transport systems are required before firms will be able to enjoy the full benefits of integrated automation.

On the demand side the Innovation Research Group identifies the cost and effort of reorganizing work, rather than technical problems, as the main constraint on the introduction of FMSs. To reap the full benefits of computer-integrated manufacturing, production has to be organized in a new way. Management reluctance to undertake this kind of fundamental review could be the major inhibitor of advances in automation. 'The major organizational problems are getting the best fit between the technology and the pattern of work organization. The sheer cost and sophistication of FMSs has forced a re-examination of organizational goals and attitudes,' says the Innovation Research Group.

The computerized integration of production blurs lines of demarcation on the shop floor and in management. Multi-skilled maintenance workers, with the flexibility to execute a number of previously separated tasks, are required to reap the full labour-productivity gains. But this means that management has to grasp the nettle of union job demarcation. Further, to reap the full potential of the new capital machine utilization has to rise. This means lower inventories and shorter queues of components waiting to be processed. The most common solution is to move to 'just-in-time' production techniques, with deliveries of parts finely matched to the production run. However, this requires management to develop new ways of checking quality and to establish new relationships with suppliers.

Finally, the integration of production functions also requires the integration of management functions. As marketing, design, production engineering, production, handling and storage all become integrated through a computerized system, so the management departments covering these areas will have to integrate. Traditional management hierarchies will have to be overturned if the system is to work at full efficiency. The economic rationale for greater and more integrated automation among small- and medium-batch producers is likely to remain strong. In the course of the next fifteen years capital costs will come down and the technology will become both easier to use and more sophisticated. The main question mark hangs over management's determination and capacity to reorganize work to realize the gains.

New technology will dramatically alter work throughout companies, from the factory floor to executive suites. The number of jobs in the economy as a whole may remain unchanged, but technology will alter the skills that are required. The welders who are displaced by robots may not have the skills to take up the new jobs that are created in maintenance and computer programming. If workers who lose their jobs cannot be trained for the jobs that are created, unemployment will go up. Meeting the demand for new skills that technology throws up will be a major challenge for national and company training programmes.

The effect of technology on skills will vary from country to country and between firms and sectors of industry, but some general trends are clear. A Manpower Services Commission report on technology and skills in British manufacturing highlights two areas where new expertise will be required.

First, new management skills will be crucial, says the report. 'Management needs greater technical skills to be able to analyse the new equipment available and decide which is best for their firms' needs, and to develop suitable new products. Attempts to enter new markets, often because of the possibilities opened up by changes in technology, have revealed serious inadequacies in marketing skills.' Negotiating change with the workforce and reorganizing work around the technology will also demand new skills in industrial relations and human resources, say the authors.

Second, new skills will be demanded on the shop floor. Instead of working directly with a machine to make a product, workers will spend more time on maintaining and checking that the machines are doing what they are supposed to do. 'The more production is automated, the more important it becomes to prevent machines from breaking down – or, if they do break down, the more vital it is to repair them and get them back into production quickly,' says Peter Senker of the Science Policy Research Unit. Experience with numerically controlled systems shows that faults can occur anywhere in the system: in the machine tools, in the computers, in the materials-handling system or in the parts being processed. The complexity of computer-controlled machinery creates an urgent need for multi-skilled workers who can both diagnose faults and repair them. Just as opportunities for multi-skilled craftsmen may expand, so those for workers on the bottom rungs of the skills ladder may diminish. A Policy Studies Institute survey found that of 34,000 manufacturing jobs lost between 1981 and 1983 through the introduction of new technology 26,000 were unskilled jobs.

For multi-skilled workers with new responsibilities life on the shop floor may become more attractive, but the OECD predicts that for others life will be much more gloomy: 'Unskilled new entrants will find fewer job vacancies. This will tend to affect particularly women and the young unskilled. The older worker whose skills have become redundant may also suffer relative to the young entrant who is more trainable.'

New Technology, Skills and Training: Ford

These general findings are confirmed by Ford UK's plans for the introduction of new technology, the reorganization of work and the generation of new skills. 'The new pressure on skills comes from the automation and computerization of the production process as a whole. We are moving into an era in which the control of the system will change, and that will require new skills throughout the company,' says UK training chief Ron Shepherd.

In future there will be fewer operatives working on machines, and those who remain will have a much higher level of skills – they will be more like the craftsmen of today. They will have to be able to understand computer data, diagnose faults and carry out simple statistical control analyses, and their work will move away from simple, routine cycles at a single machine to longer, more complex processes involving several machines working together. 'Semi-skilled operatives will more and more be a thing of the past,' says Shepherd. 'It's clear that the car industry will no longer be a large sponge for semi-skilled labour.'

Skilled maintenance staff, the craftsmen of the future, will base their strength not on rigid demarcations between skills – those of electricians or mechanics – but on multi-skilling. 'We will want our electricians to know something about mechanics and our mechanics to know something about electrics,' says Shepherd. Ford have just embarked on what Shepherd describes as a massive retraining effort to upgrade around 4,500 skilled craftsmen. Here new-technology and skills training runs into industrial relations: for the training to make sense, unions have to be prepared to accept more flexible job classifications. The latest agreement with the unions reduced the job classifications in Ford UK from 500 to 58.

Computer-aided design and manufacture are constantly changing the skills of engineers and others in professional grades. Designing products so that they can be manufactured efficiently with new technology is crucial to the containing of costs, as is the design of production systems so that they utilize micro-electronics fully. The technology in this area is changing rapidly. 'We have to keep our professionals up to date, or we will miss out on competitive advantage,' says Shepherd.

The new technology is changing not just the content of work but also the structure of working relationships, according to Shepherd. As more responsibility is passed to flexible, more highly skilled workers on the shop floor, so the supervisors' role will change. 'We are carrying out a major revision of the supervisory function throughout Ford Europe to see what kind of role it will be in the 1990s,' says Shepherd. His guess is that supervisors will become facilitators rather than directors. They will get the work done not by resting on their authority and issuing instructions but by being able to motivate relatively autonomous work teams. 'The whole idea of subordinates and bosses will undergo tremendous change if we are to use technology effectively.'

The changes affecting supervisors will be reflected higher up the structure. Ford will move away from a pyramidal management structure towards a much flatter organization. Operatives were the first to feel the impact of new technology; now wholesale change in management's role is looming over Ford. Shepherd predicts that spans of command will be broader – management will have to deal with a wider range of issues. 'This means that management training will have to be less specialized. We can't afford to have managers who are taught by doing jobs within a specific branch of the organization. They will have to be flexible enough to cope with all aspects of the business, to be much more substitutable, and that means they will have to be more generally knowledge-able.' There will also be changes in demand for specific management skills. In the past secure growth in stable markets meant that there was no premium on planning skills. 'Management was essentially extrapolating from the past. In the future we will need much more strategic leadership skills, so that our managers will be able to anticipate, and adapt to, change.'

Ford is hiring specialists in organizational development to plan the changes. Human-resources expertise in management will be crucial in the future, replacing the traditional skills of industrial relations and negotiation, says Shepherd. 'The amazing thing is that an enormous old ship like Ford, with all its inertia, can change direction. But there is no doubt that we have to change at every level if we are to stay competitive with our rivals.'

New Technology and Services

Service employment grew consistently in most major economies in the post-war era, absorbing workers who had lost their jobs in manufacturing and agriculture. The labour intensity of providing services such as restaurant food or health care is one of the main reasons for employment growth in the service sector. New technology could affect services in three broad ways.

First, machines could be substituted for people in the provision of an existing service, such as the clearing of cheques. Another possibility is that the combination of new technology and people could either produce a broader range of existing products or improve their quality. The third and most radical possibility is that the micro-electronics revolution could transform service provision by creating new products and new firms to provide them. Videotex (interactive video services) could spawn a new range of products – home banking, teleshopping and the like. This wave of new services could bring in its wake new employment opportunities.

These three effects of new technology can be seen clearly in the banking sector. 'We have come to the end of the process where automation is aimed at the displacement of labour,' says Geoffrey Miller, general manager of finance and planning at Barclays Bank. 'The aim of the new technology we are introducing now is to provide better information to manage the business.' Even if Barclays wanted to get rid of large swathes of its workforce, it could not. In common with most banks and insurance companies, Barclays introduced automation in the 1960s to eliminate labour in high-volume, routine processes – auditing, issuing statements and processing cheques. 'There are a limited number of gains we can make now in terms of either labour saving or quality of service,' says Miller.

Many manufacturing firms have responded to competitive pressure by investing in technology and reducing the workforce: technology is generally associated with job loss. For Barclays, however, technology is crucial to the bank's future competitiveness, but for different reasons. It has allowed Barclays to innovate its product range and to expand the market for financial services. Barclaycard is one obvious example; automatic teller machines are another. They provide a convenient service but they have also freed staff to concentrate on other activities such as selling services. In the next two years Barclays plans to retrain 46,000 employees in a customer-service programme. 'The introduction of technology is driven by our need to focus our activities on selling a broad range of products in the personal sector rather than on simple banking services. That is a result of increased competition in the market,' says Miller.

Barclays plans to spend £100 million a year between now and 1990 mainly on new technology for its city affiliate, Barclays, De Zoete, Wedd, and on installing small mainframe or large mini-computers in its branches. (For the first time Barclays is spending more on technology than it is on buildings to house its staff.) The new technology of mini-computers does not help selling just by freeing staff from routine jobs. It will also provide more and more information about customers, says Miller. 'In the future we would hope that if personal customers come in, we will be able to call up all kinds of personal details on the screen. Do they have a mortgage, a personal loan to buy a car, insurance, health cover? Do they have children? All this will be crucial information to allow us to know what to sell to whom.'

The growing importance of advanced computer systems, linking satellites with main branches and regional headquarters, is placing a strain on personnel, though. Miller says that general computer skills among the staff are satisfactory, particularly among school-leavers. But the real strain is on computer specialists. Citibank has 3,000 systems analysts. Barclays has just 800, three-quarters of whom are maintaining systems already in place. 'The problems we have recruiting skilled computer specialists is inhibiting our ability to expand our product range, particularly to corporate customers,' says Miller. 'Last year we had twelve advertising campaigns. We managed to recruit 100 computer specialists. In the course of the year we lost ninety-seven of them to other companies.'

The big technological leap to electronic transfer of funds from point of sale (EFTPOS) terminals, or home banking, will be slow in coming, says Miller. Though Barclays has installed some terminals to make it easier for retailers to check authorization for credit cards, at the moment there is no incentive to go for full-scale EFTPOS. The capital costs of a fully fledged scheme would be around £500 million, but only 14 per cent of the cheques that Barclays deals with come from retailers. The volume of cheques that Barclays handles is rising at 7 per cent a year. 'So EFTPOS would save only two years' growth of cheque volume,' argues Miller. This is an area in which competition in banking services may inhibit technological advance. Customers would have to pay a fee for EFTPOS, whereas with free banking writing a cheque costs nothing. 'Until the capital costs come down significantly, or until free banking goes away, EFTPOS will not make commercial sense,' says Miller.

Office Automation and its Ramifications

Banks have long been among the most intensive and innovative users of new technology in the service sector. It could well be argued that they are not representative of trends within the sector as a whole. A clearer picture of the impact that new technology could have on services in general comes from an examination of what the future holds for the most ubiquitous service providers – office workers. Offices will undergo enormous change in the next fifteen years. The long process of office automation could come to fruition with local area networks and integrated communication systems linking word-processors, mainframe computers, advanced copiers, facsimile machines and satellites.

The process started in the 1870s with the invention of the telephone, carbon paper and the typewriter. By the 1940s the earliest electric typewriters had arrived, along with duplicating machines and accounting machines. In the 1960s and 1970s mainframe computers automated many high-volume, repetitive sorting tasks, and now desk-top micro-computers are becoming commonplace. All this technological advance has been consistent with growing office employment, so why worry about the future? The evidence is that the latest wave of technical change in the office is different from past waves.

All offices essentially record, organize and transmit information through the familiar means of letters, memos, bills, invoices. Developments at all of these levels will transform office jobs in the future. Developments in data gathering and recording, using optical scanning and even voice recognition, could eliminate many routine clerical jobs. Faster processing and greater computing power, allied with new software packages, will make it easier to organize and recall information. Networking of machines, telephones, computers and remote printers will eliminate jobs associated with the distribution of information. 'The latent productivity-enhancing effects of office automation can be seen as water building up behind a dam. The dam is made up of institutional inertia and transition problems. Once that is broken through, there could be a flood of workforce reductions,' says a report entitled *The Automation of US Offices*, published by the Congressional Office of Technology Assessment in Washington.

There is no doubt that office employment does present a large target for labour-saving technology to aim at. White-collar employment in general, and office employment in particular, have grown enormously in most industrialized economies since the 1950s. Throughout the OECD white-collar employment grew by 45 per cent during the 1970s, whereas general employment grew by 6 per cent. In the USA there were 5.1 million white-collar jobs at the beginning of the century, accounting for under 18 per cent of employment. By 1950 the number had quadrupled to 22 million, or 37 per cent of the workforce. But in thirty years, less than the average working lifetime, the number of white-collar jobs has more than doubled to 52 million, 55 per cent of American workers.

Technological changes will bring in their wake a transformation of established office structures. Data entry will become a major area for productivity advances with the development of optical-scanning technology: 'More and more information will be in machine-readable form from the beginning, and computers and telecommunications technology will increasingly exchange information

between organizations without re-keyboarding. This alone will have a tremendous impact on clerical employment.' Not only will jobs be eliminated but also
many of the traditional first rungs on the ladder of a white-collar career.

The spread of technology may well increase the demand for professionals and
specialists, and it will change professional and managerial jobs. Desk-top
computers may encourage managers to do some of the routine information-
processing tasks previously handed down to secretaries, suggests a study by the
Institute of Manpower Studies, and new systems will raise professionals' productivity and give them greater flexibility, according to Dr Geoffrey Robinson,
technical director of IBM UK. Professional jobs could also be threatened,
however. Easy-to-use software programs could transfer jobs to para-professionals.
Automatic credit scoring in banking, or programs to produce standardized
legal documents, could lead to the passing down of skilled professional tasks to
former senior clerical workers.

Secretarial work is also likely to undergo enormous change. Already there is a
marked trend away from the employment of one secretary per manager. At Ford
fewer secretaries working with advanced information systems will help smooth a
reduction in the white-collar workforce. 'The traditional role of the secretary is
likely to be obsolete by the end of the decade,' concludes the Institute of
Manpower Studies. But another role for support staff may emerge.

Many of the most exciting possibilities of office automation will stem from
networking. Desk-top computers, linked by a telecommunications infrastructure, could allow much work to be done away from the office. At present
home-based office work is limited. Only about forty US corporations organize
part of their work in this way, and there may be no more than between 3,000 and
5,000 US new-technology homeworkers. But homeworking could grow significantly in the future, as employers turn to homeworking to cut the overhead
costs of large office premises and to allow more flexible management of working
time.

An even more radical possibility is offshore office work, already espoused by
one major international airline, which collects its ticket stubs from sites around
the USA and flies them to Barbados to be keyed into the company's computer
system by 300 clerical workers. Although the cost of satellite time and the quality
of facsimiles may limit this development, one of the main attractions is lower
wage costs. One executive interviewed by the Office of Technology Assessment
reported that Indian keyboard operators cost one-fifteenth the price of their
American counterparts; the saving of $58 per 10,000 characters more than
compensates for transport and telecommunications costs. The spectre of outsourcing and foreign competition that hangs over many workers in traditional
manufacturing could start to loom over office workers in the future.

So it would seem that the amorphous service sector, for so long the source of
jobs for workers displaced from manufacturing by the introduction of new
technology, might itself be the target for potentially job-displacing investments
in new technology. But, as we said in the introduction to this chapter, a group of

economists influenced by the economist Joseph Schumpeter believes that the cluster of new technologies grouped under micro-electronics could also generate many new jobs in the service sector. They argue that if advances in the technology of computers and telecommunications were combined with social changes – changes in lifestyles, patterns of consumption and institutions – a new range of jobs in information-technology services could emerge. As the storage and retrieval of information became cheaper, so demand for it would rise, and in its wake employment would expand. Advances in computer hardware and software will make computerized information cheaper and more accessible. Advances in telecommunications will make it easier for users to communicate with one another and to interrogate databases for information about shopping, entertainment, travel, legal and medical issues, news and current affairs, hobbies. 'There is no doubt that by the mid-1990s a whole new range of consumer services will be available. The question is: how big will the market be?' says Sussex University information-technology analyst Ian Miles.

In essence the home television screen, augmented by a computer linked to a sophisticated telecommunications network, could become the new market place. By 1995 34 per cent of UK households could be using some of these services, and by the year 2010 that proportion could rise to 72 per cent, according to a survey conducted in 1985 for NEDO. On this reading, new technology will not threaten service workers but will become their saviour. The massive investment required to get these services off the ground would generate jobs in the telecommunications companies that laid the cables to link the systems together; in the computer companies that provided the hardware and software to enable people to use the system; and in firms that gathered, stored and provided the information. 'Teleshopping may displace workers from the shops but there would be new jobs for them in delivering the shopping or in providing the information,' says Miles. 'The post-war boom was associated with the rise of new industries making mass-marketed consumer goods like washing machines and televisions. These were the industries that made full employment possible. In the future information technology could play this role.'

In practice, however, the problems are immense. The development of the new services predicted by the NEDO report will depend on the industrial policy decisions taken by Governments and firms.

The first problem is the massive investment that would be required to install a telecommunications system capable of carrying the information. (French plans to install a system with 1.4 million subscribers were estimated to cost £1.6 billion.) It would be the infrastructure of the information economy as roads are the infrastructure of the goods economy. Most experts agree that this would require a broad-band system of cables, able to carry digitalized information, linking homes and businesses. Most telecommunications companies in Europe plan to install these in stages up to the end of the century.

But, according to a study of the developing videotex experiments in Europe, the telecommunications companies could make or break the systems – a second problem. Godefroy Dang Nguyen, of the European University Institute in Florence, remarks: 'The lessons to be learned from the videotex experience are lessons about product innovation by a public monopoly. Instead of various types of system being tried out at a low volume, the PTTs tried to leapfrog the product-experimentation stage and to impose their own product recipe. Videotex attracted them because it was technically simple and therefore ought, in their eyes, to be a success. What they were not aware of, because they were not experienced in such matters, were the problems of marketing their playthings.'

A third shadow over the future of videotex services is international trade. Extensive videotex facilities would make many services internationally trade-able. 'There would be nothing stopping firms in the USA from setting up databases to supply market information for consumers in Britain and displacing workers here. Databases will be among the basic resources of the information economy,' says Newcastle University's Professor John Goddard.

A fourth issue is the link between being able to develop and use the new system and making the equipment for it. For some, building a strong, indigenous manufacturing base will be crucial to the development of new services. 'The better we are at making the computer and telecommunications equipment,' the more advanced we will be in providing the services, and that will give us an international edge,' says Rod Coombs of Manchester University's Institute of Science and Technology. But this approach is misguided, says Margaret Sharpe, editor of *Europe and the New Technologies*. 'The key to Europe's capacity to compete lies in its use of new technology. Governments should not bow to pressures which they meet from many quarters to establish and protect across-the-board capabilities in all technological areas. They should buy in US and Japanese expertise,' she writes in her conclusion.

The analogy with the consumer durables industries of the post-war era suggests a final, fundamental requirement if the information-technology revolution is to get a grip. The spread of washing machines, televisions and fridges was accom-panied by a tremendous social revolution: people's way of life changed. 'The provision of new services will depend on social innovations on a similar scale,' says Jonathan Gershuny of Bath University. 'It will require a new approach to all kinds of things – shopping, learning, banking, the day-to-day detail of people's lives.'

The new-technology services sound plausible. But could they really change the way we live and work within the remaining years of this century? Sceptics should consider this: in 1970 employment in the UK video industry was almost non-existent; now the industry has generated thousands of jobs in shops, factories and television studios, and it has altered fundamentally the way in which many people spend their evenings.

5. THE BATTLE AGAINST OBLIVION

> From San Diego up to Maine,
> In every mine and mill
> Where working men defend their rights,
> It's there you'll find Joe Hill.

('The Ballad of Joe Hill', US folk song)

Will we? Will Joe Hill, the spirit of unionism past, still make converts when the mines and mills are transformed into robotized plants and fast-food joints? Is the freedom of men and women still dependent on being (as a 1970s pop song put it) 'part of the union'? Or is the freedom to choose *not* to belong to a union now being exercised because it is no longer necessary, or politically attractive, or worth the money?

'The members,' says Yoichi Takahashi, president of the Hitachi Workers Union, 'are changing. We all have lots of *things*. They are losing some of their dedication to unions. They are losing their enthusiasm for corporate life and putting more emphasis on families and personal life.' And Richard Vine, an American in Paris, director of the Atlantic Institute, puts it with Anglo-Saxon bluntness: 'The political power of the unions is at an end, though they still possibly have the power to tie up Governments.'

Everyone – antagonists, supporters, themselves – are telling unions to 'change and adapt' in order to survive. But there is a real question in this – what to change and adapt *to*? To be sure, unions were being written off in the late 1950s, when unionization rates, especially in the USA and West Germany, were falling sharply; but the recovery in Western European unions (not in Japan or the USA, where rates continued to fall, though very slowly in Japan) owed a great deal to the growth of the public-sector and white-collar salariats, many of whom were unionized, using industrial unionist techniques. Now, the 'new workers' are usually in small companies, or are in secondary labour markets, where they slip in and out of jobs, or are working for high-tech companies or service companies with little or no tradition of unionism and often with personnel policies designed to keep them out. Above all, the unions do not have the assistance of (most) Governments.

Colin Crouch, a fellow of Trinity College, Oxford, points out that union strengths have fluctuated widely for seventy years or more but concedes, 'There are good reasons for seeing a difficult future for European (and US) trade unionism for some years ahead. The context of the 1970s was one of demonstrable success for union bargaining activity and of increasing incorporation of unions into national policy-making by Governments. It must be doubted whether white-collar unionization will proceed at the same pace during a prolonged recession when unions are no longer playing a central political role.'

Unions are enjoined to give up class politics, especially in those countries (like France, Italy and the UK) where class struggle has been explicitly or implicitly a feature of their activities, and it is certain that the classic confrontation that had this dimension inscribed within it – the UK mineworkers' strike of 1984–5 – has acted as a warning light, rather than a beacon, for unions everywhere. But what is their alternative? Arthur Scargill, the British mineworkers' president, was fond of saying that, in launching his men against the industry's management and the Government, he was repudiating the policies of John L. Lewis – the acquiescence, by the president of the US mineworkers in the 1940s and 1950s, in cutbacks in the workforce in exchange for more cash for those who remained. That repudiation led to sacrifices for nothing: yet today's Lewises find themselves on shifting ground too, facing tough, battered employers who want to cut both numbers *and* pay. 'They can't take the John L. Lewis route,' says Richard Vine, 'because a lot of employers want hardly any industrial workers at all, since there will no longer be a large-scale industrial process. In another twenty years you just won't have huge production centres.'

Underlying the decline of unionism (see table 8) is, of course, the rise of unemployment: that has shattered unions' industrial, social and political strength, snatched away their members in the best unionized, least adaptable areas and coralled them into often desperate, rarely well-supported protests against the scourge. The recessionary pressure that largely gave rise to mass unemployment meant that employers were usually serious when they threatened to close plants, that members were scared out of militancy, which they anyway saw as hopeless, and that the solidarity bred of self-confidence shrivelled to each man for himself.

The reason most commonly adduced, after unemployment, for trade-union weakness is the move into services and away from manufacturing because it was in manufacturing that unions first established themselves, and, it is argued, they are still rooted in that shrinking arena. In general terms, it was not misery or deprivation that created unions in the first industrialized countries but skill, craft traditions and the ability to exercise a countervailing force over that of the employer. These traditions, reluctantly broadened to include unskilled workers' unions in the early part of the century and mass white-collar unionism in the 1960s, have remained dominant – even where, as in most countries, the engineering and other skilled unions, like those of printers, electricians and woodworkers, are in a minority within the movement. This hegemony of craft and skill has meant labour movements that were, are, and may continue to be, strongly interested in the preservation of skill and skill differentials, often

Table 8 Union membership in the UK, West Germany, Italy, Japan, France and the USA, 1955–84

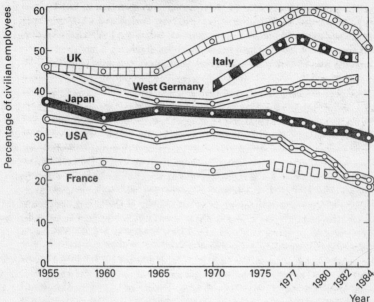

conservative in that they are resistant to changes in skill patterns, tending to be socialist or social democratic (in Italy and France, often communist) in political choice and inclined towards an inner-union democracy based on activism and strongly oriented towards male workers.

It is not inevitable that unions should do badly when the service sector grows: public-sector growth was one of the reasons why union membership grew in the 1960s and 1970s. The industrial model of unionism is well adapted to recruiting and organizing large numbers of, for example, Civil Service clerical workers – though where unions were politically high-profile, as in France, workers in the Government sector often felt, or were (as in West Germany), constrained from joining.

But perhaps unionism, by its very nature, is unsuited to organizing the confusing mix of workers who increasingly characterize the labour markets – and it is not at all suited to organizing, and has only recently and half-heartedly tried to organize, ex-workers on the dole and about-to-be workers in training schemes.

In a major and sober report on 'the changing situation for workers and their unions', the US AFL–CIO notes that, by 1990, 75 per cent of the US workforce will be in (mainly private) service industries but that only 20 per cent of its 1985 membership is already in these sectors (heavily concentrated in state and federal bureaucracies at that). The report says: 'Increasingly, workers are members of two-earner and even three-earner families in which one or more individuals work part-time; indeed, approximately 20 per cent of the workforce holds a part-time job. At the same time, more workers are employed in unstable operations whose life span is a few years, rather than several decades, and are classified as "independent contractors" or "managers" or "supervisors" rather than as "employees". These interrelated developments dilute the incentive to run the risks currently associated with engaging in organizing activity . . .'

This switch from primary and secondary manufacturing employment to services has meant that the proportion of women workers (especially part-time) has grown steadily in all countries: they, together with many new entrants into the jobs market, often find unions unappealing, daunting or even uninteresting. In many countries, with the possible exception of the Scandinavian states, unions have so far had real difficulties in transmitting their culture across the sexual division and, now, across the generation gap. Alfred Pankert, chief of the Labour-Management Relations Section at the International Labour Organization (ILO), notes that labour-market changes 'with a dynamic of their own' include in particular 'the mass arrival of women on the labour market and the quest by certain groups, especially women and young people, impelled by necessity or personal taste, for new lifestyles in which work occupies a less important and restricting role than in the past'.

The FT jobs poll found that firms with more than half their workforce organized in unions will show net job growth of only 2.8 per cent, less than one-tenth the average growth for all firms. Though non-unionized firms will have only an average employment-growth rate, they will be far less prone to job losses. Non-unionized firms make up 53 per cent of the sample but only 29 per cent of the firms projecting job losses. In contrast, while a quarter of firms have more than half their workers in unions, they make up 42 per cent of the firms expecting to shed labour. This trend is most marked in Britain, where strongly unionized firms make up half the sample but account for 90 per cent of the firms planning to cut the labour force.

Unions are under-represented in areas of employment growth. Service employment will expand more than manufacturing in every country except the USA. Outside that country services will produce net employment growth of 34 per cent compared with manufacturing growth of 4.75 per cent. But 63 per cent of firms with more than half their workforce unionized are in the manufacturing sector, while 73 per cent of service firms are either non-unionized or have fewer than a quarter of their workers in unions.

Small businesses will be a major source of job growth, but 74 per cent of them are non-unionized. In the USA 88 per cent are non-union, in France 82 per cent, in Japan 80 per cent and in Britain 65 per cent. Only one in ten small businesses have more than half their employees in unions.

New technology will be another source of job loss, according to the poll. But unions make very little difference to firms' plans to introduce new technology. Just over a quarter of the firms introducing new technology have half their workers in trade unions. Workers in firms that are heavily unionized do not show a marked resistance to technical change. Across the sample 21 per cent of firms said that their workers resisted the introduction of new technology, but only 19 per cent of heavily unionized firms reported resistance.

When Mr Takahashi, from his perspective as the company union boss, laments the decline in corporate values, he does so both for the union and for the company: indeed, like many Japanese union leaders (but not *only* the Japanese), he sees the two as essentially indivisible. Japanese managers and intellectuals devote much agonizing to this: Takeshi Ishida of Tokyo University, noting a big steel company poll that showed declining loyalty to company and union in more or less equal measure over a twelve-year period, says, 'Increasing bureaucratization [in large organizations] inevitably intensifies the member's sense of alienation and apathy and thus leads to a weakening of loyalty despite the organization's emphasis on conformity.'

All of this is happening as managements and Governments are getting tougher. In the 1980s, of all the advanced industrial countries only France passed legislation that was 'friendly' to the unions (the series of Auroux Laws, which underpinned workplace and bargaining rights) – but even this did not prevent a continued decline in union membership. In the USA the Labor Department ceased to be big labour's voice in the administration and instead became, often, its antagonist: the National Labor Relations Board's judgements on the crucial issue of union recognition were, the unions felt, generally hostile. In Japan the Government maintained its customary hands-off stance on industrial relations, but its tentative steps towards market liberalization – as in the recent legalization of contract labour companies – is seen as weakening organized labour. In West Germany the passing of 'Paragraph 116', making it more difficult for those benefiting from strikes to claim social security during a strike that lays them off, has united the labour movement in at least rhetorical denunciation of the Kohl Government and led to the unprecedented absence of an invitation to the Federal Chancellor to speak at the unions' annual conference in June. In Italy the Craxi Government succeeded in breaking the automatic indexation of wages (the *scala mobile*) in the summer of 1985 after the most rousing of campaigns by the unions and the powerful Communist Party.

Britain is a case apart. Here a powerful and proud (even smug?) union movement met a Thatcher Government first elected, in 1979, on an explicit mandate to 'redress the balance of power'. Aided immensely by unemployment, by hostile-to-unions media and not a little by union and labour movement foot-shooting (including an incredible opposition to mandatory balloting), the Thatcher Government brought in two employment Acts and a trade-union Act that curtailed the scope of industrial action, opened union funds to legal action and enforced ballots on the election of executives, strikes and the maintenance of political funds. Further, the Government effectively dismantled or froze out the tripartite bodies that had attempted to keep Britain's always rickety industrial consensus on the road: unions were scarcely listened to in public or in private, and the level of rhetorical attack, though diminishing in the Government's second term, remains high. Unions in the UK are far from out, but they remain down: and if Labour recovers its ability to form Governments, it will be little thanks to the unions.

Managements in many countries have, of course, often been as keen as some Governments to see the union movement weakened – especially in the USA (traditionally), the UK (recently) and France (very recently). But in other countries employers have not, in general, either pressed for particular advantages over unions or sought to alter the essential parameters of the employer–union relationship. It is in these countries that the union movement has continued to prosper, even showing signs of waxing in strength – and it is to these countries that the more battered union movements are looking for role models.

The first of these is Japan. When Mr Takahashi of the Hitachi union was interviewed he was flanked by three Hitachi managers, one of whom translated the conversation. No one, clearly, found the matter unusual.

The Toyota Workers Union has four basic principles: the maintenance and improvement of working conditions; independent and democratic management; the inseparability of worker livelihood and company development; and mutual trust based on friendship and loyalty. These in turn are embodied in a joint declaration between management and union, which has as its main headings: (1) 'Mutual trust is the basis for labour management relations'; (2) 'We will work for improved quality and productivity as a way both to ensure the prosperity of the company and maintain and improve labour relations'; (3) 'We will contribute to the development of the economy by helping the automotive industry to prosper.'

And over at Toyota's to-the-death competitor Nissan, Futoshi Fujii, board member for personnel, is at pains to impress on his British interviewer that the well-known resistance of retired Nissan union leader Ichiro Shioji to the investment by the company in a manufacturing plant in north-east England was not – as it would have been in the West – because of fears of foreign investment taking jobs. 'Mr Shioji was opposed,' he said, 'because it was not clear whether or not we would make a profit. He also believed that we should go ahead with passenger-car production expansion in Japan before investment in the UK.'

The examples point to a framework of agreement between the enterprise unions and the company managements in which a more or less explicit trade-off is the basis of the 'trust' to which both sides refer constantly – a trade-off between employment security and acquiescence in company goals. It does *not* produce unions that are no more than a robotized transmission belt for suppressing their members: it *does* produce an industrial culture in which the ends of both are seen to coincide and there is a real effort to be harmonious about agreeing the means.

The union movement in Japan, though its organizational structure is largely a post-war development, is rich, diverse and highly political: and enterprise unionism is not the whole story. The two big federations – Sohyo (about 4.5 million members, largely in the public sector) and Domei (2.2 million, mainly in the private sector) – are strongly socialist and social democratically oriented respectively. A third federation, Churitsuroren (1.5 million) is both wholly private-sector and politically neutral, while a fourth, Shinsanbetsu, is the last grim and tiny (60,000-member) echo of the once-dominant communist tendency within the unions.

This structure, and the stance adopted by Japanese enterprise unions, is not due merely to some indefinable national characteristic: it owes much to the national culture in which it operates and from which it springs, but it is also, more than other union movements (except perhaps the West German), the way it is because of conscious efforts by the protagonists. Labour historians often date the watershed of modern Japanese trade unionism to two events: first, the union-supported and massive protests against the revision of the US–Japan security treaty in 1959, which caused President Eisenhower to cancel a visit and ended the premiership of Nobusuke Kishi; and, second, a bitterly violent strike at Mitsui Corporation's coalmine in 1959, where the union conducted an ultimately futile struggle against redundancies.

The first of these, according to the Japanese Institute of Labour's account, 'gave the Japanese a lesson in democracy and, specifically, in the importance of gaining a public consensus through democratic procedures'. The second caused both unions and management so deeply to rethink their attitudes to each other that 'businesses were no longer able to take drastic means to cut manpower, such as through outright dismissal, nor were labour unions to attempt excessively violent action such as paralysing management and production rather than making common efforts through collective bargaining, labour–management joint consultation or complaints-adjustment procedures.' This shift away from a period in which the Japanese unions were often a byword for militancy (they were largely communist-led for some years after the war) to one in which they became the complete antithesis of that perception was underpinned by rapid growth from the 1960s onwards.

But it is certain that economic expansion in other advanced countries did not result in the same consensual approach: and when the 1973 oil shock hit energy-poor Japan as hard as anyone, the understanding between unions and management had become sufficiently strong for union leaders, after a one-year leap to recover inflationary losses through large wage settlements, to get through low wage deals and help slash non-energy costs. Ronald Dore, one of the doyens of foreign scholarship on contemporary Japan, says that the industrial adjustments to the 1973 and 1979–80 oil shocks 'would have been impossible if workers, either individually or collectively, had resisted change. In the Japanese context, however, it is wrong to place workers and unions in a secondary position in which they are made to appear always adjusting to change imposed by the Government or management. A truer picture would be to say that workers and unions actually saw the need for adjustment in roughly the same terms as Government and management.'

The vehicle for wage increases is the spring wages offensive, or *shunto*. It is a national event, preceded by a sprawling debate on the economy and the position of Japan in the world, conducted by employers, unions, commentators, academics and (obliquely) the Government. To an outsider it is refreshingly rational and transparent compared with the often hermetic and deliberately extreme positions adopted by the labour–capital protagonists in the West: both sides in Japan go a long way towards dealing with *all* the elements in the pay equation, not just those that benefit them. It is a benign contradiction in the system that the Japanese unions, while largely enterprise-based, are also capable of taking the most global of views – though their critics in and out of Japan say that view is one understandably close to the employers' perspective.

In 1986 the spring offensive was more global than usual: it was, in a sense, conducted in the glare of world attention. The unions noted with interest that the rest of the world, especially the USA, was on their side: it was seeking increased domestic demand, which meant higher wages. The unions promptly obliged their foreign allies by putting in for wage increases of up to 7 per cent: they got internal support too in the shape of the president of Suntory, the big drinks group, and (obliquely) the Government, which felt under pressure from the rest of the advanced world to expand domestic demand and growth.

The big export-dependent companies, fearful of the rising yen, carried the day: the steel companies settled for 2.6 per cent, the shipbuilders for zero; the car manufacturers offered between 4.4 and 4.6 per cent, accepted in April. By May, the settlement level was combing out at just under 4.5 per cent, with the newly privatized telecom network, NTT, paying 5.8 per cent and the private railways paying between 5.5 and 5.6 per cent. Takeo Naruse, head of research at Nikkeiren, the employers' organization, says: 'Once discussions came to micro (company) level, then the big companies, with big exports, made it clear that things were bad – and then discussion became rather reasonable.'

Being 'rather reasonable' is what Japanese unions are famed for: they are being copied in the USA and the UK. At Fremont, just south of San Francisco, the United Auto Workers at the joint Toyota/General Motors 'New United Motor Manufacturing Inc.' car plant have copied Japanese union attitudes and got jobs back for 2,500 members following a shutdown in 1983, when the then wholly GM-owned operation was swamped with disputes and a huge 20 per cent absentee rate.

This is very similar to what happened at Hitachi's UK subsidiary at Hirwaun, a bleak industrial estate just over the hill from the Rhondda Valley. There a General Electric Company/Hitachi joint venture suffered low productivity and low-quality output until Hitachi took over in 1984, agreed with the electricians' union to operate a single-union deal (to the fury of the other unions), issued identical blue jackets to everybody, tore down the status barriers, put rousing mottoes everywhere – 'We are one' is the Hitachi grand motto – and became terribly efficient.

Japan's employers know when they are on to a good thing. Takashi Kashiwagi, Hitachi's board member for personnel, emphasizes the unity of interest and the dislike of management for Western-style flexibility: 'We here in Hitachi think that lay-offs are bad. It is not that our lifetime-employment system is mandatory, rather that management and unions together evolved a practice of avoiding lay-offs. The mobility of human resources is a Western concept: here the concept is to make best use of the resources we have.'

Japanese workers very often depend on their enterprises for more than just their jobs: they depend on them for their pensions, for medical care, for housing and for many social activities. (Toshiro Nishiguchi, researching Toyota's labour relations, noted that part of the young managers' work was organizing free-time activities for employees who were placed in their educational peer groups. He quotes a weary young manager as saying: 'On Sundays I have to go to work, dragging my tired body, to do folk dancing with our young ladies. On such occasions I often feel myself foolish and pretty vacant. But I must do it with patience because the primary job of a manager is to improve the morale and atmosphere of the plant.')

It is in part because of this warm embrace – Ronald Dore calls it 'welfare corporatism' – that Japanese unions simply do not act like their Western brothers. When the two cultures meet the effect is sometimes comic. At a Ford union officials' conference in Hamburg in April 1986, Hayato Ichihara, president of the union at Mazda (with which Ford is linked), was treated with a mixture of awe and horror by his fellow delegates as he unveiled his 'vision of industrial harmony, promoting a creative contribution to automotive culture'. Mazda is to establish a plant outside Detroit in 1987. Ford sees the linkage as a way of Trojan-horsing: Mr Ichihara would, many of the delegates thought, soon be the enemy within. At the same conference the British Ford negotiators presented a report on the UK emphasizing the effectiveness of strike threats and pay-deal victories. Mr Ichihara and his colleagues smiled benignly, as if it were merely an example of quaintness on a par with haggis. Jimmy Airlie, the UK engineering union official who leads union negotiations with Ford, hardly seemed on the same planet as Mr Ichihara. But another British union official did confess: 'We would like to change, but the trouble is we've got so much political baggage we can't get rid of.'

The basics of the Japanese system are unlikely to change: indeed, the movement is towards enterprise unionism in the West rather than a Japanese move towards industrial or craft unionism. Its crucial accompaniment is economic success, and now worries are being voiced that a persistently high yen may shake lifetime employment, thus threatening the basic bargain. But for the present the lesson for unions looking for a future is clearly this: if capitalism works for *them*, it can also work for *us* – to the point where 'them' and 'us' are *we*. And we, as Hitachi would say, are one.

The same union conference at which Mr Ichihara so offended Western sensibilities was attended by representatives of Industrie Gewertschaft Metall, the 2-million-strong West German engineering union, the most powerful in the world. IG Metall members work in Ford Germany; they are also on the board. One of the main reasons why the European Ford unions cannot formulate effective policy is the tacit but powerful opposition of IG Metall to moves it sees as dangerous to the company and its position in it. An International Metalworkers Federation official attending the event said: 'The West Germans are the good part of the European company. The German unions know this and are keen to keep pole position.'

That is so. The West German union–management relationship is under strain now, but you have the feeling that it can bear it. Also the level of hostility expressed towards the Kohl Government is a little – by international standards – overdone. The steeply rising unemployment curve shocked the unions, and the Kohl Government, often prompted by its liberal partners, has gingerly trimmed a few union sails. But the central social democratic basis of the state is yet intact: as with the Japanese unions and managements (and many who know both countries remark on the parallel), the social partners deem that there is more to gain from hanging together than from hanging separately. 'Social equilibrium and social stability are the most important elements of a political infrastructure,' says Monika Wulf Mathies, leader of OTV, the public service workers' union. This, perhaps, is incontestable in all countries, but you would not hear it from (say) a British, French or Italian union leader. The shared concern is still (as in Japan) to overlay the desolation of a self-induced defeat with social peace and material success still operates; the mixed economy still functions; and the main actors still have the big parts.

Bernd Heinzemann, a senior official in the Bundesvereinigung des Deutschen Arbeitgeberverbände (the employers' association) says: 'Here the unions have a stake in the collective bargaining process. We need strong partners, so that agreements can be honoured at all levels.' The strength is only in part at national level: more important (further similarity with the Japanese) is the plant-level relationship, where the co-determination and works council system, which puts workers on the board and ingrains consultation into the industrial process, is enshrined in law. Says Herr Heinzemann: 'The workers' council leaders are a little like the princes of the old independent German states. They are more powerful in their plants than the national union leaders. The relations at plants with workers' councils function well, independent of the relations at national level.'

On the Thyssen supervisory board Hans Mayr, president of IG Metall, sits as first deputy chairman; Karlheinz Weihs, a roll turner, is one of the two deputy chairmen; Robert Baumann, a safety foreman, Kurt Kistner, a cost account clerk and Herbert Mosel, an electrician, are board members, as are three union officials. Herr Mayr and Hans Gert Woelke, the executive board member for personnel, talk often and openly. Recently Herr Woelke pointed out to his nominal superior that the union policy of enforcing the same hourly rate in the group's Emden and Hamburg shipyards made life difficult in a fearsomely competitive market. Herr Mayr said that there was no chance of changing policy.

The conversations will continue. 'Perhaps,' says Woelke self-deprecatingly, 'the example of the shipyards is not a good one. Even if we halved the wages, we would not be able to compete. South Korea [the main competitor] now functions almost as a military force.'

Both men agreed, however, on their opposition to the Government plan (presently postponed) to increase representation of managerial-level employees and non-unionized minorities on works councils – a Liberal (FDP) initiative that the Government majority party (CDU) had half-heartedly pushed. 'If it were changed, it would make my job more difficult,' says Herr Woelke. 'We would have two groups on the board competing for representation and influence.'

Over in Essen, at Thyssen Industrie, Werner Bartels chafes more obviously against the restraints but accepts the system: 'I *have* to get agreement from the unions for change. It's sometimes very difficult, sometimes very expensive. Over the past three years we've paid DM240 million in compensation for lay-offs. But I wouldn't like the US system – I know it well. It's sometimes much *more* expensive.'

Down at plant level, at Thyssen Industrie's Huller Hille machine-tool plant in Witten, Heinz Dentzen, the managing director, is categorical: 'The unions, like the management, are looking for profit because they know profit is necessary to give jobs. If we have to fire people, the works council knows it five months before and knows why.'

A shared belief in the necessity of profit, a shared memory of (or grounding in) recent trauma and thus a deliberate emphasis on harmony and stability, even a shared contempt of less well-ordered, less successful nations – these really do cross the labour–capital boundaries in both West Germany and Japan. Both are seen as models. It is clearly nonsense to say that others cannot construct something similar because both these systems *have* been constructed rather than being a timeless part of the national wallpaper. For the foreseeable future they will survive but the internal and external pressures that caused them to be formed may not be felt sufficiently strongly elsewhere to make them wholly exportable.

But the fly in the ointment in both countries is, for employers and Governments in one way and for the unions in another, the fear of an end to their internationally enviable consensus because of domestic opportunism on the part of one side or the other. Wulf Mathies, in common with almost all trade-union leaders in West Germany, is deeply hostile to what she sees as Kohl's imitation of Reagan – and Thatcher – economics. 'In developed countries a new poverty is appearing, creating rivalry between those who have work and those who have not because there will always be a person who is able and willing to take the most miserable job just to make a living.'

The denunciation of the Government, which reached a climax at the Deutsche Gerwerkschaftsbund (union federation) conference in June 1986, saw Norbert Blum, Labour Minister and IG Metall member, well on the pro-union left-wing of the CDU, get boos and whistles when introduced to the congress. It also saw a vocal commitment actively and openly to support the opposition

Social Democrats in 1987's January general election. Ernst Breit, the DGB president, told the congress that the Government's proclaimed 'turning point' (*Wende*) in economic management was 'the work of con-men. There are social engineers at work here against whom we must sell our might . . . Sand in the gears of neo-conservatism! That would be a badge of honour for us.'

This causes great anxiety among employers and on the right. Alfons Mueller, on Herr Blum's wing of the party and, with its base in the Catholic Workers Association, a strong supporter of co-determination and of unions, is particularly concerned: 'I am really worried that the socialists will gain more and more influence in the trade unions and that they have more and more influence on the SPD. We have to think how this can go on – if the DGB unions continue to act in this way and become better at attacking the Government than the SPD, I think many CDs will leave. I don't know if it will come to a split, but I do hope the DGB realizes the dangers of working within a united movement.' And he adds, significantly: 'The co-operative nature of the modern German system was a result of the Nazi experience – and the problem is that the young officials and the young company executives don't have these memories and don't have the same care.'

Rheinhard Ebert, head of the DBA's labour-market division, believes that the unions are in a quandary constructed of their own success: 'They have done a lot for their members and have helped to produce wealth. Now they must look for a different basis on which to motivate workers to join and continue to support them. Some political actions must be seen in this light: they have been taken to motivate members. But they are speaking more to themselves than to others.'

Japan's unions do not have mass unemployment to fuel their dissatisfactions, and the powerful plant union leaders, even less beholden to national union structures than the 'state princes' of West Germany, remain consensual and pro-company – so long as the companies continue to deliver full employment, the most carefully policed part of the industrial bargain. But they do have alert, ambitious left-wingers in the national union structure who are pushing for greater unity and greater militancy, among them Hiroshi Takahashi, head of Sohyo's labour-policy division, who proclaims a turning point in union wage-push tactics. 'Now that we're moving towards service-oriented industries, the unions there are playing a major role in wage negotiations, moving away from the dominant role of steel and manufacturing unions.' The Nikkeiren employers' group concedes that wage levels in services – NTT and railways, for example – are above the average.

Mr Takahashi, typically, appeals to a global view in his criticism of the softness of Japanese enterprise unions: 'Because Japanese unions are company-level, they are open to being persuaded that things are very bad when the conditions are adverse – but when times are good, the employers simply say nothing, and the unions don't take advantage.'

The employers look sourly at this and grumble, in exactly the same way as their West German counterparts, that the left-wingers are getting too powerful. But, also like the West Germans, they continue to believe that the enterprise-level unions will retain the all-important pragmatism, and in Japan at least, the politicization of unions is not obvious.

In West Germany clearly, in Japan more ambiguously, there are signs that the balanced corporatism of the post-war period is meeting large tests and that the power of the unions is under some question. Japanese employers think that the industrial-relations climate will be the most important factor influencing employment there in the next two years. Sixty-five per cent of Japanese employers say this would influence employment compared with a low of 16 per cent in Great Britain. Just as some Western unions are seeking to emulate Japanese and West German unions, so they are voicing sharp doubts about the advantages of incorporation. What remains, however, is evidence that the corporate model is more or less intact even while much of the advanced world has retreated from corporatism in the name of liberalization and efficiency.

There is always on offer in the labour movement an alternative to incorporation or oblivion: victory, variously defined as anything between a proletarian syndicalist revolution that displaces the ruling class and a state where the unions have a continuous hegemony over industry and society.

Of the advanced countries France, Italy and in a rather different way Britain have, since the war, exhibited the strongest interest in such a route. In France the biggest union confederation, the Confédération Générale du Travail, has throughout its history been largely inseparable from the French Communist Party (PCF). Even now, when the distance between the industrial and political wings is greater than before, communists dominate its ruling councils and always provide its general secretary: the present incumbent, Henri Krasucki, is also a member of the Party's central committee. The PCF, a flirtation with Euro-communism in the mid-1970s apart, remains attached both to the Soviet Union and to class struggle: when its militants engage in industrial strife – as at Renault in the autumn of 1985 and in the eighteen-month occupation of the SKF ball-bearing plant in Ivry ending in June 1986 – they are routinely engaged in pitched battles against the police, even against other (non-CGT) workers. When the occupation of Renault plants at Le Mans and Choisy-le-Roi ended in mid-October 1985 Pierre Beregovoy, the Socialist Finance Minister, told the CGT that its current loss of influence could continue only if it kept on agreeing to serve as an instrument of the Communist Party.

M. Beregovoy was not being particularly controversial: Georges Marchais, the now embattled PCF leader, has steadily put pressure on M. Krasucki to use the CGT as a battering ram against a Government from which, since June 1984, the communists have been absent and whose policies the PCF saw as class treachery. He was also right about the loss of influence: the CGT's admitted membership has declined from 2.35 million members in 1976 to 1.6 million in 1983. But no one outside the union believes these figures. The steel and mining industry employers' federation calculated the 1983 figure to be 980,000, falling to 835,000 in 1984. And in 1985 the CGT affiliate organizing merchant navy officers referred to its parent body as being 'reduced to less than 800,000'. The revolutionary route, even at a time of mounting unemployment under a Government of the moderate left, was being deserted in droves. Alain Touraine, one of the best-known of France's sociologists, says: 'The tragedy of French trade unionism is not its radicalism but its constant subordination of social struggle to political strategies. From that flows its feeble capacity to manage industrial conflict. From that comes the strong grip of the Communist Party on the unions.'

Some lessons have been learned. The CGT, in common with all other union centres, broke with tradition and gave no guidance to its membership on how to vote in the March 1986 elections. But the lessons have not gone too deep: M. Krasucki, and all other communists on the CGT executive, signed appeals to vote PCF 'in a personal capacity'.

The Italian unions suffered a solar plexus blow when, in the midst of a major strike at Fiat in Turin in 1980, thousands of workers took to the streets to demand a return to work. Says Angelo Gennari, an official of the Christian Democrat-inclined CISL union federation: 'After the Fiat strike the union veto on change was removed. It had an immense psychological impact. For the first time for fifteen years, organized workers found another force organized against them.'

The defeat of the referendum on the reduction of the *scala mobile* (automatic wage indexation system) in 1985 was a blow for the communist-led union federation CGIL (the largest) and for the Communist Party. Carlo Patrucco of Confindustria (the employers' association) says: 'This showed an increase in the maturity of the workers.' An index of the change is that the CGIL itself – unlike its Communist Party-led equivalent in France, the CGT – is willing to roll with the punch.

The unions retain their social partnership role: in Italy, as in West Germany, a common revulsion from the Fascist period still gives psychological support to an ideology that lays stress on strong and independent bodies. Indeed, the recession has seen a strengthening of national-level Government (employers) unions' negotiations over issues like the deregulation of Italy's labyrinthine labour law framework; while at plant level negotiations over increased flexibility and productivity have been pushed along by managers. Cesare Annibaldi at Fiat emphasizes that the company has always negotiated changes (but not the decision to change) with its unions – though its unionization rate was down to 35.5 per cent from 40 per cent in 1980. He concedes: 'In the past there were some plants where the power of the middle managers compared with that of shop stewards was not as it should have been.' Now, he says, the position is as it should be.

In the 1980s the automatic (arrogant?) assumption that workers were disciplinable into political camps by their unions has suffered many knocks, and has receded. The future of Italian unions, assured for the foreseeable period ahead, is none the less likely to be more modest than in the 1960s and 1970s.

Britain has never had a powerful Communist Party. In part for that reason, in part because the dominant left party, Labour, has never felt it necessary, or been able, to make the kind of theoretical discrimination between revolutionary and social democratic roads that the German SPD and the French socialists have, radical syndicalism has remained a strong strain within the ranks of a Labour movement routinely, before the 1970s, caricatured as more Methodist than Marxist, more carthorse than lion. That strain has, in the 1980s, been most ably articulated by Arthur Scargill, elected president of the National Union of Mineworkers in 1982, and the 1984–5 mineworkers' strike, in which the 'Here We Go' chant lifted from the football terraces expressed, in the heady early months of the strike, an apparently endless ambition of the aroused vanguard of the working class.

The miners' strike was the longest, bloodiest, most bitter strike since the (miner-inspired) general strike of 1926. But Scargill was wrong about its radicalizing the labour movement. Instead it forced a reluctant Neil Kinnock, the Labour leader, privately, then (after the strike was over) publicly, to draw the line between gradualism and the strategy of the coup, between reform and revolution – a service for which much (though not all) of the Labour Party seemed grateful.

In the wake of the strike the Labour Party and the unions both saw a general trend to the right in their governing bodies and policies, consolidating a movement dubbed 'new realism' that the now retired TUC general secretary, Len Murray, instituted in 1983 after Labour's slaughter in the general election – but that it took the most obvious object lessons to weld into place.

The revolutionary road, then, appears to be getting rockier. No major figure in Italy or the UK now speaks in the accents of the 1970s radicals, and in France those who do appear to be speaking from a script they find impossible to put down. In none of the advanced countries does there exist a persuasive model for the future that is, as it has been understood for the past century, revolutionary.

Is it, then, a slow decline to oblivion for those unions in the West that have not found some corporate support? Not surprisingly, exactly this perspective was put by a British miner, sacked during the strike and now turned student, to a seminar in the north-east city of Durham: 'I think unions are finished. I just don't see any future for them under capitalism.' His pessimism – or, to put it in reverse, the optimism of those who believe and wish that the decline is terminal – is presently excessive. But it is sure that those union movements faced with unfriendly Governments and tougher bosses are finding it hard work re-establishing a social and industrial base on which their futures as major social actors can be guaranteed.

In France unions are seeking to make themselves more amenable to a modern world which they see passing them by. One way is depoliticization. It has been evident, at least since the 1970s, that the strong political orientation of the

French unions has been an albatross, and the probable gainer has been the non-political Force Ouvrière, which claims a rise in membership from 837,000 in 1975 to nearly 1.2 million in 1984. The most articulate exponent of a new route for the unions has been Edmond Maire, leader of the Confédération Générale Démocratique de Travail, a socialist whose support for the Government helped the CFDT's membership fall from around 1 million in 1975 to around 850,000 in 1985. M. Maire has, especially since the March 1986 defeat for the left, pushed his own brand of 'new realism' – a mixture of support for the 'common good, and individualism'.

M. Maire's redefinition depends on the perception, common to others in other countries, that, as he says: 'The historic dynamic of the workers' movement, which sought real emancipation through collective guarantees and social security, is running down. Huge progress has been made in this area, so that while we must defend these gains in collective provision and extend them to those who don't have them, there is no longer sufficient motivation for a transforming movement [une action de transformation]. On the other hand, the change in the nature of work is an essential part of the new trade-union perspective. This is wholly new, in that it puts the individual back at the centre of the union.'

From there M. Maire moves to proposing several highly revisionist theses – among them that 'the company appears to be the main location of wealth creation'; that workers have a 'double solidarity', as producers of wealth and as union members; that 'achieving a financial result which allows a company to survive is not specifically a capitalist function'; and that 'we don't seek the total abolition of the private ownership of the means of production, nor do we wish the disappearance of market relations'. This philosophical pragmatism may be only a rationalization of what happens naturally in most enterprises anyway. At Moët-Hennessy, Alain Chevallier notes with pride that the company received an award (one of the judges was Edmond Maire) for the way in which it observed the (socialist) Government's labour legislation. Yves Bénard's Moët champagne workers are between 30 and 40 per cent unionized – double the French average – and he talks of a 'long tradition' of union–management co-operation: 'This tradition means that the representatives, even the CGT, take into account the problems of the company. Our agreement on flexible working was signed by all the unions though the CGT probably signed it against the advice of their national leaders. But the CGT has that attitude because we have fifty years of social dialogue behind us.'

British agonizing has been less elevated, and perhaps the problem is less acute. In gross terms it certainly is: where the lowest estimates put France's unions at around 13 per cent of the working population, few would seriously dispute that the UK unions organize less than 40 per cent, and conventional figures are around 45 per cent. Throughout the Thatcher period increases in real wages have remained consistently ahead of inflation, leading to a schizoid response from Government that veers from proclaiming that workers have never had it so good to exhorting them to have it less good for the sake of international competitiveness.

Many sectors, heavily unionized in the better years, remain so now with few problems. John Kerslake, general manager of Barclays' personnel division, says: 'We respect unions: we see them as part of the representative structure of the bank, and we're certainly not out to clobber them. They generally show a high degree of understanding of the pressures and the working of the industry. We wouldn't really want to develop enterprise unions – the current position is workable for both sides.' But in the areas where unions once exercised a powerful monopoly hold on their industries British employers have proved that who dares, wins. The steel unions were broken after a ten-week strike in 1980; the civil and health service unions achieved little in their prolonged disputes in 1980 and 1982; the miners were smashed in 1985. Even in national newspapers the drive for new technology and higher profits achieved success as a new newspaper, *Today*, introduced 'single-keystroke' printing (cutting out typesetting by printers) and as Rupert Murdoch's News International continued to produce non-print-union newspapers behind police lines and barbed wire.

Most unions are attempting an accommodation. At one extreme the electricians' union, the EETPU, has Japanese-style trade unionism, pioneering single-union, 'no-strike' deals that promise industrial peace for recognition and consultative councils. Their main successes have been in Japanese-owned subsidiaries, and they have found followers in the engineering union. The *FT* jobs poll shows that 42 per cent of firms say they do, or plan to, involve their workers in production decisions through meetings and discussions outside the normal trade-union channels. Joint consultative committees of some kind are most common in Japan, with 68 per cent of firms using them, followed by 62 per cent in France and 52 per cent in Britain. One-third of these firms say that these new channels of communication will become more important than negotiations with trade unions. Only 19 per cent of the British employers adopting this approach to industrial relations say it will outweigh trade-union bargaining.

In the centre of the movement John Edmunds, the clever new leader of the General and Municipal Workers, echoes Edmond Maire in identifying individualism as a horse to ride: at his conference in June 1986 he showed his members' figures forecasting relentless employment decline in their best-organized sectors and proposed a campaign to push unions as champions of individual rights – eschewing self-interested special pleading in favour of real changes for real members. On the left Ron Todd, leader of the country's biggest union, the Transport and General Workers, acknowledges that the ground has shifted irreversibly and that unions must develop 'the commitment to make sense of the new forces' – among which he counts 'the amazing power consumers have acquired to change their tastes and demands across a world market'.

But the unions, right and left, remain umbilically attached to the Labour Party, 80 per cent of whose income they provide. It no longer promises them, as it did in the early 1970s, a union-dominated Labour future. Indeed, Neil

Kinnock has sought to impress upon them that a future Government which *he* headed would retain the individual rights legislated on by the present Government and would pursue what amounts to an anti-inflationary incomes policy irrespective of their putative opposition. But the Labour Party holds out the hope at least of lower unemployment, a return to a corporatist approach, a bolstering of union power at the workplace – certainly enough, in hard times, to retain the loyalty of the union leaderships.

Some see the closeness of the relationship as a mistake. John Lyons, leader of the power engineers and a recent convert to the Social Democratic Party, concedes that the TUC should, and anyway will, retain a 'special relationship' with Labour, but insists that it should 'enter into discussions with other parties in the country that might form a future Government, or be part of a future Government. The relations will not be the same as with the Labour Party, but it is the TUC's job to influence thinking about the economy, industry, employment and industrial-relations legislation in any party likely to take part in the country's future Government.'

The battleground, then, is corporatism versus liberalism: the first promises, and already gives, unions a future; the latter is at best ambiguous about it. For the unions of France, Italy and Britain the search is on for a corporatism that encompasses the 'new forces' Ron Todd and others like him uneasily recognize and convincingly promises a more efficient delivery of the unions' side of the corporate bargain.

There can be no certainty as to the outcome of the unions' strategies. Says Colin Crouch: 'In those countries where there is a strong legacy of successful tripartite co-operation, the unions will probably be able to use that legacy to ease some of these dilemmas, and they will face little pressure for attempts by employers and conservative forces to marginalize them. But in countries lacking such traditions the unions' future will be extremely difficult. Despite the increasing integration of the world economy, there is likely to be a divergence in patterns of industrial relations in Western Europe.'

The United States is another case apart. There unionization is down to French levels – around 15 per cent – but the unions lack the corporate support that still permeates large parts of the French industrial and political establishment.

The post-war industrial-relations settlement built on New Deal and wartime policies that were supportive of unions and collective bargaining. Until the 1960s unionization appeared to be accepted as part of the American way in the industrial states. There were, though, always major companies that took the non-union route: IBM is the most famous, but also Motorola, Sears Roebuck and Delta Airlines. From the 1960s new companies, and established companies with weak unionization, increasingly adopted 'human resource management systems', which cut out or bypassed union-dominated collective bargaining by using direct communication with workers, increased (above union minima) pay and enhanced status for supervisory staff. It worked: the unions, mostly organized in the AFL–CIO confederation, did not show any corresponding innovation in their bargaining and organization strategies and were progressively corralled into their northern big-industry redoubts. By the recessionary late 1970s they were unmistakably in dangerous decline.

Matters have not improved. The Reagan administration, while its head occasionally likes to recall that he is the first former union president (of the screen actors' guild) to make it to the White House, has been unremittingly hostile to organized labour. It solved an air traffic controllers' strike by arresting the strikers, destroying the union. It made a series of appointments to the Department of Labor and to the National Labor Relations Board who were openly inimical to unions. Further, the industrial redoubts were frequently in trouble and have developed a style of bargaining known as 'concessionary' or 'give-back' bargaining, in which unions retain their organization only by agreeing to mass redundancies, (often large) wage cuts or wide-scale changes in work organization, frequently by lengthening working hours. In some cases, as at General Motors, new 'quality of working life' programmes have been instituted with union support; in others they have contributed to union weakness.

In an important survey, 'US Industrial Relations in Transition', Thomas Kochan, Robert McKersie and Harry Katz argue: 'We believe there is a central contradiction in the current operation of US industrial relations. Leaders from all parts of society are calling for an expansion of co-operative efforts at the workplace. They are also asking union leaders to support these co-operative efforts and to continue moderating their wage demands. At the same time, the dominant trend in strategic business and industrial-relations decision-making at the highest levels within firms is to shift investments and jobs to non-unionized settings. Moreover, Government policies are not creating an environment in which the labor movement can feel secure about its future as a viable force in American society.' But where labour is still organized, as in the Detroit car industry, it is powerful, and it produces and sustains a rich culture. The Ford Rouge plant in Detroit is such a place.

It looms over south-western Detroit, a mass of smoking chimneys, railroad tracks and factory after factory. The sprawling 1,100-acre Ford Rouge complex is more like a natural phenomenon than a manufacturing plant. It appeared to move to a rhythm of its own, sucking in iron ore, labour and other raw materials at one end and pumping out cars at the other. It seems inconceivable that the stroke of an accountant's pen could bring this enormous industrial machine to a halt. But, bit by bit, that is what has happened.

Henry Ford first suggested building a fully integrated manufacturing facility in 1918. The idea was to make all the components for a car within a single complex. And it still has some of the trappings of the grand design of the past: a power station that generates enough electricity to serve a city the size of Boston; over 100 miles of railway track and sixteen Ford diesel locomotives. But gone are the two iron foundries, the battery plant, the tyre factory, along with transmissions, radiators and electrical parts. 'We constantly face the threat of work being transferred elsewhere – outsourced to somewhere else in the USA or abroad. But Ford's initial idea was insourcing, and, ironically, that is what General Motors have done at Buick City and Volkswagen at Wolfsburg. But the company seems to be happy to let the Rouge go,' says local union president Bob King.

Mr King's Local 600, the United Auto Workers (UAW) organization in the area, once had a membership of 90,000 – the army of people who worked in the Rouge in the 1950s and 1960s. Now, after automation and decentralization, the Rouge employs just 16,000. Between 1978 and 1986 employment fell by half.

Since 1982, when the company came to the bargaining table looking for concessions, the union has been treading a tightrope. 'We wanted to co-operate then and we did, with a wage freeze, profit-sharing, greater flexibility and the like – and we are prepared to hold to our side of the bargain in the future. We have to be flexible. But we can never be sure that the company really wants to hold to its part of the deal,' says Mr King.

While urging on union members the new company values of people, products and profits and extolling co-operation, the management still turns all too easily to the threat of outsourcing to get what it wants in industrial relations. Nevertheless, Mr King admits some things have changed for the better. In a room down the hall from his office, union members were tapping away at word-processors on a company-sponsored training course. According to Mr King: 'That kind of thing would have been unimaginable eight years ago. The whole company training programme since 1982 has been enormously popular.' There is also greater involvement and information than there used to be. It is now much more common for the company to open up its books. And there has been investment in the Rouge plant. In the largest single-plant conversion in the company's history the Dearborn engine facility was turned into one of the most modern in the USA, at a cost of $650 million. The outlook for workers there looks rosy. But it stands cheek by jowl with plants that have not changed much since the Second World War. 'I do not think the union is going to split into two groups, one made up of the high-productivity workers in modern plants and the other drawn from workers in older plants threatened with closure. The links of solidarity are too strong in the Rouge,' says Mr King.

Yet the union has changed in the past few years. According to Mr King, profit-sharing is here to stay, as is a willingness to contemplate changes to working practices and job classifications. The union has also recognized the need to reach out beyond the Rouge to maintain its base. Of the local membership 2,000 are health workers, organized through a membership drive that last year netted the national UAW a further 30,000 new members. 'We have to be flexible, to be able to respond to the different challenges that the company is throwing us. We cannot be tied to the old rules of the past about how a union should behave.' But Mr King emphasizes that flexibility does not mean capitulation: 'The good things that we have now, like the national training programme and schemes to guarantee the income of laid-off workers, have not been bright ideas suggested by management. They have come about through hard negotiation and the union showing its strength.'

The uneasy truce between union and management, going backwards and forwards between conflict and co-operation, is likely to continue. After two years of good profits there is a growing sense in the Local that the time of reckoning has come. The concessions demanded of the union in the early 1980s still rankle, and, according to Mr King, the Local's members want to see whether the company will live up to its side of the bargain by investing in the Rouge and lifting threats of outsourcing. 'You can have as much training, employee involvement, protected employee programmes and profit-sharing as you like, but it's no good if you do not have a job. The company does give us more information, but there are tremendous threats facing this industry over the next ten years, and we have this constant worry that the company is not really addressing that issue honestly with us. It is all too possible that in ten years' time the Rouge will be just assembling cars manufactured elsewhere.'

People in the area talk of the Rouge as if it has a personality. Though a young, progressive union leader, Mr King admits to a fascination with the power of the ageing industrial giant. He started work there in 1972, having turned down a place at post-graduate law school to take up a Ford apprenticeship for the chance to work in the midst of the Rouge. And if people want to know where the *real* economy is, they should come to the Rouge, for as Wall Street goes into its daily frenzy, politicians squabble in Washington and Ford accountants do their sums in neat offices, the dirty, smelly Rouge throbs on. It is hard to believe it could be different. As one union member put it: 'It would be like flooding the Grand Canyon.'

The unions are, of course, trying to recover some ground. The AFL–CIO has formed a highest-level committee on the Evolution of Work, whose second report, in February 1985, recognized that 'Unions now face employers who are bent on avoiding unionization at all costs [the committee estimated employers spent $100 million annually on doing so] and who are largely left free to do so by a law that has proved impotent and a Labor Board that is inert.' It somewhat optimistically saw some 'seeds of resurgence' and called for a range of improvements and changes of attitude, among which the first was to abandon the sledgehammer, everybody's-the-same approach in favour of 'multiple models for representing workers tailored to the needs of different groups'. David Schecter, an AFL–CIO economist, says: 'One way the AFL is adapting to changed demands of membership is to offer them other reasons for being in the union – like individual benefits. We are about to launch a new credit-card service for members at a 14 per cent interest rate.' And John Zalusky, a collective bargaining analyst at the AFL–CIO, reflects: 'This in a sense is moving the unions back to some of their older roles as friendly societies – giving members direct benefits rather than just trying to represent them through collective bargaining.'

In the USA union oblivion is frequently talked of as not only possible but inevitable. The unions are still on their mettle to prove it otherwise.

6. 'GET SMART'

'Don't get sacked, get smart': this is the kind of motto that should be hung, as mottoes are in Japanese plants, above every production line and office area in the country. It is the injunction that has to be heeded by today's workers if they want to be workers tomorrow, and it is the motto whose adoption offers the advanced countries the best chance of not succumbing to a tide of developing-world competition from the new industrial armies of the East. Training in new technology, new processes, new ways to deal with colleagues, new approaches to customers, new ways to transfer ideas from institutions to real life – training in new ways to train, indeed: working life is, for increasing numbers, more and more resembling an institution of higher education – just as such institutions are drawing closer and closer to the world of work.

What is going is the assumption, common still to most adults above the age of 30, that education and training take place at the beginning of working life and last to the end of it, more or less. At Thyssen's Huller Hille machine-tool plant on the Ruhr the highly skilled workers are retrained *every year*, for three or four weeks, in electronics. Gunter Weigel, the company's vice-president, says: 'The products are developing so fast that it's necessary. We're spending more and more money on education every year.' 'Training,' says IBM UK's technical director, Dr Geoff Robinson, 'is now a continuing process. We have to inculcate an ethos of continuing educational and training change.' IBM already has that ethos: 5 per cent of its employees are training at any given time.

This is common across all the advanced countries, all the advanced industries – though there is a significant difference as to whom they train, and when, and how much, and in what. The FT jobs poll found that skill shortages will have a significant impact on companies' development in all major economies: 61 per cent of firms expect skills shortages of some kind to impede their growth in the next four years.

Skills shortages will be most acute in West Germany, where 84 per cent of firms will be affected, followed by Japan with 66 per cent and Britain with 60 per cent. Fifty-seven per cent of West German employers expect a shortage of professional staff to impede growth, compared with a low of 20 per cent in Britain. More than half of West German firms will be hit by a shortage of traditional skilled labour compared with a low of 14 per cent in Japan. In more than a quarter of firms growth will be impaired by a shortage of staff trained to use computers and information technology generally.

All companies need electronic engineers and software people and cannot get them; they all want their managers to gain a range of skills, especially personal skills, that were previously 'not their job'; they all want craft workers to be multi-skilled rather than one-directional, so they can look after the machines that do the work; they all want fewer simple operatives; they all want more professionals with their own training and then some more in the company's business. In short, they want to – must – raise the cultural level of all the workers except those they think cannot learn and those they want to dump. Paul Roots, Ford UK's personnel director, says: 'We have had too many people doing too few things. Now we want fewer people to do more, to upgrade their skills and responsibility.' Armand Braun, head of the Société Internationale des Conseillers de Synthèse, puts the dilemma of this last group poignantly: 'We in Europe have a population whose degree of preparation for the modern world could be represented, irrespective of the age group in question, as 20 per cent ready, 20 per cent totally unprepared and the rest only muddling through. Are we surprised, then, when we meet widespread anxiety concerning the future and the individual's place in it? People seem disoriented, deprived of the old certitudes, as they see unqualified work disappear before their very eyes.'

Millions of working men were (are) proud of their physical strength, millions of working women of their nimble fingers. When A. J. Sykes spent six months among Scots and Irish construction workers in 1969 in order to find out about their working culture, he discovered huge, competitive arrogance about how strenuous a job could be borne, carelessness over safety and health and delight in hardship and abrasive personal and industrial relations.

Now the muscles and the quick fingers are a glut on the market: the British Occupational Study Group report, in its summary of the occupations needed and those not needed, emphasizes the point: 'operatives', the jobs that need the presence of a body, are on their way out in both the manufacturing and the services sector. The only defence is to move up the skills ladder, though for older workers who have ingrained in them the rhythms of, say, foundry work – where bouts of intense physical activity are interspersed with rests – the light but continuous work on a line or the complexities of keyboarding skills (which they may have permanently dismissed as 'women's work') are hard, even impossible, to pick up.

Cesare Annibaldi, Fiat board member for industrial relations, recalls the creation of a plant at Termoli, in the Mezzogiorno. The company installed 1,000 robots and transferred workers from older factories, but it took up to ten months' training for the older workers to get used to the systems. Sr Annibaldi instances two problems: first, the need to change working mentality from one suited to operating a line to one suited to controlling or supervising a machine that operates the line; and, second, transforming mechanical or electrical maintenance workers into people with dual skills – especially difficult, says Sr Annibaldi, in the case of mechanical maintenance workers.

Raising training levels is not easy. How much is done by schools or colleges, and how specialized do they become? How much is borne by the state, how much by the employer? How can standards be maintained when training is the easiest part of the budget to cut in hard times, as the UK found when the recession hit in 1980? How far do you train manual workers to take over what were white-collar skills, how far the reverse? When do you guide children towards specialization? What do you do with older workers who have the wrong skills or none at all?

The FT jobs poll gives some indication of whether employers think that their own country's public education system is equipped to meet their needs. Two trends in particular emerge from the poll. First, Japanese employers have a crisis of confidence in the country's education and training system. Second, every employer in each country said that the secondary education system does not instil enough work discipline in young people.

Overall a majority of employers said they were satisfied with the qualities of the young workers they hired straight from school. In the USA satisfied employers outnumbered the dissatisfied by 40 per cent, in France by 30 per cent and in West Germany by 25 per cent. In contrast, 61 per cent of British employers and 64 per cent of Japanese employers said they were dissatisfied with the educational standards of school-leavers. All dissatisfied employers said that school-leavers do not have enough work discipline. The next most important factor is lack of self-motivation (61 per cent). The only exception to the general trends is in the US, where dissatisfied American employers mention basic skills as a problem, compared with a low of 30 per cent in France.

Overall 83 per cent of employers say they are satisfied with the skills and outlook of people they hire from technical colleges. In Japan, however, the satisfied outnumber the dissatisfied by only 9 per cent, while in the other four countries the margin averages 80 per cent.

Higher education gets a high rating in every country but Japan. At the top come US employers, with 97 per cent satisfied with the country's universities, followed by West Germany (90 per cent) and Britain (86 per cent). In Japan, however, 58 per cent of employers are dissatisfied. Low self-motivation and lack of relevant knowledge and skills are the most frequently quoted sources of dissatisfaction with university graduates. In Britain, however, over half the dissatisfied employers think that graduates have an antipathy to business, compared with 25 per cent of dissatisfied employers elsewhere.

Government training programmes get a lower satisfaction rating than universities or technical colleges, but 64 per cent of employers say they are satisfied with their Government's training schemes. Satisfaction is highest in France, with 85 per cent satisfied, followed by Britain (61 per cent). In contrast, a majority of Japanese employers are dissatisfied with their Government's training effort. Across all countries, including Japan, 60 per cent of dissatisfied employers say Government-training workers need retraining on joining the company. However, less than a third of British employers think that the Manpower Services Commission is doing a good job. A quarter think it does a poor job in the field of skill training.

If any country did have the answer, it was reckoned to be West Germany: its education system is the object of emulation by most of the advanced countries, and the pride of the West Germans themselves. Why?

German schools are more skill-oriented than most. Entrance to the three types – main, intermediate and grammar (*Hauptschulen, Realschulen* and *Gymnasien*) – is by examination between the ages of 10 and 12. School-leaving certificates, the necessary possession for entry into any profession, are given by all three. Some ten subjects are studied, with an emphasis on minimum attainments in a core of these, all examined together in the final year.

Of those who leave school to embark on training courses, the majority do so at 15 (when compulsory schooling ends). They then take a training course, in a company, under a master craftsman and are released one day a week to a vocational school (*Berufschule*), where both the vocational subject and general subjects are taught. Hence the so-called 'dual system' – part on-the-job training, part continued schooling – for at least three years in all occupational groups. The system does produce a highly skilled workforce: the 1978 German household survey showed that two-thirds of the workforce had a vocational or higher qualification, compared with only one-third in, for example, the UK.

Professor S. J. Prais, of the UK's National Institute of Economic and Social Research and a proselytizer for the West German system says: 'The important contrast with Britain is that for many decades there have been well-laid-out career paths involving graded courses, examinations and recognized qualifications for that broad middle section of the population that lies between, on the one hand, those who go to a university or otherwise enter a profession and, on the other hand, those who are unskilled.' At least twice as many people in West Germany have skilled worker qualifications as in the UK, and in categories like office work and retail, where skills are rare in Britain, the difference is much greater.

West Germany has developed an industrial culture in which the leadership groups – employers, unions, Government, commentators – support the training system not just formally but actively: indeed, all now see it as a weapon against unemployment. Says Gustav Fehrenbach, deputy chairman of the DGB: 'Training people beyond the immediate economic need offers much greater future flexibility and the adaptability to make continuous changes in a person's occupational career.' Because these reflexes are already in place, the system is seen as able to respond to the demands of an information age that needs its human capital stock smartened up more regularly and to fulfil a role explicitly seen as social, even moral, as well as technical. One (anonymous) employer told a researcher from the UK's Institute of Manpower Studies: 'We see no fundamental change: we need continuity within which we shall be able to manage higher levels of personal and organizational flexibility. [The dual system] must continue to supply high-quality workers to provide high-quality goods and services and to help maintain a low-crime, stable society.' The competence of the training system to tackle issues beyond the mere transmission of skills is understood by Dr Rosenmoller at the Federal Labour Ministry. 'We have to do everything we can to avoid the segmentation of the labour market into the highly skilled and the low skilled. This is one reason for a "qualifications offensive": we do our utmost to get people into the qualifications system.'

This offers something of a contrast with the USA and the UK, where (at least until recently and arguably still) employer and Government policy, or neglect, has tended to permit the development of a larger and larger 'periphery' of unskilled and semi-skilled workers, often low-paid and insecure, existing around a 'core' of skilled or professional secure and relatively highly paid employees. This two-tone labour market, whose supporters point to its great flexibility, is an object of some horror for Dr Rosenmoller, who characterizes it as a 'McDonald's' labour market, after the fast-food chain, which has a high turnover of young, transient workers tightly organized by line management. He says: 'We need *more* qualified people, not fewer. In offices now, for example, there is almost no demand for unskilled workers. Of course, the "McDonald's" labour market will continue to exist, but it is small.'

All of this is expensive. Rheinhard Ebert, who heads the labour-market division at the German Employers' Association (DBA), reckons that his members collectively spend some DM 30 billion a year on their part of the training programme and a further DM 10 billion on retraining. That represents, he says, between 75 and 80 per cent of the cost. Public provision is focused mainly on the provision of teaching and school facilities by state governments, with the federal level supporting group training centres and special-needs training. In 1980 the Edding Commission found the average annual gross cost of a trainee to be DM 17,043, though the cost of an engineering apprentice was higher (DM 23,743) than that of a shopworker (DM 14,439). Also by the end of the training period, Edding reckoned, the apprentices were 'worth' an annual average of DM 9,929 to their companies.

West German employers grumble about education as much as their colleagues in other countries: the main burden of their complaints is often centred on what they see as the other-worldly, anti-industry attitudes of German schools and universities. The Institute of Manpower Studies researcher noted: 'Dissatisfaction with the higher education system is widespread. Employers are uneasy about the quality of graduates, about the length of time students spend in higher education and about the lack of response to changing educational needs.' At Thyssen Industrie, Werner Bartels says: 'During the past twenty years the school system in Western Europe has deteriorated. There is too much education of people in the arts and in theoretical disciplines. In our best technical universities only 30 per cent finish their studies. In schools they are not motivated to come into industry. They get a negative image.'

These views are the products of industrialists who are also themselves educationalists operating something of a rival training and educational system to that offered by the federal and state system. West German training has broken down the barrier that often separates business from higher education in countries like the UK, Italy and France and that is the object of furious concern in those countries. It has done so not just by creating strong links between governments and universities (these links are proving fruitful for companies like Thyssen) but also by internalizing a large part of the higher or further educative function. And, like any public education system, it confers its own degrees and certificates. One of the many comparative studies done between UK and West German training provisions found that, in similar plants, fourteen out of sixteen UK production foremen had no qualifications of any kind, nor had served an apprenticeship, while in the German plants all sixteen were certificated craftsmen, thirteen had passed exams as *Meisters* (master craftsmen) and three were trying to become *Meisters*.

But will it work in the future? In particular, will it be able to meet the twin challenges of the rapidly growing demand for information-technology skills and the need, because of the rapid falling away of the supply of young workers, to train and retrain older workers in unfamiliar skills? Hans Gert Woelke, whose board-level personnel job puts him in charge of all of this, sees the skill needs bubbling up from his companies' divisions and subsidiaries on every side. He confesses to a 'lack of flexibility in the training system' and grumbles mildly about union resistance to change and the immobility of German workers: once trained, they resist moving to where their skills are most needed. Electronics is the keenest challenge: 'We have to give our employees different attitudes in looking at electronics. The attitude is to avoid it at all costs because it is seen as a job killer.'

At Thyssen Industrie, and at its Huller Hille subsidiary, lack of skilled workers is one of the largest production bottlenecks. Herr Bartels says: 'It's a great constraint. We're moving the production of machining centres to plants in the south, partly to be nearer to where the skills are. We must have changes in the education process because we just can't get enough skills.' A recent survey by the Prognos research group showed that over the past decade some 80 per cent of the workforce would need *some* training in information technology – only 5 per cent now had it. 'Before the present,' says Dr Rosenmoller, looking down at it from a Federal Labour Ministry office in a quiet Bonn suburb, 'you could depend to a large extent on the inter-generational changes. When grandfather retired, father continued in slightly different way, and the grandson coming in learned new techniques. But now it's train, retrain, every five years. The barriers between work and training are no longer rigid.'

The strain of shifting resources and skills to new areas is clearly causing the system to creak but not to break: it remains both a model for others and a perceived success on the part of its participants. It has still much going for it – especially, perhaps, a belief in itself.

The importance of culture is paramount. Any training or educational system depends on social relations and assumptions, both in industry and in society generally. Structured training patterns, respect for qualifications and for authority, an industrial ethic that stresses quality and 'engineers' it rather than 'inspecting' it retrospectively, managements whose responsibility for the moulding of human capital is assumed and (generally) not regarded as intrusive: all of these are to be found in West Germany – and in Japan.

Japanese companies share with German companies the characteristic of internalizing the educational functions that in other states exist only outside the factory gates. Any training system naturally transmits a company ethos as well as technical information. In Japan the transmission of the ethos is deliberate, constant and turned up to a high volume: it is probably more important than technical competence (which *is* seen as important). The intra-company exclusiveness, the corporate and collective identification, the sense of mutual obligation, of submission to a large, collective need – these values do not merely exist in Japanese industry; they are 'engineered in' from the outset of a company member's life.

Take Toyota, the world's leading car maker. Its guide to training gives a picture of a company in which individual development is directly and constantly linked to corporate performance: 'Toyota has a need to "build" men to build the better cars the world needs . . . In one form or another almost every Toyota employee continues to learn throughout his entire working career.' 'Human resources development' at Toyota has, of course, a motto: it is 'Creativity, challenge and courage', the 'three Cs' that express 'a sloughing off of conventional perspectives and concepts and exhilarating personal readiness for self-development in anticipation of the demands of a new era'.

All entrants to Toyota – in common with other big Japanese companies – are trained as soon as they enter. From the outset they find a mix of on-the-job training and structured education at institutes such as the Toyota Technical High School. From the outset too it is made clear what they are being trained *for* – not to be car workers but to be members of a company that is itself changing in response to internal needs and external pressures. 'Changes occur rapidly in contemporary society, and the information and knowledge gained in ordinary schooling is often insufficient to deal effectively with all working situations. The most important task for the promotion of future corporate activities is to develop personnel who have the basic abilities and adaptability to respond to change, are highly motivated to work and can take resolute action.'

All employees are urged to 'pool their wisdom and continually strive to carry out improvements at the work site'. Self-starting is stressed: on-the-job training is seen as a cross between supervision and learning on one's own: each employee must 'participate actively in management and have a strong motivation to work'. At all levels top company management, including the company president, lectures, demonstrates and exhorts: it also participates in the network of voluntary activities – quality circles, clubs, the 'campaign to improve dormitory life' (in which some 16,000 Toyota employees live), study groups and language (mainly English) centres – that compete for the company members' free time. 'The energetic approach of Toyota's top managers to education has continued to build a corporate climate that strongly emphasizes the development of employee competence.'

At Hitachi, Takashi Kashiwagi, board member for labour relations, says: 'The concept here is to make the best use of human resources.' He is as critical as his West German counterparts, however, of school-level education and is lobbying the Education Ministry to improve the quality and numbers of students taking engineering and advanced electronics: like every other advanced country, Japan cannot get enough of these people.

At every stage of company life Hitachi workers are trained and retrained, stretched and tested. Some 1,000 graduates are taken on from the higher educational system and between 2,000 and 3,000 graduates from the high and junior high schools: many go to the Hitachi Technical School, some to the Hitachi College, which offers a full-time, fifteen-month course of study for some 250 students at a time.

At Nissan, Futoshi Fujii is also concerned with a scarcity of electronics skills – so concerned, indeed, that he is doing the un-Japanese thing of employing other companies' workers to upgrade Nissan's skill levels. But more important is a training programme that involves climbing up a hierarchy of electronic and micro-electronic skills to fully trained status with, at each level, a grade assigned on a cartoon-spiced chart that workers carry with them. Some sixty or seventy of the British workers who will occupy the key shop-floor positions in the Nissan plant in the north of England have been trained at the company's Opama plant. 'They learn the jobs even better than many Japanese workers do,' says Mr Fujii, with a becoming show of national modesty and civility.

Companies are likely to get more like universities rather than less. Professor Kuwahara, at the Japanese Institute of Labour, says, 'The educational system in Japan is not very flexible – the transfer of students into new subjects like electronics is not adequate. So Japanese companies will rely more and more on their own training systems.'

The Japanese system, more than the West German, depends for its obvious success on *the primacy of company and collective over civil society and the individual* in key respects. It is a radical, highly organized and energetic system: it is currently building men and (a few) women to build better kinds of everything, whose flood through the world markets may be slowed by a higher yen but not halted. It is setting the standard for production workforces. Will it be – can it be – matched elsewhere?

Whether or not it can be *matched*, it is being *copied*, most of all in the advanced country with the best-developed tradition of state-level planning, France. And though this tradition is often held to be inimical to local and company-level developments, it is now clear – as it was under the previous socialist administration – that the focus in training, and in much else, is changing in favour of the company.

And explicitly too. Henri Guillaume, director of the Plan which underpins French economic, individual and social strategy, published in 1986 a visionary guide to the French future. Training was firmly located as central – and as lagging badly behind the two role models selected for emulation, West Germany and Japan. M. Guillaume points to an 80 per cent possession of a Baccalauréat (high-school certificate) equivalent in Japan, against 37 per cent in France: the report by the Commissariat du Plan on training (January 1985) says: 'Industrial-relations practice has for some time set in place in West Germany a system of managing skill qualifications that is much more favourable to industrial dyna-mism than in France . . . [In Japan] continuing training in large, medium and small enterprises is taken up not as an obligation but as a necessity for the company's progress and for raising wages.'

Says M. Guillaume: 'We have to redefine job training to adapt it to future change, whatever the difficulty of foreseeing that. This presupposes a training system that is multi-purpose, multi-skilled, taking in whole "families" of jobs rather than specializing in a single craft – and, more generally, raising the qualifications level. Companies, in the public and private sectors, cannot tolerate the level of skills training with which we've been content in France to date – in contrast to the policies of West Germany – and which does not give workers the capacity to master the range of situations they must now confront. Permanent training is, from here on, an absolute imperative, on the same level as research or investment. Indeed, it is the first investment.'

M. Chevallier agrees: among the first of his innovations when he took over Moët-Hennessy fifteen years ago was to upgrade his employees' skills. 'The pressures of quality, of competitiveness and of being in the race mean that you have to change the qualifications of your people all the time. This is so even in the so-called traditional businesses because they are no longer traditional. What we are seeing in our business increasingly is the marriage of technology with practical knowledge and skill.'

In 1984 Moët undertook a wide-ranging reclassification of jobs while at the same time introducing more intensive training programmes at every level – both measures aimed at adapting to the new production and office technologies that it was adopting and that were changing the nature of much of its work. The company report's rhetoric borrows from the Japanese in its description of this development: 'The Moët-Hennessy group relies heavily above all on people, on quality products and also on recognized principles of action that create the ambience, the style, in a word the consensus, necessary to the company's progress.'

M. Chevallier has linked with the company, through either acquisition (as in the case of Delbur, the tissue and bio-technology company) or collaboration, centres of research and study whose participation in turn requires the company to raise its intellectual sights and standards. 'We now have to have people in research who are very specifically trained and people at every level who are trained in technology. For example, the manager of a vineyard for Moët in the past had little training and grew up in a family that was traditionally in that sector. Now such a manager would come from an advanced technical school.'

This most quintessentially French business is now a science-based industry, which picks up techniques from the USA – where it has large Californian wineries and owns Armstrong Roses – and Australia, where it also has wineries. In these subsidiaries, says M. Chevallier, 'We had to rethink the process because the climate was different and the people were different. These give us new ideas, which are of use back in France. But the people back in the vineyards had to be trained in tissue culture. They had to rethink the whole process once again, to find new ways of improving the planting process and improving the immunity of the plants – but at the same time you must not lose quality.'

Greater attention to training is now paying off – even in an industry as traditional and as buccaneering as the building trade. In France, as in the UK and the USA, the trade attracts a high proportion of recent immigrants; in France too, much of it is in the black economy, the French foreman typically retaining a *caisse noire* from which to disburse funds for non-declared labour. But the French building trade is a lot better than the British: a National Institute of Economic and Social Research (NIESR) study shows that while output per French employee is generally 25 per cent higher than in the UK, output in construction is 33 per cent higher.

The study lays much of that at the door of a training system that is part of the nationwide Certificat d'Aptitude Professionelle, which commands broad respect in industry and is similar to the West German system. The system relies too on vocational schools for pupils between 14 and 17 (the UK had a similar system before comprehensivization); a 17-year-old can emerge from such a school as a craftsman with a broad range of experience. The training cuts across trade demarcations, says the NIESR study, and 'enables the craftsman to feel responsible for a whole phase of construction, and is likely to reduce defects arising from lack of co-ordination between successive stages of building'.

In West Germany and Japan, potentially in France, training has been, and is being, further developed as a tool of industrial and social progress, internalized as part of companies' routine and continually stressed as a business activity that is as important as, or more important than, any other. In each case, especially in France, with its *grandes écoles* producing business and political leaders (like M. Chevallier), elites are produced by design: in each case, especially the Japanese and the West German, workers at *every* level are also educated to a high standard, also by design.

Professor Sir James Dewar, in his presidential address to the British Association in 1902, said (superciliousness showing through the concern), 'It is in the abundance of men of ordinary plodding ability, thoroughly trained and methodically directed, that Germany has so commanding an advantage.' It still does, as do others: and the advantage shows in many ways other than simply in the skill statistics or the productivity per employee. But how do other countries respond? And is there time?

There is no question that they believe they must, with good cause, at least in the case of Italy and the UK. In Italy the number of apprentices entering industry declined from a peak in 1968 of 831,613, or 4.1 per cent of those in employment, to 554,451 in 1984, or 2.7 per cent. In Italy, as in the UK, a cause assigned to the falling away of the apprenticeship system was the relatively high wages paid to apprentices – though these fell sharply in 1984.

Besides apprenticeships, there are two parallel approaches to vocational training: the gaining of a vocational certificate or technician-level certificate through study at school, or entry to a vocational training centre, whether public or private, whether run by municipality, religious order or trade union. The vocational centres are seen as having lower status than schooling leading to college. Training is often abandoned, and little off-the-job training is generally given to apprentices.

In the UK, with its keen, even masochistic, sense of its relative decline, the problem is now endlessly rehashed. Here too there has been a precipitous decline in apprenticeships and traineeships, from 346,600 in 1972 to 150,300 in 1983. Change has come: the two-year Youth Training Scheme aims to give every school-leaver who wishes it a two-year practical training course, mainly employer-based (though there is evidence that the public sector is providing the bulk of jobs, especially in hard-hit areas – and that 'training' can mean dogsbody duties). The Technical and Vocational Education Initiative has since 1984 inserted practical training into a school curriculum formerly dominated by academic standards even where the children were non-academic.

For adults the Open University has for twenty years given people a second chance to enter higher education based in the home. Since 1983 the Open Tech has been doing the same for skills and will by the end of 1987 have some 50,000 customers.

Public provision, after initial apparent indifference by the first Thatcher Government, when training provision went down very rapidly indeed, is not now the largest part of the British problem. John Cassels, director-general of the UK's somewhat ignored National Economic Development Office and a concerned advocate of more training, says, 'To put it bluntly, the real problem is that by and large, beyond what is immediately and visibly essential, industry does not yet much believe in training.'

Mr Cassels has evidence on his side. A 1986 study by consultants Coopers and Lybrand for the Manpower Services Commission and NEDO indicated what it thought of British industry's record by calling itself 'a challenge to complacency'. In a survey of sixty large companies it showed that 'few chief executives had much knowledge of the training activities undertaken within their firm'; that it was often 'viewed simply as a reaction to other corporate decisions', and that, worst of all, 'training expenditure is . . . not seen as an investment expected to lead to an identifiable income stream, but rather more as an overhead which can, like building maintenance, be reduced when times are hard . . . The implied link between training and profitability was not often recognized.'

Ford UK is far from the worst example: it may be among the best, indeed. But Paul Roots, conceding that too many workers did too few tasks, points up the distance the company has to travel from the multi-skilled, flexible worker who is already the tradition in West German and Japanese plants. 'We have,' he says, 'been unable to organize the work to draw out fully the skills and productivity of our people.' The aim is obviously 'Japanization' – but it is a goal, not an achievement. 'We want the future workforce to be lean, flexible about its tasks, skilled with better technical competence, able to work without direct supervision, so eradicating a level of organization. We want to pass responsibility down the line' (more than an echo of the Toyota exhortation to 'participate actively in management').

Barclays is also in the skills business: like Ford UK, it spends some £25 million a year on training. It is part technology-driven, but is more than that. Like any big company aware of the need for training anywhere, Barclays shows that teaching a skill is no longer transmitting a piece of relatively timeless knowledge; it is, increasingly, training someone to be all-round smart and, in Barclays' case, nice.

John Kerslake, Barclays' general manager for personnel, says that while basic clerical skills are still important and new information-technology skills crucial, the key thing is that people will have to be more rounded. 'Selling skills will be very important – being able to interface with the customer rather than sitting at the back of the office processing forms, moving more into the retail market, rather than offering a passive service.'

He admits, 'We cannot say specifically what people will be asked to do in the future – the crucial thing is flexibility. Product development is the common denominator of skills, rather than something about the process of banking.' In moving into the packaging of financial services for its individual customers, Barclays is segmenting its market and ensuring a similar division of labour, as employees become specialists in pushing this or that package on this or that market segment – a far cry from the stereotype manager, alternately stern with the little backslider and obsequious to the big depositor. Tomorrow's bankers are being trained to be nice to *everybody*.

Sophisticated Europeans, especially the British, used to sneer at the Americans offering college-level courses in hairdressing or plumbing: it told more about what the sophisticates thought of their own hairdressers and plumbers as fellow citizens than about the Americans, whose educational system, catching up to 50 per cent of young people in further education, is still a source of strength for the economy. But vocational training has drawbacks. First, a larger and growing number of children simply drop out or drop through the educational net. The result is that some 30 million people, or 20 per cent of adults, cannot read, write, count or understand such concepts as insurance or banking. Their numbers are growing by over 2 million a year. A 1982 Labor Department study found that as many as half and perhaps three-quarters of the unemployed are functionally illiterate: some 40 per cent of black and 50 per cent of Hispanic

Americans come into this category. Vocational training is also expensive: a little industrial coatings company called Vimasco, based in Nitro, West Virginia, found that it cost $25,000 a year, or 15 per cent of its blue-collar payroll. Nationally, it is estimated to lose $6 billion a year.

Since the US Department of Education issued a highly critical report, 'A Nation at Risk', in 1983, a fierce debate about the direction of American education has raged. In the course of it, all levels of the education and training system have come under the spotlight – especially those parts meant to fit the worker-to-be for work. Says Paula Duggan, senior policy analyst with the Northeast/Midwest Coalition, 'Vocational education is in a mess: it cannot keep up with the state of the art in technology, so its job-specific training is often not very good. Surveys show that it does not increase kids' chances of getting jobs much.'

Second, the training provision is extraordinarily fragmented and often confusing. Programmes are operated at federal, state and municipal level, and there is a host of private centres. Some states – especially those with a relatively recent history of widespread industrialization, as South Carolina, Oklahoma, Tennessee and Colorado – are promoting skills training that meshes with the needs of local companies: in Oklahoma some 500 companies have made use of its 'customized' state training facilities. But others do little. Education and training programmes for new workers cost the nation some $8 billion annually, and the system runs 10,000 vocational schools, technical institutes and training colleges. Yet skill levels do not match those of the industrial competition (the Japanese). Pat Choate, senior policy analyst at the TRW Corporation and the pushiest exponent of training in the country, points to the example of 70001, the employment and training institute that has had an 80 per cent success rate in placing its unemployed, unskilled clients in jobs. 'If a significant number of hardcore unemployed youths are to find jobs, locally operated institutions must match trainees with potential employers,' says Mr Choate.

In the USA, as in the UK, France and Italy, quality on-the-job industrial training is done by big companies, who spend some $30 billion a year on it. Mr Choate says that the galloping needs of changing production, and the shift to services, will mean that the state must alter its incentives so as to encourage investment in people rather than plant. 'For every dollar of incentive the federal Government offered for investment in workers, it provided $3.2 for investment in machines and technology.'

Increasingly, business is reaching out to try to improve the training level of its workers before they come inside. In Boston the business community has entered into an alliance – 'the Boston Compact' – with the education board to link company donations with improvements in the quality of school-leavers' education. Government is encouraging these links: the Joint Training Partnership Act allocates funds to school programmes teaching occupational, work behaviour and labour-market search skills, using computerized self-learning programs, which are now available on some 130 sites nationally. One idea whose time may come is an individual training account, into which employer and employee both pay, that provides money for training and some sort of insurance against redundancy.

One of the big companies is Ford. Its management and unions looked over the abyss in 1982. More than 50,000 workers were laid off, and the company was reeling from the blows of the 'back-to-back' recessions. In March, after thirteen days of crisis negotiations, an agreement emerged that many think was the turning point for the company.

The wage pause and profit-sharing caught the headlines, but underpinning both was the new Employee Development and Training Programme (EDTP). It was, and remains, a concrete example of both sides' commitment to co-operation. The programme is run jointly, at national and local level, by union and company representatives. The initial aim of the scheme, funded by a 5 cents per hour worked contribution from the company, was to retrain these laid-off workers. 'We recognized that the scale of the lay-offs meant that we had a responsibility to those workers and the economy that they were going into to train them – a responsibility that goes beyond the interests of the company or union,' says Ernie Savoie, head of labour-relations planning. Since then 11,000 laid-off workers have gone through nine regional training centres. More than 70 per cent have got jobs afterwards.

By the end of 1983 the emphasis shifted away from managing lay-offs and towards training the employed workforce. Specific job training, driven by the demands of new production processes, continues. The EDTP provides workers with the opportunity to learn broader skills. So far 10,400 Ford workers have taken up a grant of $1,500 to cover tuition fees; 8,800 have gone through special technical courses, 3,400 on mathematics and English courses and a similar number on a special pre-retirement programme. 'We need a workforce with a good general education. Shop-floor workers will have more responsibility, so they need to be good at problem-solving. They will work in teams more, so they need communications and interaction skills. And we want to involve them in the business more, so they will need to be able to understand the broader business scene,' says Mr Savoie.

The initial focus of the programme may return in years to come. Over the next four years Ford plans to cut its white-collar staff by about a quarter. At first the programme may have looked like a special payment to the unions to persuade them to accept rationalization. But the company has returned to profitability and, according to Peter Pestillo, vice-president for labour relations, the company remains committed to fund the programme. 'If this money were spent on wages it would be wasted – it really does not make that much difference to our employees' pay packet. It's much better spent on training.'

In January 1986 a new television station started transmitting in the USA. From a small, technically sophisticated studio in Armonk, New York, IBM began to beam out training courses to employees gathered around TV sets in all parts of the country. The studio is part of a $60 million Corporate Technical

Institute that was opened last year. At the centre, like a small university campus, IBM technicians come from all over the world to update their skills in manufacturing technology, systems engineering and quality control. 'Technical improvements, driving down costs and improving quality, are what makes this industry hum, so staying ahead in the technical field is crucial to us,' says George Howie, director of technical education.

Thirty per cent of IBM's 403,000 workers are technicians, dispersed through every part of the company from research laboratories to the salesforce. But the half-life of technical knowledge in the rapidly changing information-technology industry is three to five years. So between 12,000 and 20,000 technicians need retraining each year. And the Corporate Technical Institute is like a technologist's playground. During the day the students, most of them on ten-week courses, can attend lectures in halls equipped with personal computers that double as TV screens. Any lecture can be videoed and transmitted to another room or to any one of the 205 bedrooms. These have all the normal fittings but come with a built-in personal computer that can communicate with any of the scores of terminals distributed around the building. 'A good technical image is essential to us if we are to attract the best people from universities. Technical people also have a loyalty to the profession outside the firm, so providing continuing education helps to keep them happy. And it helps us meet the challenges of change,' says Mr Howie.

IBM goes to great lengths to simulate this academic environment. Tuition fees are provided for Masters and Ph.D. research programmes, and the company even has seventy technical fellows with their own research staff. The Corporate Technical Institute will be the hub of the training programme in years to come, even if students do not attend courses there. About 11,000 employees are taking on-site courses, and in future they could receive tuition from the Institute's TV station. 'But the possibilities of the system do not end there,' says Mr Howie. 'In future we could beam all kinds of company information to our employees from there.'

Collaboration with universities plays a crucial and growing role in IBM's corporate plans. Universities have traditionally been a source of highly skilled personnel and research ideas. But, more and more, IBM is attempting to mould its greater investment in higher education in line with long-range corporate planning. Since 1980 co-operative research worldwide between IBM and universities rose from 110 studies at seventy universities to 680 projects at 205, from a multi-year commitment of less than $5m to $127.5 million today, from a fraction of IBM's sites being involved to virtually every site in North America, Europe and Japan co-operating with a local university. In 1985 the company donated $71 million in separate grants to support faculty and curriculum development, research and teaching programmes.

The rationale behind the higher level of investment is quite clear. The company fears that without it universities will be unable to keep up with technological advances in industry or provide it with graduates trained in the latest techniques. 'Industry simply must help the universities modernize their capability as a matter of its own future competitiveness,' says IBM's chief scientist, Lewis Branscomb. According to Mr Branscomb, industry has in the past led the universities into new fields but cannot afford to do so in the future. 'In 1963, for example, just before IBM announced System 360, we had thousands of people working as computer scientists. But the first advanced degree in computer science was awarded the following year,' says Mr Branscomb. And the company faces the same situation today as it moves into new areas of research into materials processing, magneto-technology and computer-aided design and manufacture. 'The strongest ties,' says Mr Branscomb, 'come from the universities' role as the source of industry's future employees. Because good education is rooted in good research, it is essential for companies to help strengthen that research base.'

A current example of where industry is leading academic research centres is magnetic-information technology. Industry has taken the fruits of basic academic research, applied them and created a sophisticated technology that has outrun the postgraduate engineering curriculum. 'In industry this is a sophisticated area of technology, where international competition is particularly active. It's a $17 billion industry. Academic engineering will need a lot of support if it is to catch up and play any leadership role,' says Mr Branscomb.

IBM has provided $3.75 million over three years to establish a graduate centre for magnetic recording engineering at the University of California in San Diego. As well as targeting funds, the company has also run a series of competitions to promote research in engineering, design and manufacturing systems design. The first was a $50 million programme to stimulate research in computer-aided design and manufacture in more than twenty universities. This was followed in 1984 with a similar competition for $25 million worth of grants for research in materials processing. 'The historic focus of materials engineering on bulk properties is clearly inadequate,' says Mr Branscomb. 'In the quest for lower cost and higher performance, the scientists find themselves using new materials – metals, glass, ceramics – in ways never tried before.' (This multi-disciplinary approach is poorly matched by the departmental organization of the universities.) On top of these programmes IBM also donates surplus equipment to university research departments. 'This equipment is not outdated cast-offs but usually machines we have used in test labs but no longer need. Universities just could not afford access to it, and it is crucial to us that research students should be able to work with the latest equipment,' says Mr Howie.

Allied to these investments in research and curriculum development are other grants to give IBM employees the opportunity to return to university. In 1985 more than 23,000 IBM employees took advantage of grants to attend courses. Almost 3,000 took up graduate work-study programmes, and eighty-two started three-year Ph.D. programmes on full salaries with tuition fees paid by IBM.

The final strand of IBM's involvement is with minority education. Here IBM's focus is not graduate research programmes but undergraduate and pre-college education. Since 1973 the company has spent $18 million supporting projects that promote career opportunities for women and minorities in science and management. In addition, 600 employees have been loaned to universities and colleges to help with these programmes.

Training in tomorrow's skills is not just getting the computer work-station manuals handed out round the offices or sending lathe operators on a basic computing course. It is engineering it into schools, colleges, training programmes and company life itself, engineering in the recognition that most working lives are being changed by information technologies and that these technologies dictate new relationships and new concepts. 'We are still,' says IBM UK's Geoff Robinson, 'basing our concepts on the nineteenth century. As we move into an economy driven by services, we think in manufacturing concepts. *That*'s what we have to educate ourselves out of.'

The evidence is that companies are taking over more and more of this role and that this will continue. The standard is being set by Japanese and West German companies that are part workplaces, part teaching places. In this, as in other areas of the world of work, the state is either ceding ground to companies or entering into partnerships with them as the old confidence in state provision continues to falter.

7. THE NEW FEUDALISM

Joseph Schumpeter once referred to 'creative destruction' – 'the endless change that incessantly revolutionizes the economic structure from within, incessantly destroying the old one, incessantly creating a new one'. Managing destruction creatively has always been the name of the biggest game in the industrial town – the destruction of raw human material and the creation of disciplined workers, the destruction of raw, inert material and the creation of finished products, the destruction of raw, diffuse data and signals and the creation of management information systems. See Ford's Rouge plant in Detroit for an archetype of a process that swallows raw materials of every kind in its huge maws and disgorges sleek Mustangs, an industrial Leviathan of vast, seemingly indestructible vitality. See IBM's omnipresent world empire for a multinational army of trained minds grabbing after information, trends, problems – and processing solutions. See the computer-controlled cellars of Moët at Epernay, east of Paris, for the acme of fermented grape-juice management systems (known as Champagne), *en route* from the chalky soil of the Vallée de la Marne to the executive plazas of Frankfurt and the City of London. See the executives of Barclays Bank trying to refashion customer-conscious sales forces bursting to sell financial services out of retiring ledger clerks and shy accountants.

Destruction and creation, endless and incessant: the tempo of management becomes quicker and quicker as competition emerges from countries regarded two decades ago as subjects only for the *National Geographic* magazine, as money markets broaden and deepen and become more demanding, as shifts in the ways of work become more rapid and complex, as information becomes at once more essential, more available and more complex.

Pat Choate, TRW Corporation's senior policy analyst, has coined the phrase 'high-flex society' for the management and production style of our times. He worries that the USA is now losing its once legendary adaptability and warns that it faces 'a future in which the shift to the technologies, production processes and management styles of the twenty-first century will proceed with few certainties and in an environment of fierce, often predatory, global competition. The pace of change, already swift, is sure to accelerate, further reducing lead times for preparation and adjustment.'

If management proceeds with few certainties, it also proceeds with more power, at least in most sectors of the advanced economies. The jobs massacre of the past decade has transformed employment into a scarce resource, and management (though its ranks too have been decimated) controls that resource much better than it did when jobs were more plentiful. There is more to adapt to but more ability to adapt to it: John Atkinson, a senior researcher at the UK's Institute of Manpower Studies, says that recessionary and competitive pressures have pushed management into a more aggressive posture in seeking changes and have 'reduced the institutional constraints on effecting such changes largely through reducing industrial-relations constraints but also through a change in management attitudes'.

Carlo de Benedetti, Olivetti's president, speaks of this change as one towards an entrepreneurialism that can, and should, exist *within* large companies. 'In the course of recent years too many entrepreneurs have become bureaucrats devoted to conserving what exists rather than to creating the future. We must give space to the entrepreneur in corporations but must also transform state bureaucrats into entrepreneurs to reduce costs, raise productivity and promote the new.'

The pressures are many. Underlying all of them is the need to adapt and accept new technologies, which means allowing computerization and its leaping capacities to flow through our systems. Jean-Jacques Servan-Schreiber, the polymathic French author and journalist, says, 'Computerization is a fundamental transformation, not only in the methods of production and consumption but also in the way of living, in the organization of the social fabric, in the definition of needs . . . As is true of each major stage of social evolution, the tremendous difficulties of transition are due to the rigidities of our mental structure.'

But there are other major issues to which managers must turn their rigid mental structures. Manufacturing companies in the advanced world must shift away from competition, which they cannot hope to beat because of the impossibility of lowering their labour costs to (say) the Korean or Taiwanese levels, and they must shift away in two directions.

Werner Bartels, chairman of Thyssen Industrie, is a doctor of engineering – not so rare in West German industry. In a learned paper for the journal $ZFBF$, he produced two graphs on whose importance he insists. The first, reproduced from Servan-Schreiber's now outdated but fascinating work 'The American Challenge', shows the rapidity of technological change – it demonstrates that where it took over a century for photography to move from invention to use, it took only a matter of three to four years for integrated circuits to pursue the same path. The second chart, his own, is simpler but more urgent. It is a wide arc traversing three areas: the first, mass production of mature goods like TVs and cars; the second, batch production of intermediate goods, like machine tools; the third, one-off production of very sophisticated, often large-scale, products or projects. The trick, says Dr Bartels, is how quickly you can evacuate the centre ground and how high up the extremes you can climb. He says, 'The Japanese will, for example, look at a video camera, and say, "How can we mass-produce this?" They are very often to be found on the mass-production side of the curve, high up. Increasingly, Third World countries will fill the gap in the middle. Brazil, for example, makes very good planes – Lufthansa has just ordered twelve of them. We are often on the high-tech side of the curve: for example, the frigates we produce are very complex indeed. It takes 800,000 production man-hours to make and almost as many (700,000) design man-hours.' On both sides of the curve is the highest of technologies: the insistent need for better systems, more automation, more sophistication in design and features.

Related to the above, companies have to shift from producing things to servicing the machines that make the things and servicing the customer who buys them. The shift from production to services is the best-known labour-market change of our times. What is less well appreciated is that the shift means, as well as people doing different things, different people doing the same things or the same people doing the same things but for different companies.

The UK's Occupational Study Group report is a fund of information on this. In sector after sector – energy, process industries, engineering, light production, construction – the report showed that production jobs were declining as the companies in these sectors rationalized and pushed more jobs previously done in house into other service companies and thus into other parts of the service sector. It is a complex movement, for while many of the jobs created in services will be low skilled, others (accountants and data-processing managers) will be at the professional end of the spectrum. The job of managing will become increasingly fragmented between highly paid and lowly paid, the centre, as in Dr Bartels's production scenario, progressively being 'hollowed out'.

All of this requires one thing from labour, one concept that has come to sum up 1980s labour management: flexibility – in manning, in job descriptions, in hours worked, in pay, flexibility to imbibe and respond to new technologies, to get away from, and on top of, the competition, flexibility to shift into services and, once there, to flex with the customers' needs and requirements.

Flexibility is seen, by Governments and by managers, as the goal that they must achieve themselves and that they must prepare labour for. Flexibility in wages is now being pursued by politicians of the right and the left as they strive to reduce unemployment rolls by 'pricing workers into jobs', and by managers as they seek to meet labour-cost competition. It is the pilgrimage on which all managers are embarked.

There is no one way, but IBM's way will be as broad as any. The world's (probably) Most Important Company has produced a corporate culture as all-embracing as anything the Japanese have devised, in that it operates ceaselessly on its people to keep them hopping. Sneakily, it uses care, consideration and kindness in this quest. Says Geoffrey Robinson of IBM UK: 'The new world of work is obviously a flexible one. IBM, the Japanese companies and others don't conform to the pattern of people popping in and out, yet do get flexibility. Clearly, it's not automatic: you can get flexibility in different ways.' In the USA the IBM parent company points one way. In five years IBM's revenue could be $95 billion; by 1995 it could top $200 billion. But such growth brings its own problems.

For many, IBM is the model employer, offering well-paid, secure employment for its workers, made possible by a rigorous system of planning and a big investment in retraining to ensure mobility within the company. 'The only way we can maintain security is by planning ahead, tactically in the short term and strategically for five years ahead. That security, our investment in our employees, motivates them. In turn that brings the profits we can use for retraining and relocation,' says Ursula Fairbairn, IBM's head of human-resources planning. This basic philosophy will remain at the core of IBM's personnel approach. The impersonal planning system, which grinds the ideals of employment security into reality, paradoxically produces intense personal loyalty among IBMers. And there is no doubt that this is crucial to IBM's continuing success.

In 1985 earnings per employee were $16,164, compared with $7,684 at General Electric and $4,612 at AT&T. The core commitment to maintain employment, which was made an integral part of company planning in 1964, is bolstered by an impressive array of employee benefits. IBM spends $6 billion annually on benefits, or about $15,000 per employee. According to a survey by the American Chamber of Commerce, most companies provide around $8,000. The IBM sickness plan, for instance, pays full salary for up to fifty-two weeks within a two-year period. IBMers are able to build up unused leave indefinitely, though this has produced its own problems. Employees show no strong inclination to take it up: the firm owes its workers 17,000 years of vacation. And one of the most innovative IBM programmes provides people about to retire with $5,000 for training in fields like property and investment management.

The second key element is a rigorous two-stage planning system, which might best be described as a system of divide, rule and reward. Each year Ursula Fairbairn draws up plans relating staff requirements three and five years ahead to profit and revenue targets. These form the basis of IBM's retraining and relocation programme. In 1981 IBM merged three marketing divisions into two and created a new customer-services division. Over 3,000 staff were redeployed to facilitate the reorganization. Three years later, Big Blue closed its last remaining computer-card plant in Washington, DC. With other changes that year, along with higher productivity goals, a further 3,000 people were reassigned. An appeal to employees at a Florida plant to take up offers of new jobs in different areas attracted 1,500 inquiries. Recruitment is always below planned targets, and peak flows of work are managed by hiring temporary staff and by contracting out.

But planning is also used to promote competition. Everything at the company is measured and evaluated. A regular survey of employee attitudes warns personnel executives of flagging morale. Everyone seems to work to quotas, which promote competition between groups of reps to reach the coveted 100 per cent club. Benevolence is based on stringent, centralized monitoring of performance. Strange, then, that so many IBM employees should talk of the sense of individuality the company gives them, of the fact that their voice counts. A 'Speak Up Campaign' encourages employees to submit complaints or suggestions for improvement. At one plant 278 workers submitted ideas that saved an estimated $1,784,550.

So IBM's planning in pursuit of employment security seems to create a benevolent circle of employee contentment and profits. To many it is a fixed reference point of good personnel practice. But can it last?

The system will come under a series of pressures in the next few years. One is the sheer size of the workforce. IBM employs 405,000 people worldwide in 130 countries. In coming years, as the company plans to grow with the industry, employment will also expand. John Ackers, the chairman, said recently: 'When you hire 20,000 people in a year, that is a lot to begin to educate in your way of thinking and doing business.'

A second pressure is diversity. From being a supplier of mainframe hardware to corporations, IBM is becoming a general information-technology and services conglomerate. It is moving into unfamiliar, more competitive markets, which require new skills. At the moment Miss Fairbairn can call up an analysis of the distribution of skills among the worldwide workforce by tapping the keys of her office computer. But she recognizes that this will be increasingly difficult and increasingly important in years to come.

Moreover, the move into new product markets has brought the company into contact with other corporations through mergers and joint ventures. In his term as head of IBM Tom Watson Jr, son of the company's founder, made just one acquisition. IBM's future strategy now relies on stakes in the Rolm Corporation and MCI Communications to challenge AT & T. And there are other established joint ventures in software, consumer services (with Sears Roebuck) and financial information (with Merrill Lynch). This makes IBM dependent on personnel unschooled in, and possibly antipathetic to, the clear, consistent principles that guide its own people.

The burden of size could also limit the monolith's ability to respond to changing markets. 'One of our basic beliefs is customer service. But to make sure we deliver that, we have constantly to keep abreast of what is going on in the market outside,' says Ursula Fairbairn. Recently the company has set up independent business units to develop new products. Further organizational innovation, to some extent fragmenting the clear company structure, may be necessary to stimulate entrepreneurship.

A final pressure is the most familiar to others but perhaps not to a company that has 62 per cent of the worldwide market in large computer systems. The computer market went through a pronounced slow-down in 1985 and competition from the Far East is growing. 'We have faced competition in the past and won, and we will win again in the future,' says Miss Fairbairn confidently. US car-company executives in the 1950s probably said much the same thing.

The downturn in computer sales prompted the company to set up a special task force to manage 'the largest redeployment of personnel since the aftermath of the oil crisis'. Once number one in the Japanese market (the second largest), IBM has slipped behind Fujitsu and NEC Corporation. Japanese tie-ups with American and European computer companies are increasing. Four million low-priced computer printers were sold in the USA in 1985. Eighty per cent of these came from Japan, and Seiko, which makes the Epson, plans to start production at a plant in Oregon. IBM is not invincible in the face of a challenge. Its smallest ever product, the PC Jr was launched to disaster, and production was halted last year despite continued company predictions of strong demand. But IBM is responding strongly: 200 executives have been airlifted into Japan to strengthen the local operation. And to stop the disease spreading, the company is investing heavily in new technology in its US manufacturing plants.

Despite the drop in sales in 1985, spending on new plant and equipment increased by a third to $6.1 billion. About one-third of the planned capital investment budget to 1989 ($45 billion) will probably be invested in new technology. New investments have modernized plants at Lexington, Charlotte and Endlicott. At the Lexington typewriter plant automation cut the human labour in each machine by 75 per cent. Three thousand employees were retrained. 'Throughout manufacturing we are having to retrain employees away from skills requiring dexterity toward computer-programming skills. In the future we are going to have to employ a different kind of person in our manufacturing plants,' says Miss Fairbairn. So it is likely that the interaction of the security of employment policy and labour flexibility within the firm will have to be even more productive in the future in the face of shifting competitive pressures. Most IBMers have a deep-rooted confidence in the company's ability to deliver. To Ursula Fairbairn the idea of reneging on the commitment is inconceivable: 'We are here to make sure it does not happen, and it will not.'

There is another way of trying to ward off managerial-level ossification in big companies: it takes a leaf from the small companies' book. There the hero of the hour is the entrepreneur, the new frontiersman who creates jobs for others and wealth for himself by taking risks and putting his judgement on the line. And yet the major economies are dominated by large corporations. In many of these big corporations management decisions are at best made by an ordered, rigorous planning process. At worst they are the output of a high-volume, white-collar production line aimed at the mass-memo market. How can the domination of the big corporations and their style of doing business fit with the new ethic of entrepreneurialism?

The path that several US corporations are treading is to stimulate 'intrapreneurship', to prompt managers to become driving, risk-taking, imaginative entrepreneurs within the harness of the big firm. The West Coast clothing firm Levi Strauss, for example, offered employees a budget of $500,000 to develop new products. Six projects were funded and three resulted in products on the market: flannel-lined Winter Jeans, Levi's Maternity Wear and Tow Horse Brand Jeans. Control Data Corporation, the Minnesota-based computer- and information-services firm, has pursued a policy of helping employees to set up spin-off businesses. Gould Incorporated of Illinois has encouraged employees to make business proposals that the company will help to fund and has decentralized its management structure to delegate more decisions to the operational level.

But perhaps the most striking example of the corporate innovator is Roger Smith, chief executive of General Motors. Mr Smith took over the ailing giant in January 1981 and since then has set about jump-starting the corporation. He has promoted a number of new ventures, which are intended to help re-energize the rest of the company through example. The high-technology 'Saturn Project' is aimed at developing new manufacturing systems and the industrial relations and management structure to go with them. The project is a laboratory for other ideas. In January 1985, when Mr Smith unveiled the Saturn prototype car, he also unveiled the Saturn Company, with its own dealer network.

Under Mr Smith's leadership GM has also reached out into new markets. The company has forged links with robot manufacturers Fujitsu Fanuc to form GMF Robotics Corporation, and it has acquired the leading computer-services firm Electronic Data Systems and Hughes Aircraft Corporation, which is developing lasers and electronic hardware. Mr Smith also has high ambitions for the General Motors Acceptance Corporation, which provides finance for people buying GM vehicles. 'I do not have any trouble seeing GMAC becoming the largest financial institution in the world. If they finance people's cars, why can't they finance mortgages, private bank accounts and everything else?' he said recently.

Critics have said that Mr Smith's approach smacks of 'brilliance unimpeded by humanity'. But there is no doubt that he has had an enormous impact on GM. And the change will continue. The Saturn project still has much to yield, but Mr Smith also talks of a 'Jupiter' and a 'Trilby' to follow. Perhaps the most important change, however, is the management shake-up. A two-year examination by McKinsey and Company the management consultants, found that pyramidal layers of management at GM had made managers risk-averse. In 1984 the company's five car divisions and its Canadian offshoot were reorganized to pass more decision-making to the operational managers, to reward the successful and to root out the unsuccessful.

What if the whole weight of culture and tradition is hostile to such a strategy? Japan is, of course, the paradigm of the 'company-as-family' culture; and, far from the common Western perception of Japanese as emotionless inscrutables, the system depends much more than the Western norm on securing an emotional response of precisely the kind that one does find in families. (To Westerners many Japanese company men also seem to ignore their real families in favour of their company ones.) Professor Tadashi Hanami, Dean of the Law Faculty at Tokyo's Sophia University, says, 'A Japanese company often refers to itself as an "enterprise family" and to employer and employees as "family members". This enterprise-family consciousness produces the total commitment of the employee to the enterprise. However, this sentimental or emotional commitment is nurtured and reinforced by the welfare policy of the enterprise.'

The welfare system is less an updated version of Victorian paternalism (which was often fairly meagre) than an internalization of the welfare state. Companies provide health care, family allowances, houses, pensions or lump-sum retirement payments; they secure school places for employees' children and even arrange marriages, a manager or company president playing the formal role of go-between. In return the company gets the flexibility that army commanders enjoy: they can post their employees anywhere to do anything. As Mr Hanami puts it, 'It gives the enterprise greater flexibility to cope with the technological changes, the introduction of new products, the expansion of the scope of business and the opening of new plants.'

One cannot and should not get too starry-eyed: working for a Japanese company can often be no better than working for any other company, and the relentless collectivism now grates on the nerves of the younger Japanese, who have caught, and value, the West's individualism. 'There is,' says Yasuo Kuwahara of the Japanese Institute of Labour, 'a narrowing of opportunities in the company (because of the post-war baby boom) and much more interest is being shown in leisure, especially as the standard of living has gone up. The young generation doesn't have such strong commitment to or belief in the companies.'

But, so far, this is fringe stuff. At Hitachi's Tokai plant only 10 per cent of the 110 trainee managers (80 per cent of whom are university graduates) will leave over the next ten years. The rest will travel up to assistant-manager rank (after six or seven years), to manager rank (in fifteen years) and then wherever their abilities take them. Those who recognize that they are not making the grade often go off elsewhere, sometimes to the small-company sector or to join the (massed) ranks of the 25 per cent of the working population that is self-employed. Some, though – the high fliers or the extra ambitious – do go to other companies, often subsidiaries of US multinationals or the few US-style micro-electronic and software companies. The US magazine *Inc*, in a report pointing to some dissatisfaction in Japanese management ranks, quoted one Hisato Gotoh as leaving the electronics company Oki for a micro company because of conservatism at top managerial level. 'If they hope to be leaders in technology,' Gotoh told *Inc*, 'they need some radical changes at the big companies.'

Mr Gotoh seems to be exceptional: the headhunting companies that have established themselves in Tokyo, mainly to serve the US and other foreign subsidiaries, find times hard. They resort to secret, conspiratorial meetings with the heads they are hunting. Often a tentative phone call will be brusquely refused, or the object of attention will loudly shout down the phone that he does not want to move from his company in order to impress his loyalty on colleagues within earshot. But Mr Gotoh's comment has the appearance of identifying a real problem: a structure in which company members move at a stately pace through the company, to the accompaniment of automatic wage rises based on age and without fear of the sack, will inevitably be hidebound, at least in some respects.

The individualistic software function is not suited to Japanese bureaucratization, and as well as developing a ring of Silicon Valley-style companies, big corporations are creating new departments in which software engineers are placed and paid more than their fellows – a breach of the norm. Professor Kuwahara at the Labour Institute links pressures in the firm to the end of a 'scale economy' in which mass production was the norm. Now, as consumer needs diversify, a company's structure must also diversify, assembling new divisions to respond to fragmented market signals, using more software to programme into production lines like those at Tokai, so that the more discerning 1980s world market may have customized features on its Datsun saloons and Hitachi videos. Says Professor Kuwahara: 'Companies now find it more and more difficult to satisfy needs by mass production. It is like the elephant and the ant. There are now opportunities for the ants.'

The pressures on Japanese companies – pressures that may disorient and introduce a degree of anomie in the country's self-disciplined labour relations – *are* growing. These include: (1) some signs of a stronger-than-usual push by unions for more unity in the fractured Japanese labour movement and for more leverage over companies; (2) the high yen, which will make exporting tougher and is already cutting the profits of the big manufacturers; (3) foreign competition, which for most Japanese means South Korea 'doing a Japan' on Japan with low labour costs, high technology plagiarized from Japan, a highly educated workforce and fanatically hard work. An (official) literacy rate of 96 per cent, an average work week of fifty-seven hours, productivity increased by 40 per cent since 1980, the capture of the biggest imported-car share in Canada, the low pricing of such electronics products as TVs and videos, the success of ships (14 per cent of the world market) and steel – Japanese executives and bureaucrats regard all this, and suck in their breath; (4) the export of capital, stimulated by the high yen, placing further strains on the loyalty of a labour force that may see work needed to preserve its own full employment shunted overseas to preserve foreign markets. The age of Japanese multinationalism will also place great burdens on managing far-flung labour forces with vastly different traditions: already American autoworkers are trying to get the reluctant Nissan workers' union to press the company into unionizing its new plant in the Deep South.

All of these strains, together with the evident pressure for a more individualistic work style and a bottleneck in company recruitment, have been adduced by some commentators as reason to believe that the Japanese 'miracle' is faltering. It is ultimately impossible to predict such a thing, and it should be said that the Japanese success is no miracle but the product of evident hard work and rational thought. It has what is seen by many as an added advantage: egalitarianism. Tadashi Nakamura, from his post near the top of the Labour Ministry, volunteers and emphasizes a final point: 'I believe that one of the most important things in

Japanese society is that there are no big gaps between the lower and higher employee grades. This makes for a more homogeneous society. If managers and others higher up the ladder said they wanted more than they get now, they would be frowned on.'

The Labour Ministry's latest survey on earnings (for 1983) bears out Mr Nakamura's point. At 22 when university graduates first join companies, they get a little less than skilled workers of the same age, a little more than unskilled workers. At 30 the differences in monthly pay are very small, skilled workers holding a differential of less than 1.1 per cent over unskilled and the managerial grades also differentiated by less than 1.1 per cent over skilled workers. Even the largest differential, between managers and unskilled workers, is less than 1.2 per cent. At 40 the differentials have widened slightly to over 1.1 and nearly 1.2 per cent between grades and to 1.3 per cent bottom to top: at 53, at or near peak earnings for all grades, it is over 1.3 per cent between grades and 1.8 per cent bottom to top. The annual bonuses show larger differentials at all grades, but even at the 53-year-old peak it is less than 2.5 per cent. This extraordinary closeness is unique among advanced capitalist states. Roy Sanderson, the UK electricians' union's official who has done more to popularize Japanese-style labour relations in Britain than anyone, points to that, together with the tradition of long and deep consultation, as key factors in the system's ability to endure.

It is different in West Germany, of course: German yuppies have many fewer constraints when it comes to getting their own company and their own Porsches, and German corporate managers are much more affected by the up-and-at-'em breeze in labour relations that blows from the West across the USA and the UK. But the constraint imposed on managers by works councils, co-determination and a general social climate that still favours consensus is real: the German 'company family' is not (in Western eyes) so suffocatingly close and exotic as the Japanese but still supports and sustains its members and expects loyalty in return. West German managers do not, officially at least, chafe at the system; they are generally anxious to be seen to support it and to stress its ability to cope with change. Says Bernd Heinzemann of the employers' association: 'Behind the structured West German system there is a lot of flexibility. The question of working time is now being negotiated by both sides, for example: they are taking the average working week of 38.5 hours and seeing what flexibility can be built round it. We have a lot of practice in doing this, and the people directly affected can do this much better at the workplace than around the green-baize tables of Frankfurt or Bonn.'

Herr Heinzemann's comments point in three directions First, there is the direction of consensus: the reflex of supporting the system-that-has-served-us-well. Hans Gert Woelke at Thyssen, comments, 'When small companies open up they must realize they have to live with co-determination. Of course, it has its drawbacks. But the new employer should engage someone to deal with these problems.'

Second, when Herr Heinzemann indicates a preference for the workplace rather than the green baize of national forums, he voices what has become almost a cliché of 1980s management: the preference for company- or plant-level negotiations rather than national-level, 'political' deals (with or without politicians). For example, at Shell UK, where the workforce has been cut by 5,000 to 15,000 since 1980 – especially in oil refining, where the manning cuts, from 12,000 to 6,500, have still some way to go – nearly all decisions are devolved to local level; only the distribution workers have a national agreement. Brian Bowden, Shell UK's personnel director, says that this decentralization of power is designed partly to make managers feel better. 'In a downturn there are motivational problems for management. There are fewer promotion opportunities, so we need other ways to motivate people. Giving local managers some say over decisions is one way.' Naturally, differentials develop in pay rates for the same job. Mr Bowden says that the differences emerge on a geographical basis, responding to local labour markets. This trend will continue. 'It will be pushed forward as a new generation of managers comes up. Older managers were used to being constrained by the bureaucracy. They were not used to being asked to take decisions.'

Professor William Brown of Cambridge University, one of the UK's most acute commentators on industrial relations, says that the trend away from sector-wide bargaining has been going on for the past two decades, with the general aim of gaining more control over the work process. There is no reason, he says, why the trend should abate. 'As well as denying the trade unions a role in the determination of broad company policy, establishment bargaining makes it possible for the management to argue that "capacity to pay" is all-important. The recently diminished power of shop stewards has provided a fresh twist. With less to fear from comparability arguments between different establishments, there has been a tendency for managements to take greater advantage of local market and bargaining differences.'

At Fiat in Italy Cesare Annibaldi, the board member for industrial relations, foresees a flow of power to his middle managers as the rigid structure of Italian labour legislation bends and relaxes, as unions are forced to do the same – and, a most important but frequently disregarded point, as individual workers express different preferences.

Carlo Patrucco, vice-president for industrial relations of Confindustria (the employers' association), says that in his own sportswear and graphic machinery companies young workers who previously balked at overtime and weekend work now ask for it. 'There's a big change in attitude among the Italian young. They're no longer all after secure jobs in big companies or in administration. They want more flexible working regimes.'

Third, Heinzemann's example is not merely random: the negotiations over working time in West German companies are one (if not the major) arena within which employers in all the big industrial countries – with the partial exception of the USA – structure their negotiations over flexibility. The West German employers, early innovators in developing flexible working time, are now bargaining over a flexible working *year*: employees and company negotiate mutually acceptable flexibilities around an individual's annual 'hours bank'.

France demonstrates clearly that these negotiations are of national interest, yet are inexorably pushed down to local, company level for final decision. Back in December 1984 all the unions, with the exception of the CGT, agreed in national-level discussions with the employers a protocol on flexibility within the legally set thirty-nine-hour week. It was broad: it covered flexible hours, redundancies, part-time and temporary working. But the national leaders were thrown over by their activists; the accord was repudiated, and no further attempt to resume the national-level dialogue was made in the succeeding fifteen months of the socialist Government.

But the pressures could not be called off, as the talks were. At plant level, companies and workers, including local-level union officials on the plant *comités d'entreprise*, *did* agree flexible working, including hours worked in excess of the thirty-nine-hour week. 'In other words,' says Christophe Boulay, editor of a string of industrial-relations journals, 'flexible working came not from on high but up from the base.'

Attempts by the socialist Government to restart negotiations at sectoral level got bogged down in the opposition, this time, of the employers. Then in the dying weeks of the administration, in January and February of 1986, in bitter struggle against a Communist Party in the lower and upper houses, the socialists managed to put on the statute book a law that allowed a certain liberalization in the statutory thirty-nine-hour week in a complex trade-off. Employers could negotiate a period of forty-two-hour-week working provided the average weekly hours worked in a given year did not exceed thirty-eight, or a forty-four-hour-week period, providing average weekly hours worked in the year did not exceed thirty-seven and a half. The Communist Party, and the communist-dominated CGT union, saw it as an attack on the rights of the working class, the employers as a sneaky way to bring in an even shorter working week.

The law is now a dead letter: a new Government of the right has different priorities. Philippe Seguin, the Labour and Social Affairs Minister, has focused on the administrative requirements to notify the Government of any redundancies that a company intends to make as a block on efficiency and has abolished them. He has further called on the unions and companies to negotiate redundancy and retraining procedures that could take the place of the old bureaucratic requirements, which he will then incorporate into further legislation. Some unions have said they will participate in the talks, but all are hostile to their aims.

The long-running battles and parliamentary crises that have attended these moves show the head of pressure that can build up over the issue as powerful movements at the base strain against the institutional and legislative infrastructure. But at company level the changes get made.

In the period of the socialist administration changes *were* made within the thirty-nine-hour week restraint. Dominique Joss, an official at the Commissariat du Plan, found, when surveying company-level responses, that while some companies simply reduced hours and did nothing more, others reduced them to thirty-nine hours or even further and introduced changed shift systems to get added productivity. Some reduced hours and, in addition, signed 'solidarity contracts' with the Government, under which they received subsidies for taking on extra workers (mostly, naturally, in expanding markets). Some were even more radical: 'There are companies that are moving in the direction of twenty-four-hour working, often in twelve-hour shifts, to utilize expensive capital equipment more fully. We see this trend as becoming more and more important. Of course, twenty-four-hour working demands new shifts, and some of these are not socially comfortable, so there must be a trade-off in terms of time off or more money.'

Etienne Crespel, a senior executive at the Compagnie Générale d'Electricité – electronics, telecommunications and power generation – says that the company's telecoms subsidiary, CIT Alcatel, reduced its working week to thirty-five hours and still had to lay off 300 people. It proposed to them that some may like to work part-time: 'A hundred were prepared to do so and so we saved fifty jobs.'

More radically, the Alsthom Atlantique power-plant subsidiary, conforming to Mme Joss's perceived trend of using costly machinery for longer, asked for volunteers to work over weekends in two twelve-hour shifts, for which they would receive full weekly pay and all the weekdays off. 'We found that many of the people interested in working these shifts were students and people who were building their own homes. In such locations the investment is so high that it can pay you only if you work it all the time. This is a strong trend.'

The impression managers now give – it is probably correct – is a vividly contradictory one. On the one hand, never has planning at the corporate level been so important: all big companies have groups and teams of strategists, policy analysts and futurologists, some largely relieved from line responsibilities, with the job of pumping ideas and projects through the company, feeding the top of the corporation with position papers. On the other hand, never has the market, with all its vagaries and uncertainties, been so stressed as the guiding spirit of corporations; never have companies, even large ones, seemed – and proclaimed themselves to be – so much like corks in a swirling, choppy sea. The paradox is very marked: the big corporations are now managing themselves more tightly than ever for an environment that is less structured than any of their managers have known it.

In Britain's particularly choppy waters the corporations with the size and scope to change are doing so as rapidly as anywhere. At Barclays, Britain's second biggest bank, the changing market is being wafted through the corridors by managers anxious to meet it. 'Change,' says Peter Leslie, the bank's chief general manager, 'takes a long time, but the pace is hotting up.'

Like its competitors, Barclays is now attempting to construct a new series of relationships with its clients. Mr Leslie says that the 'key to the branch network will be cross-selling, that is, selling a variety of products rather than just a banking relationship – for example, a competitive savings account, standard loan packages, insurance products and investment products like equities and wider share ownership'. Technology has helped: automatic dispensers take the mass-production side out of human hands, leaving staff freer to concentrate on selling to both corporate and individual customers – especially, of course to the prized A1s whose wallets can respond to the packages proffered. Says Mr Leslie: 'The ethos at Barclays will have to change: we have to concentrate much more on being a retailing organization, where all the staff have some role in customer contact.' By 1989 some 50,000 staff will have to be processed through the customer-service training programme to achieve that change in ethos. Geoff Miller, the company's general manager of finance and planning, says, 'Staff growth will be related to market growth – and the structure of the markets is driving technology change, and the need for more specialization. We are now moving into the time of the specialist. Possibly, in some areas, we'll begin recruiting people in mid-career whose skills we need, rather than taking people in at the start and keeping them with us all through their career.'

In a widely noted paper given to the Institute of Personnel Management's conference in 1983 William Brown looked ahead to see a 'Japanization' of a British union structure that had long prided itself on its militancy and its independence. He notes that, in Japan, 'the individual employee's obligation to flexible working is so great that the union's controls over the conduct of work are negligible . . . In so far as British employees and unions are moving in a similar direction, their bargaining is likely to show similar tendencies. It will become more of a vehicle for innovation in industry. *But it will also become more the preserve of a new labour aristocracy*' (authors' italics).

The spectre haunting manpower flexibility is the dual-labour market: the creation of the core of stable employees (Professor Brown's new labour aristocrats) and, around that core, a periphery of unstable, temporary, short-term workers. One manager's flexibility is another employee's insecurity. But structures are now appearing on that periphery that may mitigate, though not (foreseeably) wholly alleviate, the harshness of the plight for the temporarily employed. The periphery is organizing – or, rather, it is being organized. We are witnessing the growth of the manpower business.

One obvious sign of success: it is establishing itself in corporate Japan, where the Government has legislated to permit companies supplying contract labour to operate (under some restraint). In West Germany it often takes on an ethnic coloration, with companies specializing in supplying Turkish labour for one-off manual jobs. Most exotically, it is setting up shop in the People's Republic of China, where the Government recognizes that it must hire specialists to achieve the current modernization. When the Nigerian Government wanted to computerize its electoral rolls it sent the job out on contract – to London, where 300 contracted workers keyboarded it into shape. Worldwide more and more people are working for companies that send them to work for *other* people.

Three businesses compete for the booming trade: Manpower, which claims to be the largest, with branches in thirty-three countries and headquarters in the USA; Adia, Swiss-based, with subsidiaries in the USA and Western Europe (Alfred Marks is a UK subsidiary); and the US Kelly Girl. Mitchell Fromstein, Manpower's peripatetic president, says that his research shows that businesses become increasingly committed to the core/periphery duality. 'This ring of temporary workers will allow a firm to cover itself during work overloads and special projects as well as during employees' vacations, illness and special leave of absence. That's where we come in.' He is coming in strong: Manpower's worldwide growth is around 30 per cent a year, and sales stand at over $1.5 billion. In the UK the growth is even stronger, up from sales of £16 million in 1980 to £55 million in 1985. In that time, it has changed from being largely a blue-collar supplier to being largely (55 per cent) an office workers supplier. The other main categories are light industrial work, technical work and driving.

Manpower, like other similar companies, actually *employs* the people it hires out: it gives them four weeks' holiday a year, sickness and accident benefit and life assurance. But it does not pay them when they are not working. Tony Hoskins, Manpower UK's managing director, says that three types of workers sign up: 'There are the individuals who want to move into something but want to try it out first, so we send them to, say, an advertising company and they see how they like it. Then there are people who really like temp work, and they're increasing. They don't want to work every week; they want to pick and choose. And then there are the mothers who want to go back to work but don't want to work full-time. They want to take days off without hassle.'

The 'mission values' that Ford is starting to promulgate sound like the offspring of a marriage between public and industrial relations. At the core are the three Ps – some would say the three platitudes – people, products, profits. But it is all too easy to dismiss the programme. For Ford, home of the modern assembly-line division of labour and the pyramidal hierarchy of management, is trying to change. 'It is nothing short of an attempt to change the entire cultural values of the company,' says John Scott, until recently educational and personnel research chief at Ford world headquarters. Mr Scott has now moved to head the programme's implementation in Europe, and he is determined to succeed. 'We are not doing this because we think it's fashionable industrial relations or because we might get good press. We are doing it to survive in a competitive environment, for good business reasons.'

The mission values are encapsulated in a few short paragraphs. 'Our mission is to improve continually our products and services to meet our customers' needs, allowing us to prosper as a business and to provide a reasonable return for our stockholders.' Nothing revolutionary about that, but it is followed by an outline of the means. 'Our people are the source of our strength. They provide our corporate intelligence and determine our reputation and vitality. Involvement and teamwork are our core human values. Our products are the end result of our efforts. As our products are viewed, so are we viewed. Profits are required to survive and grow.' It continues: 'Quality comes first; customers are the focus of everything we do; continuous improvement is essential to our success: employee involvement is our way of life; dealers and suppliers are our partners; integrity is never compromised . . .'

Implementation of the new set of mission values began in 1985 with meetings of senior managers. Now lower-level management is being asked to take part in what company chairman Don Petersen calls 'a major effort to shape the culture of Ford'. In a letter to management in October 1985, Mr Petersen and Ford president Harold Poling explained the need for a common understanding of the way Ford should operate in the midst of changing international competition. 'We need a clear understanding of what the company stands for and what our priorities ought to be. We need to develop a common understanding of what the statement means, and to translate that into our daily work – our planning, our decisions and our relationships with others.'

The idea of developing a statement summing up the philosophy that should guide the company's operations, and particularly the management of the workforce, first surfaced in the mid-1970s. According to Mr Scott, it was the product of several converging factors. The first source of pressure was from progressive plant managers interested in improving industrial relations and the utilization of labour. This coalesced with senior management concerns about the growing competitive pressure from Japan. Managers came back from trips to the Far East with glowing reports about the industrial-relations climate and the way that the skills and initiative of shop-floor workers were released to improve quality and efficiency. At the same time, the union was pushing for more involvement in decision-making and a better quality of working life.

Initially, as many Ford managers freely admit, their arch rival, General Motors, was quicker and more concerted in efforts to mimic the Japanese. So by the late 1970s, and early 1980s Ford management was stung into action, introducing the Employee Involvement Programme and mutual-growth forums. 'The recession of the early 1980s may have helped us introduce these programmes. But it was not the driving force; the ideas were there for a long time before we were hit,' says Mr Scott.

It may be difficult to imagine managers and workers who have been bred on the drudgery of assembly-line work and the anger of confrontation sitting down together in a 'mutual-growth forum', but that is the plan. The first step, according to Mr Scott, is to change the whole management style at Ford. 'All our surveys show that employees are very keen on the idea of involvement in decision-making, participation, having greater discretion. It's likely that it will be with management that the real problem will lie,' says Mr Scott. In the past a brave new idea thought up at Ford world headquarters in Dearborn, outside

Detroit, would have been implemented by telexed instructions to its affiliates. But Ford intends to introduce this programme in a piecemeal way through consultation. Nevertheless, the aim will not be compromised, according to Mr Scott. 'We want to change the whole way that managers are socialized into the company – it has got to accord with the new set of mission values – and it has got to be consistent from here, to the UK, to South America.'

One of the first steps Ford is taking is to change its system of management appraisal. As an internal document outlining the plan makes clear, in the past Ford managers had a series of characteristics that generally went unaltered by performance appraisal. The list includes short-term focus, top-down decisions, quantity before quality, limited involvement with the workforce, fear of failure and an overarching interest in getting results rather than in *how* to get them. Mr Scott says there has been some shift towards a more participatory management style compatible with employee involvement, a greater interest in quality and improved efficiency. But it has not gone far enough. 'The mission values do not describe where we are now – they set us the goal of where we have to be to stay in business. We want to develop participatory management and employee involvement, not as an industrial-relations gimmick but as a day-to-day method of management. We want to give people more room to improve their own working environment, and the quality of their work, without managers pointing that out or directing it. And it should free up management to spread their experience over a wider range rather than getting too drawn into the nitty gritty.'

Of course, the idea of delegating responsibility downwards fits in with Ford's aim of reducing both its manual and its white-collar staff. And the idea of Ford waking up to the latent skills of its workforce may sound like 'too little too late' for assembly-line welders who have pumped welding guns for years and secretaries who have typed letter after letter with little hope of a job change. As one senior Ford manager admits: 'For too long we were happy to allow our people to leave their brains in the parking lot outside the plant, when in fact it's people's initiative that creates the value-added.'

But whether or not Mr Scott and senior managers at Ford are successful in reshaping the corporate culture away from the traditional mix of bureaucracy and routine assembly work and towards participation and delegation, some things will not change. 'We are still going to have to make hard decisions. Even if this is successful, there are going to be people in other companies who will be trying to run faster than us,' says Scott. 'Mission values are not a pleasant little addition to working at Ford; they are absolutely central to our future performance. They are the best shot we have got.'

We have considered the new feudalism of big companies. But there is a growing recognition that businessmen have to take account of the effects on the broader community when they make decisions within the firm. Companies are holders and providers of a scarce good – jobs. As the state has, in certain areas, withdrawn from social provision, so in some cases companies have stepped in. Is there then a developing awareness of companies' social responsibilities? And how far could this reach?

Mass unemployment has ushered in a remarkable phenomenon in most of the advanced countries that have suffered under it: the corporate charitable impulse, or 'caring capitalism'. In these countries business leaders have assigned time and money to assist the re-employment of their fellow citizens – some of whom they may have deprived of employment in the first place. The impulse is as solidly grounded in self-interest as in altruism, but that this is so merely underscores the strength of it. Says Yves Bénard, chief executive of Moët-Hennessy's champagne division (an unlikely place to find care for the dispossessed?): 'If we wish to preserve a liberal society, then it is our responsibility as employers to assist in the process of employment creation.' M. Bénard's own national traditions teach him to be wary of a *sans culottes* revolt – and Moët lost one of its largest foreign markets when the Imperial Russian Court had to give up champagne, with much else, in the 1917 revolution.

But the imperative is as strongly felt in states, like the UK, where the political traditions are gradualist. Sir John Harvey Jones, the retiring chairman of ICI, endorses the new practice of corporate concern because, he says, he does not wish to bus workers into his plants past mobs who have nothing to lose. He has witnessed, with his fellow citizens, the increasing incidence of riots and lawlessness that – while showing no clear or unambiguous link to unemployment – still appear to carry uncomfortable resonances of a movement of the rejected. Even in those countries where the post-war social democratic state has practically monopolized care for the casualties of the employment scene – as in most of the West European countries – business is now reclaiming areas that were once the preserve of the enlightened Victorians. As police chiefs everywhere order water cannon and tear gas, industrialists strive to keep those who could be the objects of these preparations off the streets. (Sometimes the two strategies for containment meet in one location. At a Thyssen plant in Wiesel steel cladding is engineered on to a Mercedes chassis to give police protection against mobs, while the same plant takes on more engineering apprentices than it really needs, in part as its contribution to preserving social peace.)

This development is momentous for its relative novelty and, still more, for what it means for the future. Once in, business will not wish to get out of an area where it can both do good and be seen to do good – and play a useful role for itself in determining some of the parameters of the local labour market. Overall, in underpinning the viability of a free-market, liberal state at a time when Governments have failed to guarantee anything like full employment, private business may be partially replacing, certainly substantially modifying, the post-war orientation towards the *state* as a source of security and opportunity with one that sees private enterprise as at least as important.

The USA led, and still leads, the way in the field. The relatively modest role most federal administrations play in the domestic social arena, and the continuing penchant, on the part of large corporations, to develop and increase their social role – often Government-pushed, as in the positive actions to promote the employment of minority groups and of women – has produced a corporate culture that routinely allocates importance, in both rhetoric and action, to community programmes.

The long-standing tradition of American corporate philanthropy underwent major change in the late 1960s. The wave of riots that swept through many major cities prompted businessmen to reassess the role their businesses could play in local communities. One of the hardest-hit was Detroit. 'The city was burning. We could hardly stand by and watch,' recalls Ken Judge, Ford Motor Company head of community programmes. With the other two major car producers, Ford helped to set up New Detroit. As an open, democratic forum for community representatives and business leaders to discuss priorities for community action, it plunged the big corporations into unfamiliar territory. 'I will never forget the chairman of General Motors being told by a seventeen-year-old black youth, "There is plenty of grass around, but your cow is eating it all",' says a senior Ford executive. Apparently, Henry Ford II was close to being outvoted for the first and only time in his career.

Ford's commitment to New Detroit continues, along with contributions to health and education programmes. And Ford has always tried to use the New Detroit model to organize its work. It rarely goes into a project without other companies and hardly ever funds something directly, preferring to work via intermediaries. 'We look upon a large part of our community contributions as "non-discretionary", almost like an annual tax which we expect to pay,' says Ron Taub, head of the Ford Motor Company Fund. The fund distributed $12.4 million in 1986, the largest chunk going to educational programmes.

Ford's contribution may look impressive, but it has slipped down the ranking of corporate donors in recent years. Near the top is IBM. In 1984 IBM contributed $145 million to charity, more than the largest private US charity. And, like everything that IBM does, the programme was rigorously planned, targeted and audited.

Corporate social responsibility is written into the ethical code that guides all IBM employees. The company's involvement in job training is extensive. In 1985 it expanded its long-running Job Training for the Disadvantaged to fund fifty-seven community training centres in inner-city areas. The programme has a placement to date of 80 per cent. IBM estimates that the 2,600 graduates of the 1984 programme went from collecting a combined welfare cheque of $5.7 million to bringing in a pay cheque of $30 million.

As well as providing direct cash funding for projects, IBM donates both equipment and personnel. One of the most innovative schemes provides employees with full salary for a year to work on social and community projects.

Ford and IBM exemplify the scale, diversity and strength of US business involvement in the community. It is an accepted part of business life, embedded within the organizations in corporate responsibility departments and in the communities. But on the back of this stability US businessmen are innovating. One of the most impressive examples of organized corporate involvement is the insurance industry.

Insurance companies' role in community affairs is stimulated by an industry-wide body, the Centre for Corporate Public Involvement. After a meeting of industry chief executives in 1981, the centre began to promulgate a set of agreed priorities for the insurance-industry social responsibility effort covering health, education, the long-term unemployed and the homeless. 'We started with a scheme to target low-income households with $2 billion special housing loans – in other words, doing something that was not that far from ordinary business. But since then we have moved into new areas and new ways of doing business,' says the centre's director, Stanley Karson.

In 1984 companies linked with the centre undertook 1,126 community projects. Arts and cultural programmes were the most popular, followed by youth and educational programmes. Thirty-five per cent of companies worked directly with the unemployed.

A second innovation in the US has come from Boston. Rather than organizing across an industry, Boston firms have started to work with the local education system through the Boston Private Industry Council. The Boston Compact that has emerged is based on a clear compact between industry and education. Industry promises priority hiring of Boston High School graduates in exchange for specific improvements in student performance. In a related initiative two insurance companies, John Hancock and New England Life, have each provided endowments of $1 million to the public schools. 'The exciting thing about the Boston Compact is that not only is business well-organized locally but it is also aiming at institutional reform rather than ad hoc projects,' says Anne Heald of the German Marshal Fund, who has followed the project. 'Rather than providing money at arm's length, business is getting into the overall design of programmes.'

US firms have also shown considerable innovation in dealing with plant closures and workforce reductions. Ford set up a joint training programme with the Union of Automobile Workers to provide laid-off workers with a route into the job market. Cummins Engine took a different approach. Faced with the possibility of trimming their workforce by half, the management established a venture capital fund within the firm to start employees on their way. Throughout, though, there is one common theme. 'Businesses are there to make profit – and we are there to help them,' says Mr Karson – or, as IBM put it slightly more philosophically, 'We serve our interest best when we serve the public interest.'

However, this approach has ensured a consistency and scale of commitment that dwarfs anything done by business elsewhere. And American business is moving ahead in this area. According to Ford's Ron Taub, this is part of a general political shift: 'I think we are having to recognize that as the state withdraws from these areas, business gets drawn in more and more. And that means we have to be better-organized and more thought-out about what we are doing.'

In Western Europe, the organized movement towards bringing business into the community is more recent – though there are plenty of examples everywhere of companies that have provided social and other amenities for their workers for a century or more and that have sought to retain a paternalist style that shrinks from creating redundancies and attempts to soften the blow. A trans-European example: Hans Renold, the Swiss-born, Paris-apprenticed inventor of the bush-roller chain, introduced into his Manchester factories a forty-eight-hour week, a canteen and a social union for welfare services – all in the 1890s and way ahead of his fellows. He was, says the Renold company historian, 'powerfully influenced in doing so by his reflections upon home conditions in the poor neighbourhood from which many of his workers came'.

But the modern variant is different – most of all in taking a corporate concern out into the community, beyond the confines of a present, or even a past, workforce. Per Gyllenhammar, Volvo's busy chairman, has pioneered innovative working practices and styles at his own plants in Sweden, and he has taken the same concern into a pan-European arena by forming a group of big industrialists (Agnelli of Fiat, Dekker of Phillips and Sir Ian MacGregor, formerly of the National Coal Board, among them) to address employment and related problems. Produced under Mr Gyllenhammar's prompting, and relying heavily on Volvo's cash, a report by the US Aspen Institute on Work and Human Values (December 1983) drew on transnational research to warn political leaderships that 'the strategy of improving economic efficiency without regard to social-political consequences is impractical – not on the grounds that it will not work but on the grounds that politically it will not be given the chance to work.'

It is perhaps less true to speak of one *movement* in Western Europe in the sense of a common strategy, as of a common alarm over mass unemployment that is evincing a series of responses, widely differentiated by tradition, industrial structure and culture, showing some similar characteristics. In Italy, for example, where the informal economy is of tremendous importance, the company-led initiatives are much less important than, for example, the co-operative movement and regional and municipal-level initiatives. In West Germany the sudden onrush of mass unemployment since 1984 has meant that the response has been later than in the UK and France. In every country the private sector's actions are intertwined in increasingly complex ways with public funding at every level and are generally highly dependent on public funds for their effectiveness. Typically, business does not commit large amounts of its own money but, rather, large amounts of time and of managerial expertise.

Typical too – and this, unsurprisingly, *is* the product of a desire to do good to others while doing good to oneself – enlightened self-interest is more or less frankly admitted to be the name of the game. On the one hand, this can be high-street store chains seeking social peace in the neighbourhoods in which they wish to sell their goods. On the other, it can be big companies establishing training programmes that can assist their internal labour markets as well as the choices of those they train in the external labour markets. It is a matter of choice, often political choice, as to how cynical one wishes to be about this: most of those who are active in the field prefer to concentrate on the results rather than the motives.

Among the countries with the most severe and intractable problem, Britain has shown that it is prepared to take some (enough?) of Mr Gyllenhammar's message. Business was drawn into the alleviation of unemployment from the first half of the 1970s as the unemployment totals grew. As Professor John Richardson, of Strathclyde University, has pointed out, this was simply an extension of its tripartite role with unions and Government at national level: 'As the economic crisis worsened, the role of the business community increased in delivering policy responses to the unemployment problem, in providing facilities for the Training Opportunities Scheme courses, in sponsoring those on job-creation courses and in providing work experience and training opportunities under the Youth Opportunities Programme (YOP) and the Youth Training Scheme.'

That role, mirrored by all businesses that had a national corporate identity, gave company executives a certain insight into, and experience of, a world that they did not generally know at first hand; but when it did begin to encroach upon their experience, and when, in the early 1980s, their friends' or their own children could not find work after school or university and, worse, when they saw coevals in the managerial ranks of other companies being laid off with little hope of a new job, then the feeling that 'something must be done' became urgent.

There was a further spur. In the summer of 1980 riots flared in Brixton and elsewhere in London: St Paul's in Bristol followed; after a four-year lull, Birmingham's Handsworth burned; and, later, riots flared again in London's Tottenham and Brixton. The scenes of burning cars, looted shops and (largely) black rioters lunging and parrying with police across high streets like medieval armies had been confined to the US or the 'special case' of Ulster. Now it was down the road.

Marks and Spencer, holding that the wealth of the high streets depends on the health of the back streets, poured time and effort into areas like Brixton, bringing over urban expert Norma Jarboe on secondment from US Citibank to assist. BAT Industries led the redevelopment of the once famed, then abandoned, Bon Marché department store in Brixton into little shops and workshops and the transformation of an old transit shed in Liverpool's Toxteth into 'managed workshops'.

One company – Pilkington – is credited with being the first to set up an organization that has become the model for others in the UK and abroad: that was, and is, the St Helens Trust, established in the town of the same name since 1978. The company, a world leader in glass-making of all kinds, had, like others, a history of paternalism, but it was the present, rather than the past that impelled the company into an activist position. It had developed, under the chairmanship of Sir Alastair Pilkington in the 1970s, the float-glass production process that allowed it to produce for its market with many fewer direct production workers. Sir Alastair, looking ahead, realized that the effect on the town would be dramatic. With other employers in the town, with the borough council, the Chamber of Commerce and the local trade-union officials, the company began to feel its way towards a role within the community.

The perceived need met a man of ideas and energy in Bill Humphrey, a former Pilkington executive who had worked for Shell, Rank Xerox and the Manpower Services Commission in London. Humphrey persuaded the committee that Pilkington had assembled that it should back him in establishing the Trust with the aim of creating real, new, long-term jobs in St Helens, primarily by energizing those in the community, both employed and unemployed, to start their own businesses. The task was huge. Pilkington's workforce had fallen from some 16,000 in the town in 1978 to some 7,000 in 1986. Rockware, another major glass manufacturer, closed its plants, as did Jefferson Smurfit and British Sidac. The General Electric Company, Beechams and Ravenhead Glass were all cutting back. In the eight years between 1978 and 1986 one-third of the St Helens workforce was made redundant, and unemployment leapt from the already (then) high level of 8.5 per cent to some 20 per cent.

David Bolt, who succeeded Humphrey as director of the Trust, says that it is 'based on the idea that started it – that we should try to get indigenous growth through helping people to have a go and making it easier to have a go'. The Trust is a centre for expertise of the kind that an entrepreneur needs – knowledge of what money is available at local, regional and national level in the public and private sectors, knowledge of what the land and the buildings are and which are suitable, the ability to tailor company plans to the needs of the business and of the investors. Pilkington funds about half of the Trust's £120,000-a-year running costs and, with other companies, provides seconded management.

Anthony Pilkington, the company's and the Trust's present chairman, believes that his efforts have slowed the tide of unemployment, if not turned it. Significantly too he believes the Trust has been able to overcome the factional bitterness that the issue inevitably engenders and that has in other communities produced stasis. 'I make only one condition for the board of the Trust – that all of us leave our politics outside the meeting. Once you enter the room, you're only here to create jobs.' The Trust has. Mr Bolt says that some 450 companies have been started, many in manufacturing: fewer than fifty, he says, have failed. Most are very small, but they are getting bigger. Ten have an initial capitalization of £100,000, and many are expanding and outgrowing their first plants, with some sixty companies doubling in size since 1985. 'We have', says Mr Bolt, 'to run fast to keep up with the rate of redundancies, but I think now we may just be turning the corner.'

As the Trust was getting into its stride in the early 1980s, so the Confederation of British Industry (CBI) was signalling its alarm. It could feel too the cold wind of disaffection: in a document produced in January 1980 it warned, 'If the existing system were to lead to socially and politically unacceptable levels of unemployment, then free enterprise itself could be under threat.' Later that year the Special Programmes Unit was launched to assist companies to place YOP trainees. After conducting research into the specific problems faced in areas of high unemployment, the unit called for the creation of more local agencies (of the St Helens type) that could manage and co-ordinate Government funds, promote training and assist in start-ups.

Since then, the CBI has remained wedded to the active promotion of business-led community involvement – stimulated, from time to time, by the pleadings of its more active, or more conscience-stricken, members. At the 1981 annual conference, hard on the heels of the London riots, Christopher Bailey of Bristol Channel Ship-Repairers proposed an action group on unemployment (set up early in the following year). In 1985 more riots in Brixton and Handsworth helped to produce a chorus of concern that was translated into a CBI demand that the Chancellor allocate £1 billion to employment-creating measures in his next Budget.

But it was Business in the Community (BIC) that made the real change. Its parentage, oddly, included a Labour Cabinet Minister. Peter Shore, when Environment Secretary in the Callaghan Government, worried by the growth of inner-city crime and unemployment, saw public and private partnerships working on the US West Coast and brought his experience back to London to begin discussions between companies and local authorities. Labour left office, but the initiative blossomed into a conference at Sunningdale, from which came a working group that in turn established BIC as the 1980 riots flared in the course of their sessions. BIC in turn took off when a member of its board, Stephen O'Brien, sold off his money-broking company, Charles Fulton, and was persuaded to devote himself full-time to the project. Mr O'Brien, an energetic and committed man, had already started Project Full Employ while in the City, aimed at providing traineeships for youngsters of the kind who were not much in evidence in Threadneedle Street – unskilled, under-educated, often black – so he had a track record.

Mr O'Brien quickly lifted the organization into a high-profile group that won the trust of Government (which liked self-help) and business (which wanted a vehicle for activity). He forged a relationship with the Prince of Wales, who suggested more work to help the young black unemployed. He organized a further conference in Windsor in November 1984, which brought captains of industry into seminars with the foot soldiers from the black neighbourhoods, to the surprise and benefit of both.

BIC used existing institutions – like local enterprise agencies – to build partnerships between public and private projects. Through Cathy Ashton, formerly a vice-chairwoman of the Campaign for Nuclear Disarmament who joined Mr O'Brien in the spring of 1983, it began to overcome the distrust of Labour local authorities, unions and politicians. Now Norman Willis, the TUC general secretary, launches BIC appeals, and local left-wingers sit under the BIC aegis to talk about job creation with yuppie managers. 'Only BIC could do that,' says Miss Ashton, 'because we insist that all sides consult with each other and reach agreed ways forward.'

The movement in the UK is now diverse. The companies that have done most and/or been longest in this field – Marks and Spencer, ICI, Shell, Barclays and the other clearing banks, BAT, Boots, the big brewers, British Steel Corporation, the National Coal Board among them – have been, and are being, supplemented by newcomers trying to catch a popular tide. They are becoming inventive too. Shell offers £350 to any employee, or employee's wife or husband, who can invest it in a community group of which he or she is a member. Boots gives its surplus equipment to voluntary groups and has set up a trust in Nottingham to assist them.

Barclays' Quaker origins have always inclined it to charity, but the unemployment crisis, and Mr Michael Heseltine's Merseyside initiative in 1981, drew it more deeply than before into job creation, through both staff secondments and donations of around £400,000 a year, much of that going to some 100 enterprise agencies and to Project Full Employ. Colin Harman, head of the bank's social responsibility group, says that he concentrates on youth unemployment and on areas where the state does not have a direct role that it might supplant. He is frank about the bank's enlightened self-interest: 'The bank has to get out and make sure that people know what we are doing and that we are acting in a responsible way, rather than just being associated with big profits and South Africa.'

The National Coal Board (NCB), on the other hand, had been for the forty years of its existence a state corporation with defined duties to its workers and the environment but with no formal concern for unemployment or the community in a broader sense. But in early 1985, as the year-long miners' strike drew to a close and as a result of prompting from Peter Walker, the Energy Secretary, it established NCB Enterprise in order, in the words of Merrick Spanton, its chairman, 'to assist in the creation of long-term job opportunities in the coalfield areas of the UK and hence to assist in wealth creation for the country as a whole'. The funds allocated to it from Government, initially £5 million, have been quadrupled to £20 million. The rise is not unconnected with the very large pit-closure programme that has followed the end of the miners' strike. Its accent has been on helping the unemployed to start up in business for themselves through creating places in managed workshops and through training in new skills. It is also looking out for new investment, both domestic and foreign. In its first year of life it managed to create 500 job opportunities a month; it doubled its target to 1,000 for 1986.

All of this activity, as well as seeking to assist entrepreneurs, is giving birth to its own in a full circular movement. Peter Whates, a former development officer at the Volunteer Centre who set up in 1986 as a 'corporate social responsibility consultant', makes a living from his home near Milton Keynes. He helped to develop a programme called Crossover (funded by the Rowntree Trust), which eases employees into early retirement by setting them new goals in the voluntary sector. The programme recognizes that people retiring in their sixties or early fifties have twenty to thirty years of active life ahead – a further working lifetime in which the desire to do something useful can meet the huge need for useful work to be done.

For all of this, the British experience is in many ways still quite shallow. Executives are still treated with deprecating sneers for 'doing the socially responsible thing'. 'It may,' says Mr Whates, 'turn out to be just the Eighties thing, like quality circles and workers' involvement.' But the roots are growing deeper and stronger.

French employers, too, have seen riots – notably in Lorraine – as well as continuing inter-communal and racial tensions in the cities, especially Marseille. And, like the British, the French Government has sought to supplement grudging private benevolence with public generosity by establishing programmes like 'Chômeurs Créateurs' (the unemployed as entrepreneurs), which seeks to give a self-start boost to the jobless. The previous socialist Government was initially doubtful about the role of the private sector in unemployment relief, and its doubts were more than matched on the private sector's side. But in the latter part of its term of office, and now under the centre-right coalition Government of Jacques Chirac, more encouragement is being given, and business feels it incumbent upon it to prove its social *fides*.

The underlying problem, says Etienne Crespel, a senior executive of the Compagnie Générale d'Electricité – the electronics, power and telecommunications group – is the continued drop in industrial employment, with 1 million industrial jobs lost over the past ten years. 'Just as we had a rural exodus in France, so now, even as that exodus is continuing, we have an industrial exodus too. No big industrial group can avoid the consequences. As our productivity rises [by 8 per cent in many of CGE's activities] faster than our sales [around 4 per cent], so the difference is people who must go. The trend will continue for at least five years. Beyond that we don't know.'

In January 1983 M. Crespel was seconded to begin CGE PI (Promotion Industriel), now composed of a team of youngish managers in the solid CGE headquarters who advise and chivvy the group's affiliates – like the power company Alsthom Atlantique, the telecommunications group CIT Alcatel and the cable-makers Cables de Lyon – into assisting the unemployed. In part it is there to stimulate self-employment – 'People may have a good idea or a new technique but lack money or expertise: we can bring all these together'; in part it is trying to tempt companies, French and foreign, into high-unemployment areas.

It is slow and hard work, but it has had some results. The Italian Pacchetti company set up a precision forge, through its French subsidiary ATS in Alès, with 50 jobs at the end of 1985, and the Norwegian company Tandberg employs seventy-five people to make computer terminals in Lannion, north Britanny. M. Crespel has taken a route similar to Shell's in encouraging people to lend a hand: Jacques Billaud, a manager at CGE's optronics laboratory, got a week's cruise to the Antilles for two from CGE for his part in attracting the Pacchetti investment – a bonus that is available for all who do likewise. M. Crespel voices a credo common to managers in his position among the 'enlightened' companies: 'When your plant has been in a community for decades – to be sure, it has paid its taxes and brought wealth, but it has also *taken* wealth and skills and education from the place – so we have a responsibility to give it back when we get out.'

On a bigger scale Elf Aquitaine, the oil and chemicals group, has set up structures to assist the start and growth of small and medium-sized companies both to assist employment and to support Elf's chemical plants. Early in the field, it created several regional investment funds in the mid-1970s and technical support centres in the 1980s. Activity centres on the Aquitaine region, where the company's natural gas resources are running down. Henri Deriès, business manager of Elf's regional finance company SOFREA, says that since 1981 the company has had a hand in providing technical and financial aid for more than 800 companies, arranging millions of dollars in loans and helping to create, or save, 20,000 jobs. The results, says M. Deriès, 'give a new dimension to the traditional relationships between large corporations and small businesses'.

But in France, as elsewhere, the efforts of managers often beat feebly on the door of economic and industrial restructuring, forces whose power dwarfs their efforts. Yves Bénard, from the Moët base at Epernay, the capital of champagne country, says that the town's two other industries – timber and car-seat manufacture – have declined and closed down following industrial disputes. At 11 per cent, the town's employment is 2 per cent over the national rate – 'but champagne has created a high-wage economy, and companies who come in offering low wages find wage claims pushing them beyond what they're willing to pay. Workers here won't work for lower wages and, besides, companies and institutes prefer to move south, where it's warm.' M. Bénard has started a programme of apprenticeship training for young people in vineyard culture and, through an association of young managers of which he is a member, has set up a finance company to assist struggling young entrepreneurs who have ideas and nothing else. But his activism is coloured with a certain pessimism: 'We have the responsibility to prove that a liberal society can be dynamic and, at the same time, care for those who are laid off. If we don't do that, then I don't know what kind of employers we would be.'

West German employers were late at the social responsibility starting gate, in part because unemployment has hit them late, in part because they already have a form of 'social responsibility' in the country's admired training system and co-determination practice, which has worked relatively well and to which all parties, albeit with less enthusiasm than in the past, remain committed. Some industrialists, like Thyssen Engineering's Werner Bartels, dismiss the notion of employment-creation curtly: 'We don't see it as our job to help people start up their own companies.' But at the company's Duisburg headquarters Hans Gert Woelke, the Thyssen board member for personnel, takes a more sanguine view. The company employs some 31,000 in its steel division, but that is down 20,000 from its late 1970s peak. Unemployment in the town now stands at 15.2 per cent.

Herr Woelke had a meeting with a group of the town's ministers in 1986 and confesses to having been shocked by the effects of long-term unemployment on their flocks and his ex-workers. 'I heard things I scarcely could believe were true. There are men who have been unemployed for years – they leave their homes early in the morning and come back at five o'clock in the evening to give their children the impression they are working.' Herr Woelke says that the company is about to take an active interest in their fate. 'We are prepared, to a certain extent, to put money into this.'

But in large measure it has been through the apprenticeship system that West German companies have played the social role so far by staffing up with more apprentices than they need. At Thyssen the crude numbers of apprentices in the steel division has remained the same – around 3,000 – while their proportion of the rest of the workforce has grown from 5 or 6 per cent to 12 per cent. 'If we didn't do this, we'd increase unemployment even more,' says Herr Woelke.

In Wesseling Mayor Alfons Mueller is looking at an unemployment rate of a relatively benign 6 per cent, less than half that of neighbouring Cologne (13 per cent). This low figure has meant that only one of the town's three big chemical employers has felt impelled to dabble in community schemes (they have some 400 young trainees among them) – though Herr Mueller himself has set up a training school for young workers, run by the Rheinische Beruf Akademie, and the Catholic Workers Association, of which he is president, runs another training institute for youngsters with 110 places. 'The trouble is,' Herr Mueller grumbles, 'the young often lack motivation.'

West Germany's next problem, not so far down the road, is a possible labour shortage as the population shrinks in the 1990s and beyond. This approaching people famine limits employers' desire to act on the present surplus – though there are the beginnings, strong especially in the suddenly unemployed Ruhr towns, of a willingness to give assistance to entrepreneurs. Siemens, the country's biggest electrical manufacturer, has for several years assisted the unemployed to start small businesses, sometimes using company patents and technologies. The challenge for both private companies and public authorities, says Christopher Hull, a researcher at West Berlin's Science Centre, is 'to conceive and implement strategies of intermediation between firms in need and institutions with problem-solving resources. What is required is not so much to throw money, advice, etc, at the small-firm sector in general as to improve the mechanisms whereby the available resources are effectively relayed to the individual firm.'

The notable absentee from concern of this kind among the leading industrial economies is Japan. Caring capitalism has so far been given short shrift in that bustling country – or, rather, it has been thriving *within* the confines of the large companies. The lifetime-employment system, though limited to the big, so far expanding companies, is the glory of the employers and the unions, and both work hard at retaining it, which means tolerating (to date) the rigidities it has imposed. An unemployment rate of around 3 per cent does not dictate a change of attitude, though the Japanese will, on occasion, admit a tendency to be indifferent to those they define as outside the 'family' – whether the real family or the company one. The still evident stability will have to deteriorate sharply before they rethink their industrial culture.

It is possible to argue that those countries where corporations are doing most to develop community programmes – the UK and France, following the US lead – are those where corporations were anyway lagging behind in demonstrating the kind of welfarist approach that Japanese and West German companies have espoused for decades, and where the corporate culture has been only sporadically public and ambitious enough to lead and shape social issues. But this is likely to change. Alain Chevallier, Moët-Hennessy's chairman and an *énarque* to his fingertips, makes large claims for the scope of the private sector: 'In a period in which the unforeseeable dominates, corporations are the organizations that are closest to reality, so they're an indispensable factor in establishing coherence. The company doesn't claim universal knowledge, but it knows its job: it knows where it has to go.'

According to this claim, the corporation, rather than the Government, has both the superior grasp of detail and the more informed vision of the future and thus is better able to construct a 'coherent' universe in which change is managed more efficiently than by vote-seeking politicians or haltered bureaucrats (of which M. Chevallier was one). It is a potentially dangerous vision if pushed beyond the confines within which the Moët chairman would expect it to reside – but a seductive one for companies, nevertheless. The corporate plunge into society has at least helped in addressing, often inadequately, the largest social problem of the day. It has left some executives exhilarated by the experience, unlikely to wish to come out of the water yet awhile.

8. THE GROWING FRINGE

In the 1960s film *A Kind of Loving* Alan Bates walks to work with his screen father. They part on a railway bridge. Bates goes to work as a draughtsman in a nearby factory; his father departs for the railway yards. The scene sums up many of the dominant images of work from the period. Bates's white-collar job in a large factory spells security, long-term employment; his job as a draughtsman indicates the growth of technical and white-collar occupations. His father's work represents the old and declining world of industry based on coal.

One of the most popular British films of 1986 was *My Beautiful Laundrette*. The protagonists run a small business in the service sector. One is an Asian entrepreneur. In contrast to the homogeneity, predictability and stability in *A Kind of Loving*, this film conjures up images of diversity, enterprise and uncertainty. *My Beautiful Laundrette* reflects two developments in the labour market in the 1980s: first, the expanding role of small businesses in generating jobs and, secondly, the fact that around the world of secure employment with big companies a fringe of informal work is growing. Some of this informal work is not new but remains largely unrecognized – the domestic work mainly carried out by women. But some seems to be new, a response to the rise in unemployment. In particular, the advanced economies are witnessing a rapid growth in their black economies. As our poll shows, big businesses are the major source of job losses. If jobs are to be created, will they emerge from new organizations – small businesses, self-employment – rather than from 'employment' as we traditionally understand it?

Small may still be beautiful, but, more important, it now spells dynamism, vitality, efficiency, competitiveness and, above all, jobs. Having once been bit players on the big stage dominated by the big firms, small businesses are now the rising stars, fêted by politicians throughout the OECD.

In the 1960s and 1970s prosperity seemed to be delivered mysteriously from above. The grey, impersonal machine, which brought together macro-economic demand management and the big corporations, churned out growth. In the 1980s that approach has been overturned. Prosperity, we are told, will well up from below. The know-how of skilled technocrats has been replaced by the raw energy of thrusting entrepreneurs. In the 1950s and 1960s European industrial policy encouraged mergers and rationalization to create firms large enough to compete with the American corporations. Now attention has turned to fostering small businesses as the most important source of new jobs. Future prosperity will be fed by an enterprise culture that will breed successive generations of entrepreneurs. They will drive the economy on, pulling together resources to use them more efficiently, creating new products, new markets and new firms.

Rags-to-riches entrepreneurs have always been folk heroes, but now they have been given the role of saviours. Individual businessmen and women, grafting away to make sure their firms survive, look rather weak in the face of mass unemployment. But the new gospel of enterprise says that, taken together, these efforts will generate a new economic vitality founded on risk-taking, profit-seeking entrepreneurialism.

The sweeping rhetoric is all very well, a challenge to the comfortable assumptions of the 1960s. But should our economic hopes be pinned on something as intangible as 'enterprise culture'? Is small-business growth the best and possibly the only route to future jobs? Are we witnessing a permanent shift towards smaller units of business organization? Or is their growth the only straw in the wind politicians can grab at in the face of declining public-sector and big-company employment?

Sorting out what role small businesses have played in employment growth, and what role they may play in the future, is a far from simple task. Half the firms that form the UK small-business sector will not be around in five years. To predict the kind of employment that small businesses will create means accounting for the 750,000 small firms that will be formed in the next five years.

Small businesses generate jobs through two routes. The most obvious is growth. For some the key is not small businesses in general but the minority that will grow into the big firms of the future. An extensive small-business sector may not matter as much as the quality of small businesses. The second route is businesses that start small, stay small but stay in business. Start-ups employing five people may be more important than the occasional firm that grows. So, to assess the contribution small businesses have played in job generation and might play in the future we need to look at both the extent of the small-business sector and the way in which firms grow out of that sector.

There has been some drift towards concentrating employment in smaller enterprises, according to a report by the OECD employment secretariat, though only six OECD countries provide data for small-firm employment across the entire economy. Small-firm employment has risen in four – Austria, Belgium, France and Japan. OECD evidence for the manufacturing sector, which covers a broader range of countries, shows that small-business employment has also risen in the UK and Denmark. The OECD says that the overall impression is stability in small-firm manufacturing employment, but 'where the share of small firms has risen the change can best be described as marginal, being less than 3 per cent'.

The growth of the small-firm sector, however, has to be considered in the context of the changing structure of the economy. It is generally thought that the growth of the service sector has stimulated small-business activity. Nearly 60 per cent of service-sector employment in Japan is in small businesses, compared with

47 per cent in manufacturing. In the seven countries for which data are available firms employing fewer than twenty people account for more service jobs than large firms in every country except Sweden, according to the OECD. So some of the recent growth of small-business employment is attributable not to a burst of entrepreneurial spirit but to the continuation of a slow shift in the structure of the major economies. As this trend continues, so more employment will be concentrated in small firms. Moreover, there is mounting evidence that large firms are contracting out peripheral elements of their operations, like cleaning, catering and security, to smaller firms. Hence the growth in small-business employment may be not so much job growth as job redistribution.

A recent report by analysts at the National Federation of Independent Businesses (NFIB) in Washington confirms that this development has played an important role since 1979. 'If you look at the relationship between consumer spending on services and service employment, it remains fairly close till 1979. Then, with no apparent increase in consumer spending, service employment goes up. This means that extra demand for services must have been coming from somewhere, and the natural explanation is big business contracting out,' says the NFIB's William Dennis.

However, not all the growth in small-business employment is due to the expansion of the service sector. In Austria 77 per cent of small-business jobs have come through smaller units in manufacturing, in Belgium 53 per cent and in France 54 per cent. 'In some countries there has been a trend in recent years towards a growing employment share in small enterprises which is not fully accounted for by shifts in the structure of output towards services. Apparently, the average size of enterprises is falling in these countries,' says the OECD.

The growing share of employment taken by small businesses has to be set against the poor performance of larger firms, however. Small-firm employment in the UK, for instance, rose from 13.5 per cent of total employment in 1968 to 21.1 per cent in 1982, but the absolute level of employment has varied very little, rising from 981,000 in 1968 to 1.9 million in 1976. It has remained stable since then. Since 1976 large-firm employment (firms employing more than 1,000 workers) has fallen by over 1 million to 6 million. Between 1977 and 1981 twenty corporations were responsible for 22.8 per cent of all redundancies in the UK (264,200). So the recent rise in the share of small-firm employment is almost entirely due to the downturn in big businesses.

Even if small-firm job growth has not kept pace with labour-shedding in big firms, the small-business sector does seem to have weathered the recession more effectively. In the 1974–6 recession the death rate of small businesses rose by 50 per cent, to 158,000 in 1977. However, in the recession of the 1980s the UK small-business death rate hardly rose at all, staying steady at around 9 to 10 per cent. It seems that the small firms of the 1980s are more robust than their predecessors. So there has been some shift towards smaller business units, independent of the impetus given by the growth of services. As the OECD notes, there are signs of a dynamic small-business sector developing in several countries, which could be a source of employment.

One of the reasons for this is flexibility: small firms have to adapt production to changing market conditions, but they also gain flexibility through the kind of jobs they create. If in the future more jobs are to be in small firms, what kind of jobs will they be?

The smaller the firm, the lower the wage, according to the OECD. The differential is widest in the USA where small-firm employees get 57 per cent of the wage of comparable workers in a large firm. In Japan the differential narrows to 77 per cent, and in most of Europe it is narrower still. Health-insurance plans were available to 35 per cent of American small-firm workers in 1983 and pension plans to just 17 per cent. Over 85 per cent of large-firm workers had access to these benefits. The OECD concludes that a worker is more likely to be fired from a small than a large firm. Average job tenure with small firms was four and a half years in 1983 compared with nine years in large firms. Although the evidence is limited, it is enough for the OECD to suggest that 'jobs in small firms are not of the same quality as positions in larger firms'. So a growth in small-firm employment may give rise to wider wage differentials and a more unequal distribution of company welfare benefits. But a more extensive small-firm sector may inject greater flexibility into the economy as a whole.

At first sight, comparing the UK and Japan, a more extensive small-business sector is associated with better all-round economic performance. Japan has more manufacturing employment in small businesses than any other major economy and the best unemployment record. The UK, on the other hand, has a relatively limited small-firm sector in manufacturing and a high unemployment rate. However, a report by small-firm economists at Newcastle University, 'Small Firms and the Process of Economic Development', shows that these are extreme cases. 'There is no evidence to suggest that countries where small firms are dominant do better than countries where large firms are more important. Indeed, once the UK and Japan are excluded, it appears that among other OECD economies those who are more dependent on small firms do worse,' says one of the authors, Steven Johnson. The report outlines three types of small-business growth that have been particularly important in recent years.

The first is exemplified by a traditional area of manufacturing employment: the UK's West Midlands. The area lost a quarter of a million manufacturing jobs in just five years. According to the Newcastle team, this has significantly enlarged the pool of people who are pushed to become entrepreneurs. The severity and depth of the downturn has meant that skilled craftsmen and managers with the expertise to start their own businesses have found themselves on the dole. But relatively few of these entrepreneurs set off to found 'growth' firms. The rise of small businesses in the West Midlands is both a response to the decline of the big manufacturing firms and a reflection of it. 'What is noteworthy about the rise of small firms in the West Midlands is not the alleged injection of dynamism and growth into the UK economy but rather the opposite. They are the visible expression of economic decline and industrial restructuring in the UK: individual response to mass redundancies,' says the Newcastle report.

However, a recent report prepared for the UK Department of Employment found that unemployment has become less of a force driving self-employment growth or small-business start-ups. A survey of over 300 small businesses found that between 1975 and 1980 unemployment was the major reason for start-ups. But the survey reveals that small businesses in the 1980s are much more likely to be started by ambitious proprietors interested in securing their independence than by redundant workers with no other option.

The West Midlands experience is in stark contrast to small-business growth in Boston and Bologna, which has spawned firms that are internationally competitive. Twenty years ago, the New England economy was dominated by traditional industries such as textiles, footwear and clothing. But in the last five years of the 1970s the area created more jobs than the whole of Europe. The driving force has been a highly competitive, wealth-creating sector of small firms. These mainly high-technology firms have grown on the twin pillars of defence spending and the concentration of university research institutions in the area. They have directly created relatively few jobs, but their success in international markets has brought high wages and profits, which have boosted the rest of the economy. (A similar set of high-technology firms has developed around the university city of Cambridge in eastern England.)

The third example of a set of internationally competitive small firms comes from Italy. Their competitiveness in traditional low-tech sectors like clothing and shoes stems from modernization and investment. Between 1973 and 1978 investment in small firms rose by 169 per cent, compared with a 64 per cent rise in large firms. In 1972 the ratio of fixed investment per employee in small firms was 3 per cent lower than in large firms; by 1980 it was 16 per cent higher. Central and north-eastern Italy is dominated by small firms: around 65 per cent of employment is in firms with fewer than 100 workers. Moreover, these areas have enjoyed much faster growth than the rest of Italy. In the ten years to 1981 employment in these traditional sectors grew by 8 per cent across Italy; in the central and north-eastern regions employment grew by 21 per cent. While traditional sectors in other OECD countries have been battered by growing imports from the less developed countries, the Italian share, produced mainly by small firms, has remained fairly stable. According to the Newcastle report, this ability to compete internationally is built on the production of high-quality goods, a unique system of co-operation and sub-contracting between the small firms and the legacy of peasant production.

The small businesses in Val Vibrata, a valley on Italy's Adriatic coast, are excellent examples of Italian success. Leo Micante, for instance, is furious that he had to throw away his entire artichoke crop because of fall-out from Chernobyl. But his main worry has nothing to do with his three-hectare smallholding, which supports, besides the radioactive artichokes, a few pigs and an excellent sparkling wine. Sr Micante is preoccupied with his other business, which makes leather bags mainly for the West German market. The West Germans, he says, are showing signs of switching their favour to Eastern Europe. So he is a little anxious as he bustles round his workshop (a former restaurant), where his nine workers, mainly women, sit looking through an open window on to a field of ripening corn a few feet away.

The workers are cramped, but seem happy enough. Like Sr Micante, they each have a plot of land, which they work when not making leather bags. No doubt their families are much like his. His father is a building worker; his mother works in a shirt factory; his sister makes pullovers; his son works in the family business; and his grandmother is on a pension. For Sr Micante's enterprise is typical of the 15-kilometre-long valley, which has become a model in Italy and beyond for successfully moving from an agricultural to a light industrial economy. In making this transition the valley has blended the family-based work regime that characterizes smallholdings with the different requirements of small businesses. The valley still looks largely agricultural to the casual eye. Yet it contains about 1,600 businesses employing more than 11,000 people, working mainly on textiles, leather goods and furniture. Some, like Euroflex, with its 180 workers, $5 million turnover and sales of its holdalls throughout Western Europe and in the USA, are sizeable concerns. But most are, like Leo Micante's, tiny businesses in small workshops often built on to family homes.

Antonio Angelini, president of the Val Vibrata Development Association, reckons that fewer than fifty of the valley's businesses employ more than 100 people. Even when they succeed, they grow more often by increasing their network of sub-contractors than by increasing their direct employees. Thus Sr Angelini's own knitwear company employs only twenty-two people, yet has about thirty sub-contractors working for it, the largest of which itself has thirty workers. There are practical reasons for this pattern of development. Each sub-contractor can specialize in making one product for the larger companies, relying on them for financial help for specialized equipment. Moreover, the relative scarcity of even medium-sized companies means that the valley is not disfigured by too much factory building. Sr Angelini stresses too that the flexible working afforded by small businesses suits the local way of life. 'They get up early, work from five to ten in a workshop, spend ten to four on the beach, return home and do another four hours' work, then have the evenings free and the weekends for their plot of land.'

No doubt many of the small companies fall through the net of Italy's burdensome taxation system and rigid labour laws, though a majority, and certainly virtually all of the bigger ones, are now firmly out of the black economy. At Euroflex, for example, Mario D'Eustachio, the president, emphasizes that his workers are paid according to the rates laid down nationally by unions and employers. The unions have worked hard with the employers to make the valley a success, moving quickly to resolve difficulties such as those that arise when a company has tried to pay below the nationally agreed rates. Sr D'Eustachio says the unions in his plant spend more time talking about the company's problems than about the workers' grievances.

The signs of success are many. Some companies are moving up-market technologically: Euroflex, for example, has just introduced a major programme of computerization. The valley is now feeling the need to market its products under one brand name. And, perhaps most impressive for a rural area, people are moving back; the population of some of the valley's mountain towns has increased by as much as a quarter in the past decade. Government bodies charged with developing the rural south now look on the Val Vibrata as a more promising model than other attempts to prod large companies to locate major plants in rural areas – the so-called 'cathedrals-in-the-desert' approach. So too, to judge by Sr Angelini's visitors, do some other countries anxious to help their rural areas make the leap from agriculture to industry. These have recently included delegations from China, Yugoslavia and Bulgaria.

'All three cases show that it is not the absolute number of small firms that counts but the quality of those firms. In Boston and Bologna small firms have grown because they have become, and have remained, internationally competitive. In Birmingham they have grown because large firms have failed to maintain their competitiveness,' says Steven Johnson. So the prospects for job growth in the 'stay-small' business sector are mixed. There has been some drift towards smaller business units supporting more employment. But the OECD warns that it would be 'superficial' to read into this great job-creation potential. Moreover, if small businesses are to create the wealth to generate the jobs of the future, it is their quality that counts rather than their quantity. Small-business growth may be a partial answer to job-shedding by large firms, but it is not necessarily the flowering of the entrepreneurial spirit.

To answer the complicated question of what role small firms could play in job generation it is not enough to look at the small-firm sector. Snapshots of the share of employment taken by firms of different sizes revealed by periodic Government surveys may give a very misleading picture. If, for instance, at the time of the initial survey a firm had ten employees but then grew dramatically to employ more than 100, it would no longer count as a small business. This would show up on the snapshot as a loss of employment from the small-business sector, whereas actually a small business would have created more than ninety jobs. To avoid these difficulties many researchers have concentrated on tracing individual firms through their life-cycle to find out whether employment growth comes from small firms that are getting larger or from firms that are already large.

The most striking evidence for small-firm job generation comes from a report by the American economist David Birch. In 1979 he reported on a survey of 5.6 million firms, which found that, between 1969 and 1976, 82 per cent of US private-sector employment growth was generated by firms that had started by employing fewer than 100 workers. A similar study by the US Small Business Administration found that between 1980 and 1982 all the employment growth in the USA came from small firms.

However, these studies have been challenged by other work. A report from the Brookings Institution found that between 1978 and 1982 half the new jobs came from medium-sized or large firms. Mr Birch himself has lowered his estimates of small-firm job generation to around 70 per cent in the 1980s.

Nevertheless, it appears that while employment in US small business stood at 40 per cent in 1977, the contribution they make to job growth is much higher, in a range between 53 and 82 per cent, over the long run. Similar results have been reported from elsewhere. In the ten years to 1984, 64 per cent of net private-sector jobs in Canada were created by small businesses, according to a Canadian Government report. Analyses of firms' contribution to job growth from France and West Germany found that only small businesses enjoyed employment growth during the 1970s. In the UK only firms employing fewer than 100 workers in 1971 showed any net job growth, according to the most authoritative study, by Colin Gallagher and Hugh Stewart at Newcastle University. However, medium-sized firms also created a large number of jobs, as well as suffering job losses. The authors conclude: 'No one size of firm is responsible for the majority of job generation in the UK.' But small firms have been an important new source of jobs, particularly compared with larger firms. 'We are a long way from establishing unambiguously the precise extent of the contribution of small firms to job generation, but the trend during the past ten to fifteen years in the OECD countries has been one of major reduction in employment by large firms, with the small-firm sector generating job growth,' says Steven Johnson.

The FT jobs poll shows that small businesses will grow strongly in the next few years, but they will not be the only job-creating firms. The poll confirms that job losses will be concentrated in firms employing more than 1,000 people. The small-business sector as a whole will generate new employment growth in 37 per cent of firms, compared with the average net growth rate for all firms of 20 per cent. American small businesses will put in the best performance, with 43 per cent net job growth, followed by 40 per cent in Japan and 37 per cent in Britain. In contrast, the big-firm sector will show no net employment growth in the years to 1990. Employment in firms with more than 1,000 workers will decline by a net 33 per cent of firms in France and 9 per cent in Great Britain. In the other countries employment in big firms will grow at below the average rate. Big firms make up a quarter of the sample as a whole, but 41 per cent of the firms project job losses. However, small business will not be the major source of job growth in the USA, where employment in medium-sized firms will grow most strongly, by 59 per cent net. This reflects the buoyant employment outlook of US manufacturers. In the UK the small-to-medium-sized sector will outgrow the small-business sector by 5 per cent.

What explains the sharp difference between the employment outlook of small and large firms? Small firms are far less likely to introduce new technology than big firms. Overall 44 per cent of small businesses said that they had introduced new technology since 1980, compared with 79 per cent of large firms. In the sample as a whole 45 per cent of firms said that they had plans to introduce new technology. Only 31 per cent of small firms have these plans, whereas 60 per cent of big firms plan to introduce micro-electronics.

However, the evidence from Japan and Britain shows that even when small businesses introduce new technology, they can still generate jobs. The Japanese sector will generate net employment growth in 40 per cent of small firms, even though 57 per cent of small businesses plan to introduce new technology. Employment in the British small-business sector follows a similar pattern. French small businesses are the most technologically advanced: 34 per cent use high technology compared with 31 per cent in West Germany, 27 per cent in Britain, and just 3 per cent in Japan.

Small firms are far more likely to be non-unionized than large firms. A little over half the firms are non-unionized, but this proportion rises to 74 per cent among small businesses and falls to a low of 21 per cent among large firms. In the USA 88 per cent of small firms are non-union, in France 82 per cent, Japan 80 per cent and Britain 65 per cent. Small businesses are far less likely to have more than half their employees in trade unions. Overall a quarter of firms have more than half their workforce unionized, but this figure falls to a low of 10 per cent among small businesses and rises to a high of 39 per cent among large firms.

Companies planning to sub-contract some of their work to other firms will provide very low net employment growth in 3.8 per cent of firms. Large firms are far more likely to contract out than small firms. Forty-five per cent of large firms have contracted out in the last five years, compared with a little over 20 per cent of small businesses.

Almost half the new firms formed each year fail within four years. Most of those that survive hardly grow at all in terms of employment. 'Employment growth is concentrated in very small, young firms,' says David Storey, editor of 'Small Firms and the Process of Economic Development'. 'It is not clear that the recent increase in new firms will increase the number with growth potential,' he notes.

The characteristics and ambitions of the proprietors of these growth firms are particularly important. It is their drive, their ability to find gaps in the market and to organize efficient production, that is crucial. Politicians throughout Western Europe have set out to transform the economic culture, to instil a new set of values that respects risk-taking entrepreneurs rather than professional managers of big corporations. And it is the American example that most of these politicians are attempting to follow. As Nigel Lawson, the UK Chancellor, said in a television interview in 1986: 'The way forward is the American way. Enterprise culture is the way ahead.'

But what is the 'enterprise culture' of the USA, and what has created it?

'What most astonished me in the USA was not so much the grandeur of some undertakings as the innumerable multitude of small ones,' wrote Alexis de Tocqueville in 1840. A similar observation could be made today. The small-business birth rate has risen from 90,000 a year in the 1950s to 600,000 a year in the 1980s. 'What lies behind this growth is a reversion to the traditional

American values that dominated the pioneering society in the nineteenth century,' says William Dennis of the NFIB. At the root of the high level of business start-ups is a widespread public respect for business and the people who start them, he claims. One US survey, for instance, found that over 87 per cent of respondents would approve of their sons or daughters starting their own business, and a study by Dutch researchers found that American small-business owners felt significantly more highly respected by the public at large than in any other country. But it is easy to over-emphasize the American love of small business. The US survey mentioned above found that people still thought that big businesses were the most important source of jobs, and teachers and farmers rate much more highly than small-business owners or entrepreneurs. Most significantly, around 70 per cent of people thought it difficult to start a business, and 77 per cent thought it difficult to found a business that would grow.

Undoubtedly there are deeply held American values, like respect for the individual and personal independence, that are conducive to entrepreneurialism. But they have been around for decades: why would they explain the recent growth in small-business entrepreneurialism?

According to small-firm expert David Birch, a crucial characteristic of the American enterprise culture is acceptance of failure. 'This is a country that is very forgiving of failure. If you start a company and fail, you are seen as innovative, gutsy, a great guy. So what if you failed? You tried and, in the process, learned a lot,' says Mr Birch. The second key characteristic is acceptance of change, says Bob Friedmann of the Corporation for Enterprise Development. 'All countries have faced changes forced on them by a shifting world economy. America has responded better than some because we adapt to change much more quickly. We have less to root us to the ground.'

But other developments have underpinned the small-business boom. One is the working through of the cultural revolution of the 1960s. The rebellious generation of twenty years ago, which campaigned against the military-industrial complex, has founded many small businesses, according to William Dennis. 'These people were campaigning against the overweening power of big business. But not only were the big corporations morally tainted; they could not offer good jobs. Promotion ladders were clogged. So, for a variety of reasons, the baby-boom generation became intensely disenchanted with the big corporations.' The small-business boom started in 1970, just when the first of the baby-boomers were passing 25 and entering the prime age for starting a firm.

Another trend of importance has been the growth in female participation in the labour force, says Mr Dennis. As women have come into the labour force, they have been an important source of labour for small firms, many working part-time. They have also become important business starters. The rate of business start-ups among women is eight times that of men. The participation of women in the labour market has also generated a need for new service firms to provide laundry, cleaning and fast food.

So underlying cultural factors have combined with demographics and social change to produce small-business growth. An additional factor has been the Government's role. 'Direct Government policy has had hardly any effect on small-business formation, and entrepreneurship,' says Bruno Maur of the Presidential Commission on Industrial Competitiveness. William Dennis puts the point more directly: 'The Small Business Administration is more or less irrelevant. It does good work collecting information, but that's all. Anyway, entrepreneurs worth investing in do not need a Government to tell them where the gaps in the market are.' However, certain Government measures have been important to small-business growth, particularly deregulation.

Firms in deregulated industries are employing an increasing percentage of the American workforce. Almost a quarter of the 12 million jobs created in the USA between 1976 and 1982 came from deregulated industries. Small firms accounted for 82 per cent of this growth. And small firms in deregulated industries also withstood the recession. In the deregulated trucking industry, for instance, firms employing more than 500 workers shed thousands of employees between 1980 and 1982, while firms with fewer than twenty employees generated more than 60,000 jobs. But the importance of deregulation goes beyond opening up particular markets, weakening the power of near-monopoly large firms. 'Governments can best encourage entrepreneurs to come forward by sending out consistent signals that they want more entrepreneurship,' says Bob Friedmann. 'Government cannot tell a society that entrepreneurialism is good in computers but bad in steel, good in transport but not in retail. It cannot let one area go and help plan another. You cannot have selective entrepreneurialism.'

In contrast, 'Small Firms Policies in the UK', published by the Centre for Urban and Regional Development Studies, Newcastle University, in 1986, urges the Government to adopt a much more selective approach to supporting small firms. The authors argue that Government reform of employment legislation, easing the burden of red tape and providing financial assistance through the Enterprise Allowance and other schemes, aimed at the wrong target. Moreover, the report concludes that the kinds of small business that the Government's policy encourages create relatively few jobs in depressed areas or for those who are registered as unemployed. The authors advocate support of key growth firms that will generate most small-business-sector jobs. For instance, one criterion of assistance they suggest is that firms should be able to show an ability to sell outside the UK. For Friedmann and many other American analysts, however, such a change would be a mistaken attempt to mould small businesses in the images of the big businesses they are replacing. 'The vision of the entrepreneurial economy cannot be restricted to high-growth firms that generate big profits so that people can drive around in big cars. We have to recognize that entre-preneurialism must also be able to answer social problems,' says Mr Friedmann.

The final factor that has spurred American small-business growth is the nature of the financial sector. In 1982 there were 14,451 commercial banks in the USA, one for every 15,676 people; in the UK there was one bank for every 1.6 million people. 'The decentralized banking system is crucially important to give people access to funds. Loan capital is not a major problem for small businesses; it is access that counts rather than cost,' says the NFIB's Mr Dennis. But for others the quality of financial aid is much more important. 'Firms that are crucial to job generation are those that are growing. It is they that have changing needs and run into difficulties with the banks. So we have not solved the financial problems yet,' says Mr Friedmann.

Whether or not Western Europe will be able to create its own enterprise cultures with this combination of cultural values, social change and institutional support is as yet unclear. But while small businesses may not offer a solution to unemployment, they will play an increasingly important part in shaping the future of work. The attractions of self-employment, the shift towards the service sector, a continuing trend towards contracting out among big firms, the applicability of new technology to small-business production, the growth of the European venture-capital industry and the interest of politicians of left and right should ensure they will retain a crucial role in future developments. Yet the clearest result from all the studies of small-firm job generation is actually the converse: big-firm job loss has been the source of rising unemployment. It may well be that only when the big firms start hanging out the vacancy signs will unemployment start to fall again.

The official economies of Western Europe may be in reasonable shape. But, cheek by jowl, their hidden economies are going through a period of sustained growth. It has become increasingly clear that most developed countries have not a single economy but at least three: the official, formal economy of legal firms that make tax returns and are governed by employment legislation; the black economy, which ranges from tax avoidance and pilfering at work to fully fledged black-market factories; and the informal economy of odd jobs, household and volunteer work. For several decades these three economies have enjoyed a stable relationship. The households provided firms with workers to produce goods and services. The workers in return got a wage, which they spent on officially produced goods. The black economy was kept to the margins. Now that stable relationship is being destabilized by a range of pressures, from sustained mass unemployment to the increased availability of 'domestic capital' that allows more people to 'do it for themselves'.

This development raises serious political dilemmas for Governments. Should hidden-sector workers be lauded as standard bearers of enterprise or stamped on as parasitic tax fiddlers? Can Governments anxious to cut unemployment afford to see jobs swallowed up by the hidden economy? Or should informal work be seen as a way to augment formal jobs? The development of the informal economy also throws out a challenge to societies based on the centrality of paid work. In principle, a growth in informal patterns of work offers a solution to the unemployment crisis: the lack of official jobs for all who want them. But much informal work is based on an explicit rejection of the rules and ethics of 'proper jobs'. Can informal work be encouraged without forging a major change in social values and attitudes?

Various pressures are pumping up the informal economy. One pervasive, long-run force is the greater availability of sophisticated 'domestic capital', which raises domestic productivity and displaces service workers in the formal economy. In *The New Service Economy* Jonathan Gershuny and Ian Miles show that an increase in this kind of self-servicing could curtail the growth of service-sector employment. The Gershuny/Miles model is very simple. People have a basic set of needs that they have to satisfy, like eating or laundering. They can either pay someone to provide these services (for instance, by going to a restaurant) or do it themselves (by popping something in the microwave). As more sophisticated domestic capital becomes available at lower and lower cost, it becomes more attractive to provide these services for oneself. Domestic work is more cost-effective. If the price of bought services in restaurants or laundries does not fall, through productivity gained or wage restraint, demand for them will be reduced, and service-sector employment will suffer. So work will shift out of the formal economy of laundries and restaurants and into the informal economy of private kitchens. And those industries and countries that produce domestic capital goods will enjoy a steady demand for manufactured products and employment. (One estimate has suggested that the average home now has more capital than a small nineteenth-century factory.)

Commenting on a detailed analysis of changing patterns of demand for domestic goods and services, Gershuny and Miles say, 'Households have been shifting away from the traditional labour-intensive modes of provision, away from the purchase of final services, and towards good-intensive modes of self-provision. During the 1970s people were buying fewer laundry services and more washing machines, fewer cinema tickets and more TVs, and fewer travel tickets and more cars.' The growth of self-servicing in the household economy has important implications for the future of service employment. 'Many people have assumed that the services would soak up workers displaced from manufacturing industry. But the attractiveness of self-servicing, using domestic capital, is placing service employment under increasing pressure,' says Ian Miles.

The second pressure that is raising the level of informal economic activity is disillusionment with the world of formal work. Sustained high levels of unemployment and disillusion with unsatisfying jobs in big companies are both seen as fuelling the hidden economy. This has led some to suggest that informal work offers a solution to the unemployment crisis. Simply, informal household work, odd jobs and volunteer work all keep people occupied by providing others with goods or services they need. This area of work could expand much more rapidly than the formal economy and could soak up the unemployed. To get back to full employment we need to change our idea of what a job is. 'We have to recognize that we are not going to create jobs as we knew them in the past. There will always be plenty of work to do, but increasingly people will do this through a mixture of part-time work, work for cash, odd jobs here and there and voluntary work,' says Professor Charles Handy. 'This is all work, and we need to give it a high social status to encourage people to do it rather than treating it as second best to a proper job. In the future there just will not be enough proper jobs to go around.'

Others see even larger possibilities in the informal sector. For James Robertson, author of *Futurework*, industrialization spells specialization. The private social world of the household becomes a refuge from the harshness of dissatisfying work in the big machine. Mr Robertson argues that advanced societies should build on the qualities of household and unpaid work and move 'from economic growth to human growth; from increasing specialization to increasing self-sufficiency; from increasing dependence on professionals to increasing self-reliance; from increasing centralization to increasing decentralization'. So, for Mr Robertson, informal, unpaid work offers an alternative to a society that constantly generates a need for employment that it cannot satisfy. His vision of self-reliant modern artisans is part of a more general attack on the values of the modern world.

Even advocates of the new informal economy recognize that there are immense problems associated with translating their visions into reality. The informal sector may nurture a new flowering of human values and self-reliance, but it also spells insecurity, instability and low social status. If people are to forgo a formal job and weave instead through various kinds of work in the informal sector, they will have to be persuaded that they will not forgo the key benefits of formal employment: social status and a stable income. Societies will not be able to maintain cohesion unless informal work is given higher status and formal work is downgraded, says Peter Kelvin, Professor of Psychology at London University. 'Unemployment must become accepted as a normal rather than a deviant condition. In strictly quantitative terms, for a substantial number of ordinary people work will not take up a large slice of their lives; it will not therefore be so central to their self-concept as work is today for many people,' he says.

To translate this shift of values into everyday reality, most advocates of informal work argue that the state should provide a basic income for all people of working age. A guaranteed income attached to informal work would bring not just personal satisfaction but also security and a new social status. Revenue for such a scheme would have to come from taxes levied on firms and workers in the formal economy. Even if this did not sap the vitality of the formal economy, it would undoubtedly provoke continuing political controversy.

Another problem for advocates of informal work as a way out of the unemployment crisis is that such evidence as exists suggests that the unemployed are the least likely to undertake informal work. 'Most unemployed men do not have access to the facilities necessary to initiate productive informal activities themselves,' says Ian Miles. Whereas 60 per cent of employed men have access to an electric drill, only 10 per cent of men unemployed for over a year do, according to a study he completed in 1983. Only 10 per cent of unemployed men have access to garden tools or a car, whereas between 70 and 80 per cent of employed males have access to these tools. Moreover, he found that work contacts were crucial to generating opportunities for informal work. A similar study conducted in London found that those most likely to undertake informal work were those least likely to suffer unemployment. 'Our data provide unequivocal evidence that unemployed people are not more likely to provide for themselves or to offer themselves as a source of informal labour for others,' says one of the report's authors, Professor Ray Pahl of Kent University. Further, while some of the unemployed may find opportunities for work if they live near relatively affluent areas, it is not clear that informal work can be stimulated within an area of very high unemployment.

Despite these findings, there are strong signs that the black economies of Western Europe are not just prospering but are becoming more entrenched and better organized. There are ways to measure a hidden economy. One method is to look at the use of cash in the economy on the assumption that the black economy is largely cash-in-hand. Another is to compare income and consumption measures of GDP to prise out discrepancies due to unrecorded activities. Neither of these measures is entirely reliable, but nevertheless there are various official estimates of the size of the black economy.

The West German black economy is now worth DM180 billion (£52.6 billion), or 10 per cent of GNP, according to the Federal Labour Office. Up to 600,000 people are thought to be involved in undeclared economic activities that cost the exchequer DM50 billion in lost tax revenue and improper social security payments. The most recent estimates of Italy's well-established underground economy suggest that it accounts for 20 per cent of goods and services and involves over 3 million people. The US hidden economy could account for 10 per cent of GNP, according to a report by economists at New York University. In France there are between 800,000 and 1.5 million people in the black economy, according to an ILO report. About 2 million French families employ domestic servants, but only one in eight are on the country's social security rolls. In the UK the Inland Revenue suggests that the hidden economy accounts for between 6 and 8 per cent of GNP. These estimates include all forms of economic activity that should be declared to the authorities but go unrecorded, so simple tax avoidance may make up a major part of the hidden sector.

According to a recent OECD report, in the USA the average four-person household spent $2,730 on black-economy goods and services in 1980; in West Germany, DM5,800 ($3,190 at the 1980 exchange rate); in the UK, £960 ($2,240). Some of the black-economy workforce comes from among the unemployed. Thirty-six per cent of London's unemployed youth work part-time for cash in bars or restaurants. At the other end of the spectrum early-retirement programmes have also swelled the hidden-economy labour force. But most reports suggest that the main participants in the black economy are those who already have a job but do a little bit extra on the side.

The more organized forms of economic activity are attracting attention. Many politicians seem to believe that the rise of the hidden economy shows that enterprise can create jobs and that people are prepared to go out and look for work. 'The existence of the black economy indicates that where people find a direct relationship between the money they get in their hands and the work they do, they not only do that work but they go out to find it. The enterprise is still there,' Margaret Thatcher said in 1985. So politicians are in something of a bind over the black economy. The lost tax revenues hurt the Exchequer, and black-economy job creation does little to reduce the official unemployment count, but it can be held up as a standard of enterprise. The OECD report warns against over-stating the phenomenon. It suggests that national accounts under-record economic activity by only around 3 per cent of GDP. 'Hidden activities may not be large relative to total GDP,' the report says.

The fringe economy displays an astonishing diversity: from social-service volunteer work to back-street sweatshops; from the self-fulfilment of pursuing life-long hobbies to the insecurity of illegal foreign workers; from the simple act of cooking a meal to building a house. It is a shifting target for policy-makers to aim at. If volunteer social work is encouraged with a new social security payment, then why not other forms of informal work, like housework? If some black-economy enterprise is to be praised, then why not all? What is clear is that, increasingly, policy will be unable simply to ignore or suppress the informal economy. The persistence of high levels of unemployment, the rising real incomes of those in formal work and the drift towards self-provisioning will ensure that the informal economy will continue to play an important role.

There are two ways in which the informal economy could develop, according to Jonathan Gershuny. The state could try to ignore it. But this would imply sanction for large numbers of people to work in a parallel economy, unprotected by employment legislation and without social security benefits. The scale of the informal economy and the seeping effects it would have on the rules, ethics and organization of the formal economy would eventually force the state to take action to suppress informal activity or reform it. Suppression would be too costly and too messy, says Mr Gershuny. Eventually Governments will have to start taking a more constructive approach to work in the informal sector. This will require relinquishing the goal of creating full employment in the formal economy and replacing it with a new vision. 'In the future we could look to the formal economy to provide efficient material production and to the informal economy to provide services,' argues Mr Gershuny. 'This would involve the state in the active promotion of community-based services in such fields as child care and care for the elderly and the sick. It would involve the modification of laws relating to very small companies, to relieve them of administrative and heavy tax burdens. It would require a change to social security to remove high marginal tax rates on low wage-earners and to provide some form of protection for those working exclusively in the small-scale, informal sector. And, most important, it would involve the state in taking action to encourage people to participate simultaneously in the formal and informal economies.'

Giving the informal economy a realistic role in future employment strategies could be one of the most important challenges of the next fifteen years.

9. POLITICS

The expression of concern about unemployment is a necessary component of the political rhetoric of our days. At the very least, it is the tribute that vice (or policy vacuousness) pays to virtue (or remembrance of a full-employment past). Of the major industrial economies only Japan does not suffer from high structural unemployment; only the USA, with an unemployment rate of 7.1 per cent, has actually reduced its jobless. The big West European states, especially the UK, are caught in the grip of unemployment.

Much of the agenda of international policy formulation derives from this concern. The Tokyo summit in May 1986 provided a forum for further pressure on Japan and West Germany to reflate in order to supply jobs in Teesside and the Mezzogiorno. The European Commission's debates on lowering the barriers to market freedom within the Community are couched in the language of labour-market efficiency designed to create employment. Debates on the immorality of South African apartheid swirl around the rock of the objection that effective sanctions mean loss of jobs in the industries of its trading partners. Government ministers, including Prime Ministers, fly about the globe to act as super-salesmen (and women) so that they may announce that their timely intervention with the king of this country or their special relationship with the president of that one has created or saved a thousand jobs among their own voters.

The expenditure on employment measures and the inventiveness of Government responses have been unparalleled in history. In part this is because all Western European countries had adopted social insurance and other welfarist programmes when unemployment was seen as a largely frictional and residual problem; now these entitlements are proving hugely costly to service. No Government can afford simply to pay the benefits and wait for the day – relatively distant in some cases – when demographic factors will rescue it: all must actively intervene in their labour markets to make work, raise the training level of the unemployed and encourage new relationships between public provision and the private sector. It is not a movement that can be much distinguished on political grounds. Tony Hubert, a researcher at the European Centre for Work and Society in Maastricht, says, 'It is difficult to ascertain differences between so-called right-of-centre and left-of-centre Governments not only in the amount of public finance they have devoted to this field but also in the changing nature of their approaches.'

The two radical political figures of the West in the 1980s have been conservatives: Ronald Reagan and Margaret Thatcher. 'I believe,' said Mr Reagan in January 1982, the second year of his presidency, 'that we have started government on a different course, different than anything we've done in the last half century since Roosevelt began with the New Deal.' Five years into her premiership, Mrs Thatcher said, 'I believe that five years ago the British people made me Prime Minister primarily because they sensed that socialism had been leading them into a life of debilitating dependency on the state when what they really wanted was the independence and freedom of self-reliance and responsibility.'

Though both politicians, especially Margaret Thatcher, are controversial and at times divisive figures – particularly, in recent times, on foreign policy issues – they have seen under their leadership the development of a reluctant consensus on at least some issues of their domestic policy, and nowhere has this been more evident than in the employment field. In the USA, and more particularly in Western Europe, where the labour market has been more tightly regulated and structured, the rhetoric of free enterprise, individualism and anti-statism has been ingested not just by political debate but also by policy formulation and even by the language and programmes of Opposition parties.

It is the left that has felt the heat over the past few years of unemployment growth, the left that has made, or has been forced to make, the largest change of ground. In none of the six major advanced countries does a party of the left hold power – even in Italy, the right has the largest share of the governing coalition. This hegemony of the right coexists with a groping bewilderment on the part of the left as to what it would do with the economy in general and the unemployed in particular.

Daniel Bell, the Harvard sociologist, says that a Democratic administration pledged to a liberal (leftist) programme is impossible while that programme is not seen to have a coherent answer to US domestic issues, including employment change and industrial policy. In the last presidential election a union-backed Walter Mondale came a poor second to an incumbent President who won many union members' votes. This was a vivid display of the loss of authority by a group that may be unable again to find a Democratic (or a Republican) candidate who will campaign on the issues that attract organized labour. They include import controls, high public spending, support for declining industrial areas, opposition to state-level right-to-work (anti-union shop) laws and support for collective bargaining. Of recent presidential aspirants only Mr Mondale and Edward Kennedy have made these concerns a part of their programmes; no one on the horizon is likely to do much more than genuflect towards them. Americans have not become less socially liberal overall (*pace* the moral majority), but, as Brian Girvin, a historian and commentator on conservative politics, notes, 'The rejection of economic liberalism, which is associated with inflation, has been the motor for Reagan's success.'

In Western Europe the most recent and most notable socialist experiment was that undertaken by the French socialists, voted out of office in March 1986. Their combination of Keynesian expansionism, redistributive taxation, enlarge-ment of the state sector and reform of collective bargaining held at bay unemployment – but it also contributed to a thrice-devalued franc, rising inflation, a balance-of-payments deficit and a swing to the right. France was pursuing demand-led growth at a time when all other major market economies were retrenching. As Robert Lekachman of New York's City University, a friendly commentator on the country, put it, the lesson was that 'socialism in one medium-sized country is unworkable if that country's major trading partners pursue substantially different national policies.' Dr Lekachman pushes the thought a little further, noting that the necessary conditions would be co-ordinated moves to the left in Western Europe, together with a left-wing Government in either the USA or Japan, the only economies large and rich enough to go it alone – and the most conservative. 'Socialism, in short, has its fairest prospect where it is least likely to occur.'

These thoughts provided the basis for reflection within the French socialist party – still the largest in the Assembly – during the Chirac Government's honeymoon period. The debate taking place within and around the party (contrary to the lurch to the left of the British Labour Party after it had lost power in 1979) is very much within the framework of the centre-left: the period of austerity that the socialists administered in the last three years of their Government has not provoked widespread charges of treachery from within – though these charges are being made by a presently failing Communist Party.

Indeed, some of the strongest arguments come from the right of the party, where former members of the Government are seeking to find an accommodation with socialism and a base of supporters no longer conforming with an undiffer-entiated description of 'working class'. Among those who have taken the lead in this debate is Paul Quiles, Defence Minister in the last year of the socialist Government. For him the party's commitment, in its 1971 declaration of principles, that the majority of workers should abolish class and take for themselves the means of production and exchange, is old hat. Says M. Quiles: 'Who would still define the socialist party by reference to the notion of the "class front", the up-to-date version of the class struggle? Social classes exist, certainly, but economic, cultural and technical changes have altered French society to the point where its social structure depends not only on who does what but also on how and for whom.'

Further discussion has been somewhat muted because of the need to support the embattled socialist President Mitterrand until the next elections. But at the party convention in the Paris suburbs of Pré-St-Gervais at the end of June 1986 something of the same current emerged. Laurent Fabius, the former Prime Minister, told the conference that the party must now be responsible in its criticisms – 'For we are no longer condemned to govern for a few months every twenty or thirty years. We have become the alternative party of government;

without abandoning our objective of transforming society, we must refuse to take an all-or-nothing attitude.'

M. Quiles's message was taken right into the party itself: on 22 March soon after the socialists' (narrow) defeat, he told the executive committee of his party that concepts such as the class front, a break with capitalism and workers' control ('autogestion') were no longer relevant and had to be dropped. 'Some utopias cannot be flourished any more,' he told them, 'even if they were forces for mobilization before 1981, *because we have confronted them with the proof of power.*'

The need to rethink and re-order the priorities of socialism spreads throughout the democratic socialist movement of Western Europe: all parties of the left are seeking to reassemble a political/ideological base. Donald Sassoon, a historian at London University, says that the right's electorally successful critique of the state has 'contributed to the crisis of left politics and engendered a welcome wave of self-criticism'. Mr Sassoon distinguishes three responses to the 'crisis'. From those socialist parties in power or with a share in it (as the Spanish and Italian) has emerged a centrist strategy that 'ends up by accepting most of the neo-liberal critique of the welfare state and, in particular, the concept of over-loaded government'; from sections of many parties, a continued fidelity to class politics and hope in the ultimate collapse of capitalism; from two major parties, and sections of all, a 'Europeanist' option that accepts the case that socialism cannot be attempted in one economically isolated country and that a European community, at once strengthened and democratized, is a necessary companion to future left-wing progress.

The Italian Communist Party and the German Social Democrats have constructed an improbable 'alliance' around this last current. Achille Ochetto, a senior official of the PCI, willingly cedes that 'no coherent left exists as yet' and that 'the conservative offensive has established a new agenda for the debate between free marketeers and social reformers.' Sr Ochetto challenges the European left to put itself at the head of necessary modernization, which 'can be achieved only if it is prepared to abandon its traditional defensive and sectarian attitudes. Then, and only then, could it open a debate with a section of the strong – those, for instance, involved in the new technology, the new professional classes and those forward-looking entrepreneurs who are willing to work towards employment and growth in the context of a new framework of industrial relations and democratic control of the economy.' Sr Ochetto emphasizes the PCI's adoption of a democratic socialist position and its rejection of a class-struggle strategy.

The German SPD has, since its loss of power in 1982, moved to incorporate some of the concerns of the Greens (it proposes now to pursue economic growth within ecologically defined guidelines), become more overtly responsive to the needs of the Third World, taken a more sceptical stance on Nato nuclear policy (while still maintaining a large and hostile distance from unilateralism) and emphasized the trans-European nature of future policy. Peter Glotz, the party's secretary general (and a member of the federal Parliament) has in his 'Manifesto for a New European Left', published in the autumn of 1985, gone farthest in proposing a European strategy that recognizes the shifts in support, and the loss of national sovereignty, with which the left must come to terms. Says Herr Glotz: 'The left must grasp this once and for all. The minimum return that must be offered to investment-seeking capital – to make productive investments and job creation possible – is less determined today by the policies of individual nation states than ever before.'

This modesty in aims and conception of powers affects the British Labour Party too – a party more battered than any of its European comrades over the last few years by internal struggle and electoral drubbing at the hands of the right. Pulled into the centre to find votes and to recognize precisely those economic and social factors that now engage the Continental left, the Labour leadership has responded with a pragmatism unthinkable in the early, left-galloping 1980s. Neil Kinnock, the party leader, has served notice that he means to preserve a Conservative law which enforced ballots for union elections and before strikes, while at the same time conducting a guerrilla war on the far left and taking time to commend the Japanese industrial system. Roy Hattersley, his deputy and shadow Chancellor, has, in a range of speeches, advanced a highly revisionist definition of socialism that accords a large place to markets. Mr Hattersley concedes, 'Our [Labour Party] attitudes towards markets have sometimes been wrong' and joins the European left chorus in agreeing that 'socialism is in desperate need of a reassertion of its basic philosophic position.' His tentative propositions are that 'a substantial market sector is essential both to the promotion of efficiency and to the maintenance of a free society' (this last a leaf from the Conservative book – though not invested, as he says, with their 'moral significance') and that 'markets cannot in themselves guarantee either the optimum distribution of resources or the maximum satisfaction of individual desires and needs', though 'in some sectors of the economy they can contribute to both ends.'

All this is closer to Europragmatism than to Euro-communism or -socialism: it is founded on a common sense of loss of base, a common analysis that the 'working class' is no longer automatically 'our people' and that some at least of the advances made by the right have to be preserved (and may even be worth preserving).

Common too is a tacit acknowledgement that the 'dirty work' being effected by Governments of the right would have had to be done, or already has been done, by Governments of the left. The UK Labour Government's adoption of mild monetarism, the German SPD's repatriation of guest workers, the French socialist Government's austerity programme, the Italian socialist-led coalition's de-indexing of inflation-proof pay rises – all of these furnish the main left-wing parties in Europe with the 'proof of power' and have moved them away from any residual utopianism.

Those who again take power will probably find the terrain as rocky as before, though the German Social Democrats would benefit soon both from demographic changes and from an existing corporatist framework. A future Labour Government, however, would find a debilitated union movement, a virtual collapse of the tripartite forums, a largely privatized economy and – perhaps worst – wage increases still running ahead of inflation because one of the goals the Conservative Government has *not* achieved is bringing down wage rates in order to assist job creation.

In Britain, as elsewhere, parties of the left criticize the creation of a society where the majority have found security and rising living standards in work but where the minority out of work, or only occasionally in it, is both relatively and absolutely more impoverished than before. Peter Glotz calls it the 'two-thirds society', in which the majority quietly accepts the degradation of the lower third. The democratic problem is, of course, that two-thirds can always outvote one-third: thus how can a new deal be struck between the haves and the have-nots that gives the latter some hope and the former something to vote for?

Charles Handy makes the point in the context of the UK: 'This, then, is the most crucial choice which the 80 per cent of the relatively fortunate in Britain have to make. Will they hang on to what they have and devil take the hindmost in a cruel world, or are they prepared to give up part of their jobs and, with it, a part of their income, for a fairer society?' It is not a choice that will be presided over by Governments of only one political stripe.

'We need a mixture of deregulation of the labour market and state intervention in it.' Gianni de Michelis, who launched a debate about the future of work in Italy while Labour Minister in the Craxi Government, is, with these words, pointing to an intriguing marriage of ideas about work normally found at different points of the political spectrum. Governments should break down the barriers that have sprung up in the path to a more freely running labour market. But they should not be afraid to step in and help things on their way if they fail to reach their destination: full employment or something like it. In other words, any formula to combat unemployment must come in two parts: measures to encourage more flexible working patterns and to channel jobs in directions (like Italy's depressed south) where they would not naturally flow.

This two-pronged treatment proposed by Sr de Michelis flows from a two-fold diagnosis of the causes of unemployment: the slowdown in growth among the major economies, plus the inability of ossified working patterns to cope with new social and technological demands being made of them. 'What we considered work ten years ago was very different from what we will consider work to be in the future,' Sr de Michelis says, citing two examples of these changes. 'The model of work used to be of a secure job in a unionized workplace,' he says. But not any longer: workers will have to become more used to switching jobs and employers. 'We will have to think more of job rotation and less of job satisfaction,' Sr de Michelis argues. He also sees more self-employment as the most radical sign that secure jobs in large organizations are in decline. In Italy, even excluding the small businesses that fall through the official net, more than a quarter of all workers are already self-employed. He goes further to talk of a blurring of the distinction between employed and self-employed, just as there has been a merging of blue- and white-collar work. In Italy the networks of small entrepreneurs who do work on contract for the giants like Benetton have some of the characteristics of employees (complete dependence on one company) and some of those of the self-employed (flexibility in their own working arrangements).

Sr de Michelis is a socialist, yet he welcomes the trend away from the large, regulated, unionized organizations with which the left has traditionally felt most comfortable. 'Our problem is to accept these changes and to accelerate them. We need to reduce the gap between the job destruction in the old industries and job creation in the new industries,' he says. Only thus, he believes, can we lay down the conditions for what he calls 'the twenty-first century's full employment'. He emphasizes two initiatives that run with the grain of these changes: deregulation and flexibility. 'Until a few years ago our labour market was completely regulated,' he says. And not without exaggeration. Italian laws are still rigid in areas like hiring and firing. When recruiting new workers, companies must take those offered by the state labour exchanges. If they lay workers off, they have to re-hire the same ones if they expand later.

Negotiations between the Italian Government, employers and unions have begun the painstaking task of chipping away at these laws. 'We want deregulation, not for ideological reasons but because it will help changes in our labour market. We are on the road towards flexibility,' he says. Put at their lowest, the aim of these measures is to persuade the black, 'submerged' economy to surface: more ambitiously, they are designed to encourage new patterns of work throughout the Italian economy.

Sr de Michelis is keen to encourage young people to start their own businesses, partly to dent the 30 per cent youth-unemployment mountain in Italy but also because he thinks there is a gap here in enterprise creation. In the past, he says, most small businesses in Italy were formed by workers leaving larger organizations to go it alone: the 'work-to-work' route, as he calls it. He wants to encourage young people to move straight into small businesses: the 'school-to-work' route. He has developed aid packages for that purpose.

Yet side by side with these liberalizing, free-market initiatives, Sr de Michelis and the Italian Government are busy operating employment schemes of the more traditional kind, such as a panoply of measures to help the Mezzogiorno, the depressed south. Does this pragmatic blending of measures from both camps – the liberal and managed views of the labour market – offer a way out of the ideological warfare of the 1970s and 1980s?

Mass unemployment and labour-market revolutions have produced more changes in the political superstructure, though, than *Angst* on the left. As important, it has invited the participation of corporations in the labour market *and therefore*, *inevitably, in the political market.* This is not, of course, new in itself. The private sector has played a political role for centuries: indeed, one of the origins of mercantile capitalism lay in financing Governments. But in our own times we have accepted a *de facto* division of labour between the state, as provider of education, social security and even full(ish) employment – all areas into which private enterprise has now trespassed and will continue to do so – and private, entrepreneurial activity. We have seen how business has come into the community, seeking to defuse social reaction to its own strategies of retrenchment and to do itself some good. But the concept of business as the guider of the nation's fortunes, while comprehending these initiatives, goes beyond them.

Alain Chevallier of Moët is a particularly frank exponent of this theme. He says: 'The really positive factor here is the coming together of private initiatives. Governments are exhausted and without imagination. Besides, there are in Europe enterprises, centres of research, investors, innovators and problem-solvers. A space in the West where private initiatives can act and express themselves is in the process of being formed. It is unified space, driven by the markets and the forces of exchange. I no longer look to politicians and to their programmes as capable of getting us out of our present problems in a rational and voluntary way. We're moving towards a more or less feudal society. In coming years concentrations of power, action and decision-making will appear. They won't be substitutes for the existing political powers, which are usually territorial: they will be concentrations of economic forces.' The new feudal baronies, will, in M. Chevallier's view, effect a transition from an economic world dominated by macro-economic concerns to one dominated by the micro-level solutions. It begs huge questions, but who can say that the lines of development leading to such a society are not to be detected in place?

Japan (with a real feudalism in a more recent past than most advanced societies) can be said to be there already. The big companies, with internally cultivated managers the toughest of whom rise to sit on company boards, where they find little challenge to their authority from the representatives of the shareholders, already operate small welfare states within their boundaries. They co-operate closely with the bureaucracies, especially Miti, and spend lavishly to ensure the constant re-election of the Liberal Democrats as the governing party. Their actions overseas, as the export of Japanese capital speeds up, will change the policies and politics, the industrial relations and labour movements, of the states in which they operate.

But companies will not be able to operate a new feudalism untrammelled. The moves in that direction, if confirmed, will meet opposition or modification in those parts of society that corporations cannot control and for which Governments must continue to take responsibility: the barons will find more or less powerful kings, or Governments, willing to curb their powers. The multiplicity of pressures on businesses in environments where more is expected of them is well illustrated by that long-time multinational corporation, Ford.

'In the past, to be a good businessman you had to be interested only in cost and price. In the future the good businessman will also have to be a good politician.' Competitive pressures on business are growing not just in the labour market and the car market but also in the market for political acceptability, according to Pete Pestillo. Mr Pestillo is Ford's vice-president responsible for developing the company's new co-operative labour-relations strategy. But his job goes beyond the hard graft of handling union–management relations. 'Labour relations is just a part of communications and persuasion. Unions are just one coalition that we have to deal with. In the future we will increasingly have to deal with claims from Governments, other businesses, consumers and environmentalists – a much broader coalition of interests.

The pressures on businessmen to become more politically adept come from within and outside the company. Ford has developed a new approach to labour relations, particularly in the USA, which centres on the Employee Involvement Programme. This mimics Japanese quality circles, which have the same aims of enhanced efficiency and quality. Ford executives think that the programme is essential to the firm's future competitiveness. But, according to Mr Pestillo, it carries far-reaching implications for the running of the company. 'In the past we used to pay high rates to dolts because they were easy to manage. Now we have to include people much more in day-to-day decisions about production, and we hope the system will spread through our operations. The next stage of employee involvement takes us into the question of who runs the company, of governance, the arena of a truly jointly run business,' he says.

But the politics of involving the workforce are compounded by pressures to cut employment. Since 1981 Ford US has laid off 53,000 hourly paid manufacturing employees. Over the next few years it plans to reduce its white-collar staff by about 20 per cent. In the past these workers would have left with no more than a pat on the back and special unemployment benefit. But, according to Mr Pestillo, the company now has to recognize a responsibility to them, their families and the economy outside Ford. 'This kind of change can have such an impact on the individuals involved and the economy outside that we have a responsibility to try to control the dislocation to ensure a soft landing through retirement and retraining programmes. The recognition of the responsibility not just to cast people aside is something new.'

Decisions affecting the local labour markets in Michigan or Genk are at one end of the spectrum of political pressures on Ford. At the other are decisions about its multinational operations: outsourcing and joint ventures. These decisions, which may once have been straightforward matters of profit and loss, have turned into political footballs; companies can no longer afford to be politically naïve and passive. Outsourcing of production has introduced much needed competition into labour costs, says Mr Pestillo. But that benefit has been won at the expense of plunging Ford into politics.

The economic logic of the industry will continue to drive companies towards joint ventures, but their extent will be limited by what is politically acceptable.

Overcoming these political obstacles is not just a matter of good lobbying. 'To be a successful, accepted company it is no longer enough just to provide a good product at the right price,' he says. 'For instance, we do not have a strong manufacturing presence in Italy. Would we sell more if we produced more there, if we provided more employment? Would we be seen as more of an Italian company? These kinds of factor affect sourcing decisions, not just labour costs.' The choice between making cars at Halewood in the UK or at a new plant in Portugal at a wage rate of $3 an hour is a hard one, says Mr Pestillo. 'We are making a very good Fiesta in Spain, with people who used to be onion farmers. But could we afford to lack a manufacturing presence in a major market and run into all the political problems of switching production? I do not think we could, even if it made business sense.'

So, in the pursuit of efficiency, multinational businessmen will have to turn themselves into politicians to ease social and political constraints on their business actions. 'In the past Governments played the crucial role, mediating conflicts of interest. In the future we as a company will have to deal with interest groups directly to be successful,' says Mr Pestillo. 'We will have to deal with national and local politicians, consumer groups, the unions, environmental groups. Businesses will have to deal with these broad coalitions as well as workers, suppliers and consumers.' And this will require a revolution in the way that management sees its role. In a shifting economic and political environment just keeping things ticking over will no longer be enough. 'In the future executives will have to provide more than good business management. We will have to provide something altogether different: leadership. That is something we have been very bad at in the past.'

The European Round Table, the six senior businessmen brought together initially by Per Gyllenhammar, chairman of Volvo, is one of the best examples of the new stab at Mr Pestillo's goal of social leadership now being made by business. Its latest report, 'Making Europe Work' shows the industrialists grappling not just with familiar topics like Government aid and public purchasing policy but also with demography, education and social division. It does not signal inhibitions about intervening in what was once the guarded preserve of politics; instead it poses central questions to which European policy-makers in Government and business must address themselves. Can this tide of unemployment be made to turn? Can we marshal our endless analysis of the causes of the crisis, and our piecemeal experience in dealing with it so far, into an effective programme? The use of 'we' puts the industrialists inside the policy debate explicitly, as the subjects rather than the objects of policy formation. It is not a position they are likely to cede.

From this flows a number of questions. If the corporation is strengthened as a part industrial, part political actor, what is the role of Government and of trade unions? How far can a private initiative, inevitably partial and ultimately inevitably self-interested, replace a political process that gains legitimacy, at least in theory, from the popular vote? How far will private intervention be regarded as legitimate? How far will it set up new tensions – especially between the corporations and their members and those who find themselves outside the feudal walls?

There are no global answers to these questions, nor even some common to the advanced states. As we have seen, developments within their industrial cultures show differences as well as similarities. Further, we should be wary, as some forecasters are not, of being determinist about a future because industrial and technical changes seem to dictate a certain model. Ian Miles, a senior research fellow at the UK's Science Policy Research Unit, says, 'The mass-consumption model, the growth of public education and welfare services, increased wages and leisure time, were all achieved through political processes, reflecting changes in class structure, etc., rather than passively flowing through from changes in production.'

In Japan, West Germany and, to a lesser extent, Italy the corporatist model that is seen (at least in the first two) still to be serving the country's economy well, will retain a political attraction for the foreseeable future.

In France, the defeat of the left has given new encouragement to liberalization tendencies at a time when the union movement is particularly weak and defensive. The issue is dramatized by the current split within the Patronnat, between its president, Yvon Gattaz, who favours a flexible, somewhat anti-corporatist style that would, implicitly at least, further downgrade the unions' social partnership role, and Yvon Chotard, who (with the backing of the present Government) wishes to retain some balance in industry so that change can be negotiated and mediated. On 11 July 1986 Gattaz, seeing that Chotard's approach was gaining ground, resigned.

In the UK economic liberalization since 1979 has helped greatly to reduce the power and influence of the union movement to the point where the main Opposition party, Labour, must detach itself somewhat from it in order to look credible as a potential governing force. But the unions remain relatively strongly organized in most sectors and have been able to defend (without much of a fight, in most cases) their members' living standards.

In the USA a corporate industrial style that includes the union movement is not seriously on offer, but general political concern will continue to be focused on Japanese and other Far Eastern competition and on the ability of US workers to make improvements in educational and productivity standards to compete.

A final, unifying paradox: as all the advanced states, in one way or to some degree or another, have had to become more active in labour markets, so their parties of left, right and centre have recognized, often explicitly, that the social and industrial fragmentation that we have witnessed in these markets has also meant political fragmentation. Shirley Williams, former Labour Minister and herself a prime mover in the fragmentation of British politics when a founder member of the Social Democrats, comments that the unemployment that hit the advanced world in the 1930s bound together whole working-class communities, which created a bedrock for socialist and communist parties, but the solidarity that survived the Second World War weakened as incomes grew in real terms, as the occupational structure favoured technical, professional and white-collar jobs, as women entered the labour force. '"Proper" jobs, full-time, traditional jobs, turned into zealously protected quasi-monopolies of the employees and overheads for the employers. The losers were part-time workers, the young and those, like many married women, who moved in and out of the formal labour force. Often those lucky enough to be employed did not want to be told about those without jobs. While those employed in blue- or white-collar jobs strengthened their defences and improved their material position, the unemployed became poorer.'

An 'employment underclass' is not new, but its composition has greatly changed. Yesterday's labour aristocrats, once contemptuous of those on the margins like women, now find themselves on the scrap heap as women keep and get jobs, the middle-aged and elderly find no prestige attached to age, the unskilled young find that no one wants their muscles. This is the greatest challenge to democratic politics: how to continue to ensure material progress without using a larger or smaller victim class that acts as a now mute, now rebellious support for the advance of the rest. It is being thrown up acutely in our times and will be so in the future: no answer has yet been found.

10. CONCLUSION

How can we sum up the forces that are changing work? And what can we say of the question that we raised at the beginning about the need for a new public philosophy centred on work?

In the introduction we outlined a minimal three-part definition of the role that work plays in the advanced economies. Work is part of the system of production, an economic resource; it is a source of income, which gives people the capacity to consume; it also has a tremendous social significance. 'What do you do?' is still one of the commonest conversational openers. A person's occupation gives all kinds of clues about him or her: educational background, income, possibly politics and so on. Beyond this, work also provides people with a structure for their time and a source of social contact with others. Factories and offices are tremendous social as well as economic institutions.

The exchange that millions of people take part in — exchanging labour for income — is fundamental to all economies. When it changes, much else changes in its wake. So what can we say about the elements of this definition that have changed in the last few years?

First, the overwhelming conclusion of this book is that there has been, and will continue to be, a tremendous waste of work as an economic resource. Unemployment now stands at 31 million throughout the OECD area. All those people could be working, making goods and providing services that would make the advanced economies better off. As a society we would benefit from the output that the unemployed would produce if they were working. The persistence of mass unemployment is evidence that the advanced economies are badly malfunctioning. Second, the supply of labour has changed, and will have to change further, dramatically. Workers are coming from new sources. Of particular importance is the growth of the female workforce, especially among married women. Third, in both manufacturing and services new methods of production are making heavy demands of education and training. Thousands of workers, in companies as diverse as Ford, IBM and Barclays Bank, are having to be retrained to ensure that they remain usable economic resources. The importance of education and training is felt not only at the level of the company; there is a growing recognition in the United Kingdom, for example, that the quality of a nation's education and training system is a crucial determinant of an economy's capacity to grow.

One of the main pressures on the education and training system comes from the introduction of new technology. To reap the full gains of new technology it is not enough just to introduce islands of automation. Entire production processes have to change and, with them, the work that people do. Japanese manufacturing success is related not to replacing large numbers of people with small numbers of machines but to combining people and machines in more efficient ways. At Ford UK, for instance, new technology is having a sweeping effect on the skills required of managers as well as those of production workers. To remain valuable, economic resources workers have to be retrained and reorganized. But what of those who are laid off, those whose skills have been discarded? How will they gain the skills they need to keep their heads above water? For if they are to find new jobs, it is certain that they will need new skills.

Some suggest that new technology deskills workers; they become button pushers. Jobs that once required skills of touch and sight are now carried out more efficiently by computer-controlled machines. All the evidence suggests that the effects of new technology on skills cannot be read off from the design of a machine. Management plays a crucial role in deciding how to organize work and skills around the machines that are installed. And the power of workers in the labour market also counts. Those who are least powerful in the labour market (young people, women, ethnic minorities) are the groups least likely to be able to influence the direction that new technology takes. Those who already have some power (skilled men, often in professional associations or trade unions) are more likely to be able to influence the direction of change and the benefits that accrue to them. The effects of technological change are not determined by the make of the machine: they are refracted through the allocation of power in the labour market.

New technology will not change just the skills required by individual groups of workers. To reap the full gains of new technology, entire production systems have to be changed. Many observers believe that we are on the verge of the development of a new concept of production. The motor-manufacturing industry spawned just such a revolutionary production concept in the 1920s and 1930s, when Henry Ford combined flowline production processes with a rigid division of labour and a pyramidal hierarchy of management. The routine tasks of production workers are, for many, what sums up working in factories. However, the introduction of flexible manufacturing systems and computer-integrated manufacturing will change that. More and more workers will move away from direct production and will become indirect maintenance staff. They are likely to be multi-skilled, able to carry out a wide range of tasks and to follow a complex production process rather than merely to oversee a routine operation. The rigid division of labour that characterizes so much work in factories may be breaking down. These multi-skilled operatives and craftsmen will be the new-technology labour aristocrats. Most studies suggest that these craftsmen will be given greater autonomy on the factory floor. The old authority structure of foremen and supervisors will change. So it is not just that new technology will demand new skills: it will also promote a different organization of the production process. And with that will come new ways of working and new divisions of labour.

A final point about work as an economic resource is that work and workers are being matched up in different ways. Evidence from the UK and elsewhere suggests that labour markets are becoming segmented between 'core' and 'peripheral' workers. Whereas once it was taken for granted that work meant full-time work, now it often means self-employment, part-time working, short-term contracts or homework. In recent years there has also been a growing interest in the informal economy. In households, voluntary organizations and the black economy people are working to produce goods and services without being formally employed. The rules of exchange in this economy are often very different from those in the formal economy. Most people who work for an employer do specific tasks for a specific wage. In the household economy a wide range of tasks is carried out for a general (and often not substantial) return of services in kind. Money and prices play no clear role in this economy.

In these and other ways, then, work and workers as economic inputs are undergoing tremendous change. This obviously has an effect on the second basic aspect of work: as a source of income. Again, the most significant point must be the persistence of mass unemployment and, through much of Europe, of long-term unemployment. For 31 million people throughout the OECD area employment is not the main source of income. Many part-time workers and the self-employed have to face fluctuating, uncertain incomes. The Western economies are also seeing the growth of their black economies, in which work yields an undeclared livelihood. These developments, and particularly the rise in unemployment, suggest growing inequalities in income. The growth of long-term unemployment means that millions of people have come to accept that the state, rather than an employer, will be the source of their regular income.

In tandem with this development those in secure jobs have benefited from periods of low inflation. In companies where prospects now look brighter after the recession of the early 1980s the evidence suggests that wage bargaining has returned to its old path. For the employed labour force in economies that are growing by between 2 and 3 per cent a year economic conditions may not look very different from those of the 1970s. The key difference is that now there are much higher levels of unemployment. In the UK there is growing concern that earnings are rising by around 7.5 per cent a year despite massive levels of unemployment. Classical theory, which suggests that the unemployed should be able and prepared to bid down wages and that companies should take up their offer to work for lower wages, has not been borne out. Increasingly, labour-market economists seek to explain what is happening to wages by looking at the conflict between 'insiders' and 'outsiders'. The 'insiders' are workers and managers of firms who sit at the pay-bargaining table. The 'outsiders' are the unemployed who find it very difficult to influence pay bargaining directly. The evidence suggests that pay is not determined by the state of the general labour market. As our poll shows, despite record numbers of people out of work, employers think that unemployment is the least important factor influencing pay. Rather, pay is set in line with the internal needs of companies.

The division between the 'insiders' and the 'outsiders' is not created simply by the income gains that those in employment have made. For substantial numbers the form that their remuneration takes is also changing. Increasingly, the simple wage packet is being augmented by bonuses, pension entitlements, share-option schemes, profit-sharing and other new forms of remuneration. In the USA some companies are now considering forms of 'cafeteria compensation', which allow workers to design their own mix of wages. The association of employment with wages is slowly changing.

A final point about the relationship between work and income comes from the economists James Meade and Vassily Leontieff. They warn that if there is greater use of new technology, the returns to capital may rise faster than the returns to labour. In other words, the share of national income taken by profits will grow at the expense of wages. As Meade says, there is nothing objectionable about this as long as capital ownership is broadly based; then the gains from the increased returns to capital will be spread through the economy. Without a broader ownership of capital, the economists warn, the introduction of new technology could lead to a long-run increase in income inequality. To this end others have suggested moves to widen share ownership through the market or to set up wage-earner investment funds to manage investments for workers. There is also growing interest in income-maintenance schemes that would provide people with a state-guaranteed basic income regardless of whether they were in work. Proponents of such a scheme argue that this would help to remove the stigma of unemployment, that it would be a way of providing people with income security while they suffer the uncertain prospects of employment.

The link between income and work is changing and will continue to change. With the change in work as a source of livelihood and work as an economic resource will come change in the social significance of work. The significance of paid work has been made all the sharper by the lack of it for so many. It is clear that unemployment denies millions of people many of the basic social benefits that are associated with work: a sense of purpose, a role in the public world, social contact with others, a structure for the week. What is as yet unclear is the impact that the persistence of mass unemployment will have on the value of work. Some argue that work ethics will have to change. A society that treasures work, yet denies it to millions of its citizens, cannot maintain cohesion, they claim. To cope with mass unemployment our values will have to change: we will have to remove the pain of unemployment by weakening the desire for work.

How likely is this in a society where employment brings such benefits? Work undoubtedly still exerts a strong pull over the unemployed, though they may feel its loss more strongly than the need to find work. The unemployed may have accepted, or acquiesced in, their joblessness – but if this is a new ethic, it seems to rest on dejection, depression and fatalism. There are few signs of a culture of unemployment spreading beyond the unemployed.

A new social ethic of work would not, of course, be simply a matter of mass moral conversion. It would require an entirely different view of how the economy works and to what end. A new work ethic that praised sharing or even abstention from work to provide others with opportunities could be based only on people seeing jobs as society's rather than individuals' property. Explanations for unemployment that stress either personal frailty (laziness) or the mysterious workings of the world economy would have to be replaced by explanations that stress society's control over, and responsibility for, unemployment. Such a transformation in public thinking about work will take an enormously long time.

In the last few years the very idea of what it is to be an employee has undergone enormous change. At the lower end of the labour market we have part-time and temporary workers with uncertain legal rights. In the UK hundreds of thousands of youngsters are being put through the Youth Training Scheme. Their legal rights are enshrined in a series of leaflets, but are they trainees, apprentices or employees? Just as these workers find that their relationship with their employers is becoming more problematic, so at the higher end of the labour market there is also change. There are growing signs that employees are becoming incorporated into the companies for which they work: through profit-sharing and employee-involvement schemes workers are being encouraged to identify more with companies and their commercial aims.

Another challenge to the assumption that work means employment comes from the interest in entrepreneurialism. People are being encouraged to reject dependence on an employer and to go into business on their own. There is a new cachet and social status attached to being an entrepreneur.

Along with these changes have come pressures on the trade unions, which have been battered both by the rise in unemployment, particularly in manufacturing, and by Government policies aimed at freeing up the labour market. The UK Government has taken the most aggressive approach to reforming the trade unions through a rolling programme of legislation since 1982, which has dramatically altered the unions' legal position. But it would be wrong to think that Government policy is the only source of pressure on the unions. Many of the new jobs that are being created are in small businesses, whereas trade unions prosper in larger concerns. The advanced economies are moving away from the manufacturing heartlands of trade unionism. The unions are slowly coming to terms with the changes and finding new ways in which to organize workers in the rising industries.

The shifting structure of the economy is also creating a new culture of work. Industrial towns like Sheffield, built on old industries like steel and coal, have a culture of work entirely different from new towns, like Basingstoke, which are dominated by service industries. The collective ethos created by the industrial machines that once sucked in thousands of workers a day is disappearing. In the new towns it is being replaced by antiseptic office-block estates that do not spread noise and grime across the town. Without romanticizing the 'communities' based on the old industries, there is a greater sense of atomism in the growth towns like

Basingstoke. As jobs providing services take over from jobs making things, so the point of work, the conditions of work and the culture of the institutions where people work will change.

As we said in the introduction, work – in the sense of full employment – was central to the post-war consensus. The commitment to, and the provision of, full employment was the foundation of the social democratic public philosophy of the era. With that commitment gone, or at best unlikely to be fulfilled in the near future, what new public philosophy will be promoted by these changes in the character of work?

One of the notable characteristics of the current period is its ambiguity. Take the widespread 'acceptance' of the fact that unemployment will not be reduced. This could be translated into acceptance that nothing can be done about unemployment and very little for the unemployed. In the UK we could find ourselves yielding to the notion of 3 million unemployed as the concomitant of security for those in work. But acceptance of the likelihood that there will not be a swift return to full employment could also lead to recognition that we need to adopt new policies towards the unemployed. It may be that a period of mass unemployment is part of a necessary adjustment in the advanced economies. But the people who bear this burden of adjustment are chosen relatively arbitrarily. In the UK, for instance, most of the burden of high unemployment has been carried by a growth in long-term unemployment; it is not that more and more people have become unemployed but that, once unemployed, people now stay out of work for a long period of time. The recognition that mass unemployment is likely to last for some considerable time may lead to new policies designed to 're-integrate' the unemployed into general social life. Such policies would have to embrace new measures for income distribution and new ways of providing the unemployed with work outside formal employment.

Another ambiguity surrounds the growth of informal work, early retirement and 'atypical' forms of working. For some the growth of part-time and informal work offers the hope of a new model of work that combines paid employment with personal pursuits, hobbies and leisure. To some, then, the growth of new ways of working offers the hope of liberation from the pursuit of full-time work, greater freedom in the choice of how and when to work. Yet for many the growth of part-time working is a second best. Far from offering greater choice, it spells insecurity, instability, uncertainty.

There are other uncertainties. New technology could lead to a regeneration of the productive base of the economy. It could spawn new products and industries, just as the new technologies of the 1930s did. But at the moment those displaced by new technology are joining an already large pool of unemployed in the OECD. New technology seems to be aimed at promoting rationalization in the production of existing goods rather than creating new products that will bring new jobs in their wake. New technology could lead to re-skilling and up-skilling. It could give some workers on the shop floor of factories and in offices new responsibilities and new autonomy, but it may de-skill and routinize the work of others. There is nothing inevitable about the way that new technology will affect work and workers; its effects will depend on how it is introduced and with what aim.

A final example of the uncertain direction of change is the area of profit-sharing and employee ownership. There is growing interest in this from all points of the political spectrum, from the wider share-ownership policies of the Thatcher Government in the UK to the wage-earner funds set up in Sweden.

In short, there is great uncertainty over where changes in the character of work may lead the advanced societies. There seem to be at least two extremes we could pursue. One is a relatively benign public philosophy, which would include a long-term commitment to ensuring greater equality of access to jobs. If the advanced economies have to bear the burden of unemployment, that burden could be more equally shared. It would include too some longer-term commitment to attempting to restore full employment. This benign approach would also entail some measure of income redistribution towards the poor, the unemployed and those in insecure jobs. Their uncertainty offers companies and the economy as a whole greater flexibility. This approach would try to ensure that flexibility was not necessarily accompanied by loss of protection. New ways would have to be found to combine flexibility with security through measures of income support and new legal rights. Within the firm the line between management and workers would blur, thanks to new methods of participation and employee involvement backed by a wider spread of capital ownership.

But realism demands that another general public philosophy should be taken much more seriously: a new, divisive one that stems from the way that the character and distribution of work have changed, and will continue to change, the distribution of power in the advanced economies. New social divisions are opening up around work. The rift between the employed and the unemployed is the starkest. But within the world of work there are also new divisions. There is growing evidence that sub-contracting and the use of temporary and part-time workers are erecting a new feudalism. 'Core' workers, the key skilled personnel that a company needs to retain and motivate, are inside the walls, defended both by the firm and by unions or trade associations. 'Peripheral' workers come and go through the gates. The unemployed are on the outside. Admittedly, as we have shown, there is some evidence that firms are adopting a larger social role in the communities in which they operate. There is a greater sense that companies have to assume responsibility for the effects that their actions have beyond the walls. This is most pronounced in the USA and is growing in the United Kingdom. But the extent of this movement should not be overstated. The primary task of coping with the effects of redundancy and unemployment still rests with the state.

Nevertheless, it appears that at the level both of the firm and of the economy as a whole the pursuit of flexibility and the burden of adjustment to new economic circumstances is being borne by the weaker competitors in the labour market. At the same time those in work have relative stability and security. As the OECD puts it: 'Should high unemployment persist, the unskilled minorities, youth and other weak social groups will bear virtually all of its social cost without much effect on the wage bargaining of core experienced workers.' Whatever developments we see in working structures and practices, whatever the effects of the introduction of new technology or greater profit-sharing, it is the insiders who are likely to gain and the outsiders who are likely to lose.

The social democratic philosophy of the post-war era, which was based on the aim of employment for all who wanted it, is no longer practicable. The societies that are now facing widespread unemployment must construct a new consensus, founded on fresh policies that address the challenges posed by a world of work that will increasingly be characterized by formal inequalities but may be complemented by informal opportunities for those who are not part of the labour force.

APPENDIX 1.
THE *FT* JOBS POLL

This book has raised a series of questions about the availability and nature of work in the future. In an attempt to provide partial answers to some of these questions, in 1986 the *Financial Times* commissioned the polling organization Gallup to conduct a special poll of employers in the five major economies: the USA, Japan, West Germany, France and Britain.

Interviews were conducted mainly by telephone; in some cases the questionnaires were returned by post. About two hundred companies in each country were polled. The samples were chosen at random from published directories of companies to give a cross-section of respondents. Although the final samples do not exactly mirror the structure of each economy, they do give a wide spread of companies according to their sectors of operation (primary, manufacturing, services), the number of people they employ, whether they use high, medium or low technology, their rates of unionization and the like.

By cross-tabulating responses and comparing them, we were able to draw a picture of the pressures affecting employment in these different economies. We could also explore whether there are common trends in the pattern of job losses and job gains, though the poll does not provide anything like conclusive evidence about the factors that will influence future employment prospects.

In this appendix we consider some of the main findings of the poll. More specific conclusions – for instance, those related to training and education, macro-economic policy, and new technology – are to be found in the chapters that deal with these topics.

Throughout we use one vital measure of job growth or loss, which is based on the balance between firms that expect employment to pick up and those that expect employment prospects to dim. (For example, the poll found that in the sample as a whole 37 per cent of firms expected to take on workers in the next two years, while 17 per cent expected to shed labour. This means that a balance of 20 per cent of firms expected to take on more labour in the next two years.) The balance can be used as a measure of optimism or pessimism, but it needs to be treated with considerable care. For if (as we found) most of the job losses come from large firms, while a sizeable proportion of the job gains comes from firms with a small workforce, then a positive balance of firms expecting job growth does not imply that there will be job growth of that magnitude or even at all.

It is impossible to correct for this without more detailed information about the extent of job gains and job losses among these firms. So, though the poll results allow us to trade in the attractive currency of percentages, its results should rather be taken as pointers to overall trends. In a number of areas we found enough divergences and common trends to allow us to make clear statements about the factors driving changes at work. These are the main results.

Which countries have the brightest employment outlook?

- Overall 78 per cent of employers think that employment in their country will worsen or stay at the same level over the years to 1990.
- But a balance of 11 per cent of companies think that unemployment will worsen (32 per cent believe that it will get worse, whereas 21 per cent believe it will get better).
- Japanese employers are the most pessimistic: a balance of 41 per cent of employers believe that unemployment will get worse. In West Germany a balance of 30 per cent of employers think that unemployment will fall, while in Britain a balance of 24 per cent think that unemployment will get better.

However, a look at employers' plans for their own recruitment and labour-shedding reveals a very different picture.

- In the sample as a whole a balance of 20 per cent of companies expect to take on labour in the next two years (37 per cent expect to take on labour while 17 per cent expect to shed labour by 1989).
- There will be net job growth in 40 per cent of companies in the USA, 22 per cent in Japan, 17 per cent in Britain, 15 per cent in West Germany and just 5 per cent in France.

In which sectors of the economy will these jobs come – services or manufacturing?

The poll's findings suggest that service-sector employment will expand more than manufacturing employment in every country except the USA.

- The US manufacturing sector shows net job growth in 49 per cent of companies. This compares with an average net job growth of 4.75 per cent in the manufacturing sectors of other countries.
- Across the sample as a whole the service sector shows job growth in a balance of nearly 35 per cent of companies. In Britain, West Germany and Japan, for instance, service-sector companies make up 38 per cent of the sample but account for half of the firms expecting job growth. Banking and finance will be among the leading employment-growth sectors, with 83 per cent of British firms expecting employment growth and 60 per cent of Japanese companies.

Will small companies be the predominant source of new jobs?

- The small-business sector will represent the largest proportion of companies expanding employment in every country except the USA, where medium-sized businesses will generate most jobs.
- In the small-firms sector a balance of 37 per cent of companies expect to expand employment in the next two years. This compares with net job growth in 20 per cent of companies overall and no net job growth in the large-firm sector.
- The US small-business sector leads the way with 43 per cent net job growth, though US medium-sized businesses show even better job growth, 59 per cent. In Japan a balance of 40 per cent of small companies will provide employment growth, while in Britain 37 per cent will.
- Across the sample as a whole, companies employing more than 1,000 people will not show any net employment growth. In Japan, the USA and West Germany employment in big firms will grow at rates well below the average, while in France big firms will show net job decline in 33 per cent of companies and in Britain a 9 per cent net decline.
- Big firms will be responsible for more than their fair share of job losses. They make up about one-fifth of the sample but account for about 39 per cent of the job losses.

Will profitability be the route to higher employment, or will labour-shedding be the route to profitability?

- Sixty-nine per cent of the companies expect to be profitable in two years' time. The main exception to this is Japan, where only 24 per cent of companies expect to be showing a clear profit by 1989.
- Firms expecting to be profitable make up 69 per cent of the sample as a whole but account for 74 per cent of the job gains and about half the job losses.
- In the sample as a whole 12 per cent of firms that expect to be profitable also expect to shed labour, whereas in Britain half the firms that expect to be profitable also expect to shed labour.

Will new technology create as many jobs as it destroys?

- The high-technology group of companies in the sample will show net growth in 16 per cent of firms, below the average of all firms of 20 per cent.
- Outside Britain companies using low technology will show stronger than average job growth – a balance of 24 per cent.
- Overall 45 per cent of firms said they have plans to introduce new technology that will affect employment in their firms within the next two years. Japanese firms will lead the push, with 68 per cent planning to bring in new technology, followed by Britain with 59 per cent.

• There is a clear link between the introduction of new technology and employment prospects. Firms expecting to introduce new technology make up 45 per cent of the sample but 64 per cent of the companies expecting job losses and only 37 per cent of those expecting to take on more workers.

How will the trade unions fare?

• Non-unionized firms are far less likely to suffer job losses than firms with more than half their workforce unionized. Non-unionized firms make up 53 per cent of the sample as a whole but only 29 per cent of firms projecting job losses.
• A quarter of the firms surveyed had more than half their workforce unionized, but they account for 42 per cent of the firms forecasting jobs cuts. The trend is most marked in Britain, where heavily unionized firms make up a little more than half the sample but account for 90 per cent of the firms planning to cut their workforces.
• Across the five countries firms with more than half their workforce in unions will show a net job growth of 2.8 per cent, a fraction over one-tenth the average growth rate for all firms.

Will there be a big shift towards firms establishing a core of secure, regular employees combined with a periphery of more casual employees, and will firms adopting 'flexible patterns of working' show stronger than average employment growth?

• Sub-contracting will be a major source of job loss or job redistribution. In five years' time 55 per cent of firms will be sub-contracting some of the work normally done in house. This ranges from a high of 82 per cent in Japan and 61 per cent in Britain to a low of 34 per cent in West Germany.
• In the sample as a whole a balance of 20 per cent of firms will show job growth, but among firms contracting out only a balance of 3.8 per cent will provide employment growth.
• Across the five countries 34 per cent of firms said they expected to seek greater functional flexibility by compressing job classifications, eroding demarcation lines and introducing multi-skilling. The range was from 50 per cent in France and 35 per cent in Britain to Japan and the USA in the mid-20s per cent.
• Firms intending to compress job classifications and introduce greater flexibility over tasks show employment growth in a balance of 11.8 per cent of firms, well below average. This trend is strongest in Britain, where the move to simpler job classifications is a factor in 59 per cent of the firms expecting to shed labour. In contrast, in France and West Germany greater flexibility at the workplace will promote strong job gains as well as strong job losses.
• Overall 64 per cent of firms use part-time workers; 38 per cent use workers on fixed-term contracts; 32 per cent use workers from temporary agencies; and about

7 per cent use homeworkers. West German firms emerge as the most flexible – 42 per cent of them use some form of peripheral workers, compared with an average of 27 per cent in companies elsewhere.

● There will not be an enormous growth in part-time and other forms of flexible working. Only 3 per cent of firms expect to increase their use of peripheral workers, while 7 per cent expect to reduce their peripheral workforce.

● Firms employing part-timers show below average employment growth: a balance of 16 per cent of companies employing part-timers expect to take on more employees in the next two years.

What measures would be most effective in expanding employment?

● Only 13 per cent of companies say that nothing would induce them to expand employment. A tax concession linked with the hiring of new workers is the most popular measure: 40 per cent of companies report that this would lead them to expand employment.

● The abolition of minimum-wage legislation consistently ranks as the least effective measure, with only 7 per cent of firms across the sample saying that this would lead them to expand employment.

● After a tax concession related to the hiring of new workers, expansion of demand is the next most effective measure overall, with 35 per cent, and the most effective in Britain, with 48 per cent.

APPENDIX 2.
THE AMERICAN MODEL

Only one country has enjoyed a fall in unemployment since 1975 – the USA. This fall in unemployment is widely attributed to the US economy's capacity to generate new jobs. For many politicians it is to the USA that Europeans must turn to learn how to generate new employment. Some on the European right stress characteristics of the US labour market that, they claim, have been at the heart of this job growth: wage moderation, occupational and geographic flexibility, low unionization and limited Government regulation of the labour market. Social democrats, on the other hand, hold up Reaganomics as an example of modern-day Keynesianism. They argue that the growth in US employment is due largely to the enormous expansion of fiscal policy over which Mr Reagan has presided in the name of supply-side economics, a policy that has been described as 'sound money and lots of it'.

Amid these competing views it is easy to lose sight of what is being debated: what does the American jobs miracle amount to?

First, it is worth looking at the USA's unemployment record in the long run, for it is only recently that Europeans have envied the USA's performance. In the mid-1980s the US unemployment rate looks quite attractive by comparison with many European economies, but that is largely because European unemployment has worsened so much since the 1970s. In the 1950s and 1960s the USA's unemployment rate was high relative to other economies. In the period 1956–66 it was 5 per cent, double the rate in the UK and well above the rates in West Germany (1.4 per cent), France (1.5 per cent) and Japan (1.7 per cent). Between the end of the 1960s and the 1980s unemployment rose in the USA in line with rises elsewhere, though it was still relatively bad. In the 1980s, however, unemployment elsewhere has risen dramatically, whereas in the USA it has declined slightly. So, after a long period during which the USA did not have an enviable unemployment record, it now has a better international standing. But, despite enormous job growth in the last few years, unemployment has rarely dipped below 7 per cent. While the problem is being held at bay, it is far from conquered.

Second, employment growth in the USA is not a recent phenomenon. The job creation of the 1980s is the continuation of a longer-run trend. Between 1959 and 1985 about 42 million jobs were created in the USA. From the recessionary low of November 1982 to February 1986 around 11.1 million jobs were created.

But the job generation of the 1980s does not look impressive by historical standards. In the ten years from 1959 the number of jobs grew by 1.9 per cent a year, 14 million over the period. In the 1970s 20 million jobs were created, at an annual growth rate of 2.2 per cent. In the period 1979–85, however, employment grew by only 1.3 per cent a year, or 8.5 million. So employment growth in the USA has been a long-term phenomenon, spanning changes in Government economic policy and diverse economic shocks. But unemployment growth was fastest at a time when the American unemployment rate still looked unattractive by international standards.

Third, it is not so much the US economy that has generated jobs but a few sub-sections of the economy. Employment growth has been highly concentrated. In particular, wholesale and retail trade (12 million jobs) and other business services (15 million jobs) have provided most of the employment growth since the late 1950s. Between 1959 and 1985 they provided 65 per cent of the job growth, but in the last seven years they have been responsible for 99 per cent of all employment growth. So employment in the USA is expanding at a slower rate than it did in the 1970s. Nevertheless, it has expanded enough to allow a slight fall in unemployment when unemployment elsewhere has risen and stuck at very high levels.

Many European economists and politicians claim that the long-run job generation of the US economy, which has spanned changes in political and economic regimes, must be due to the decentralized character of the American labour market. In the US economy employer and union federations do not dominate wage determination, as they do in Scandinavia; national wage patterns are not set by a *shunto* (bargaining push) offensive – a principle by which all pay negotiations take place over a limited period – as they are in Japan; wages are not affected by minimum-wage laws, as they are in France; arbitration tribunals play no part in wage setting, as they do in Australia; and the Government rarely intervenes directly in the labour market to influence wages. In particular, European policy-makers have focused on the apparent real-wage flexibility that this decentralization is thought to have produced.

In a 1986 paper Richard Freeman, of the US National Bureau of Economic Research, showed that while real wages (money wages expressed in terms of what they can buy) fell between 1973 and 1985, this was partly a result of a change in the way that real wages were calculated. Freeman's estimates of money wages, expressed in terms of the Consumer Price Index, showed that on one measure the real wage fell by 1.8 per cent in the twelve years up to 1985. However, until 1983 mortgage interest payments were calculated in such a way that the Consumer Price Index rose rapidly in the 1980s compared with the Wholesale Price Index. As a consequence, it looks as though the purchasing power of money wages fell quite dramatically. But for the employer the important real wage is the wage expressed in terms of what the firm will make in revenue from any new hirings. Freeman suggests that the Wholesale Price Index is a much better measure of the real wage that faces the employer. This measure shows that between 1973 and

1985 the real wage did not fall but rose by 9.2 per cent. Freeman claims that the rise was close to long-term rates. 'Whereas over the entire period of twelve years it is reasonable to attribute some of the employment performance of the US economy to roughly unchanging costs of labour, it is not reasonable to do so for the period 1980–85.' Nevertheless, Freeman shows that between 1970 and 1983 real hourly compensation in the USA rose by 10.7 per cent. In France over the same period it rose by 76.8 per cent, in West Germany by 66.8 per cent, in Japan by 60.6 per cent and in Britain by 54.3 per cent.

So over the longer run the USA has enjoyed a relatively modest rise in real wages, underpinned by the comparative stability of money wages paid to workers. Extensive research by American economist Jeffrey Sachs and Israeli Michael Bruno indicates that, compared with European economies, money wages in the USA respond very slowly to price changes and relatively quickly to rises in unemployment. This means that when inflation rises, US money wages respond to higher prices only after a considerable time lag, but when unemployment rises, money-wage growth falls quite rapidly in reaction.

In sum, then, Freeman finds that in the long run the flexibility of US labour does lead to wages being more responsive to changing economic conditions, and he suggests that in some sectors of the economy this wage flexibility has been very important in generating extra employment. In particular, the increase in the number of young people seeking work in the 1970s was accompanied by a widening of the differential between adult and youth wages. Freeman says that this accounts for the relatively lower youth unemployment in the USA compared with many European economies. The same is true of the wages of female and educated workers. He shows that as the US labour force became more educated in the 1960s and 1970s, the premium paid to those with a college education declined, reflecting the higher supply of educated workers. However, he also notes that there are large sections of the US labour market that do not display this kind of flexibility. In particular, wages in large firms and in the unionized sector have risen without there being any apparent competitive pressure driving wages up.

Yet at the aggregate level Freeman suggests that the key to explaining US job growth is not the latent dynamism of the US economy but the lack of it. Although wages have shown consistently modest growth, it is difficult to attribute all the rise in employment to this; rather, he says, the key lies in the USA's poor productivity record. From 1970 to 1983 real GDP grew at similar rates in the USA and Europe, but productivity in the USA grew at less than one-third the rate in Europe. 'Had the USA had the same GDP growth but with European productivity growth, the American employment record would have looked like the European record,' says Freeman.

In the recovery from the depressions of the early 1980s the USA has had a better growth rate, productivity record and employment growth than the European economies, but it remains to be seen whether higher growth in Europe will close the gap. Freeman says that the key is the link between productivity growth and real-wage growth. One explanation might be that, given the growth in output, real wages grew only modestly to ensure high employment growth. The combination of high employment growth and low growth in overall output led to low productivity. But another explanation could be that low productivity led to low real-wage growth, which in turn led to higher employment, given GDP growth. Whichever way round the explanation runs, Freeman argues that the relationship between wages and productivity is at the core of the USA's strong job growth. The movement of real wages alone cannot explain what has happened to US employment.

BIBLIOGRAPHY

Economics

Artus, J., 'The Disequilibrium Real Wage Rage Hypothesis: an Empirical Evaluation', IMF, *Staff Papers*, Vol. 31, No. 2, 1984

Bank of England Academic Panel, 'Employment, the Real Wage and Unemployment in the UK', Paper No. 24, 1984

Beckerman, W. (ed.), *Wage Rigidity and Unemployment*, Duckworth, London, 1986

Blanchard, O., *et al.*, 'Employment and Growth in Europe: a Two-handed Approach', Centre for European Policy Studies, Paper No. 21, 1985

Blanchard, O., Dornbusch, R., and Buiter, W., 'Public Deficits and Fiscal Responsibility', Centre for European Policy Studies, Paper No. 22, 1985

Brittan, S., *The Role and Limits of Government*, Temple Smith, Hounslow, 1983

Bruno, M., and Sachs, J., *The Economics of Worldwide Stagflation*, Harvard University Press, 1983

Chouraqui, J.-C., and Price, R., 'Medium-term Financial Strategy: the Co-ordination of Fiscal and Monetary Policies', OECD, *Economic Studies*, No. 2, 1984

Coe, D., 'Nominal Wages, the NAIRU and Wage Flexibility', OECD, *Economic Studies*, No. 5, 1985

Curruth, A., and Oswald, A., 'Wage Inflexibility in Britain', *Oxford Bulletin of Economics and Statistics*, Vol. 49, February 1987

Davies, G., 'Governments Can Affect Employment', Employment Institute, London, 1985

Dornbusch, R., 'Macroeconomic Prospects and Policies for the European Community', Centre for European Policy Studies, Paper No. 1, 1983

Economica, special issue on the international rise in unemployment, May 1986

Gowland, D., *Money, Inflation and Unemployment*, Wheatsheaf Books, Brighton, 1985

Gregory, M., Lobban, P., and Thomson, A., 'Wage Settlements in Manufacturing 1979–84: Evidence from the CBI Pay Databank', *British Journal of Industrial Relations*, Vol. 23, No. 3, 1985

Jackman, R., and Layard, R., 'A Wage Tax, Worker Subsidy Policy for Reducing the Natural Rate of Unemployment', Centre for Labour Economics, LSE, Discussion Paper No. 226, 1985

Jackman, R., and Roper, S., 'Structural Unemployment', Centre for Labour Economics, LSE, Discussion Paper No. 233, 1985

Johnson, G., and Layard, R., 'The Natural Rate of Unemployment: Explanation and Policy', Centre for Labour Economics, LSE, Discussion Paper No. 206, 1985

Kaldor, N., *The Scourge of Monetarism*, Oxford University Press, 1982

Layard, R., *et al.*, 'Europe: the Case for Unsustainable Growth', Centre for European Policy Studies, Papers Nos. 8 and 9, 1984

Layard, R., and Nickell, S., 'Unemployment, Real Wages and Aggregate Demand in Europe, Japan and the United States', Centre for Labour Economics, LSE, Discussion Paper No. 214, 1985

Layard, R., and Nickell, S., 'Unemployment in Britain', Centre for Labour Economics, LSE, Discussion Paper No. 240, 1986

Layard, R., Nickell, S., and Jackman, R., 'European Unemployment is Keynesian and Classical but not Structural', Centre for European Policy Studies, Paper No. 13, 1985

Marris, S., 'Deficits and the Dollar: the World Economy at Risk', Institute for International Economics, Paper No. 14, 1985

OECD, *Economic Outlook*, various issues

OECD, *Employment Outlook*, various issues

OECD, 'Perspectives on Macroeconomic Performance in the 1970s', *Occasional Studies*, No. 2, 1983

Oxford Review of Economic Policy, special issue on the labour market, Vol. 1, No. 2, various articles

Price, R., and Muller, P., 'Structural Budget Indicators and the Interpretation of the Fiscal Stance in OECD Economies', OECD, *Economic Studies*, No. 3, 1984

New Technology

Arnold, E., and Guy, K., 'Lessons from Abroad – What the UK Can Learn from Foreign IT Policies', Report to the Alvery Directorate, Science Policy Research Unit, 1985

Barras, R., and Swann, J., 'The Adoption and Impact of Information Technology on the UK Insurance Industry', Technical Change Centre, London, 1983

Barras, R., and Swann, J., 'Adoption and Impact of Information Technology in UK Local Government', Technical Change Centre, London, 1985

Barron, I., and Curnow, R., *The Future with Microelectronics*, Frances Pinter, London, 1979

Benson, I., *Intelligent Machinery*, Cambridge University Press, 1986

Bessant, J., *et al.*, *New Information Technology Products and Services: Technological Potential and Push*, National Economic Development Office, 1985

Blanchard, F., 'Technology, Work and Society – Some Pointers from ILO Research', *International Labour Review*, Vol. 123, No. 3, 1984

Brady, T., 'New Technology and Skills in British Industry', Manpower Services Commission, 1984

Burgess, C., 'The Impact of New Technology on Skills in Manufacturing and Services', Manpower Services Commission, *Skills Services*, No. 1, 1986

Clark, J. (ed.), *Technological Trends and Employment: Basic Process Industries*, Gower, Aldershot, 1985

Commission of the European Communities, *New Technology and Social Change, and Manufacturing Automation*, Brussels, 1986

Connor, H., and Pearson, R., 'Information Technology Manpower into the 1990s', Institute of Manpower Studies, 1986

Cooper, C., and Clark, J., *Employment Economics and Technology*, Wheatsheaf Books, Brighton, 1982

Ebel, K., 'Social and Labour Implications of Flexible Manufacturing Systems', *International Labour Review*, Vol. 124, No. 2, 1985

Engleberger, J., *Robots in Practice*, Kogan Page, London, 1980

Freeman, C., *The Economics of Industrial Innovation*, 2nd edn, Frances Pinter, London, 1982

Freeman, C., Clarke, J., and Soete, L., *Unemployment and Technical Innovation*, Frances Pinter, London, 1982

Freeman, C., *Technological Trends and Employment: Engineering and Vehicles*, Gower, Aldershot, 1984

Futures, 'Technical Innovation and Long Waves in World Economic Development', Vol. 13, No. 4, 1983

Ginneken, W. von, 'Employment and the Reduction of the Working Week: a Comparison of Seven Macroeconomic Models', *International Labour Review*, Vol. 123, No. 1, 1984

Guy, K. (ed.), *Technological Trends and Employment: Basic Consumer Goods*, Gower, Aldershot, 1983

ILO, *Technological Change: The Tripartite Response 1982–85*, Geneva, 1985

Kaplinsky, R., *Computer-aided Design*, Frances Pinter, London, 1982

Leontieff, V., 'The Distribution of Work and Income', *Scientific American*, September 1982

Loveridge, R., *et al.*, 'New Technology in Banking, Retailing and Health Services: the British Case', Technology Policy Unit, University of Aston, 1985

Marstrand, P. (ed.), *New Technology and the Future of Work and Skills*, Frances Pinter, London, 1984

Miles, I., 'Information Technology and Service Activities: Two Scenarios', Working Paper, Science Policy Research Unit, 1986

OECD, *Microelectronics, Productivity and Employment*, Paris, 1981

OECD, *Microelectronics, Robotics and Jobs*, Paris, 1982

OECD, *Industrial Robots and their Role in Manufacturing Industry*, Paris, 1983

OECD, *Science and Technology Outlook*, Paris, 1985

OECD, *Software: An Emerging Industry*, Paris, 1985

OECD, *Science and Technology Indicators: R and D, Innovation and Competitiveness*, Paris, 1986

Office of Technology Assessment, *The Automation of America's Offices*, Washington, DC, 1985

Sharpe, M. (ed.), *Europe and the New Technologies*, Frances Pinter, London, 1986

Smith, A. (ed.), *Technological Trends and Employment in the Commercial Service Industries*, Gower, Aldershot, 1986

Soete, L. (ed.), *Technological Trends and Employment: Electronics and Communications*, Gower, Aldershot, 1983

Soete, L., and Dosi, G., *Technology and Employment in the Electronics Industry*, Frances Pinter, London, 1983

Standing, G., 'The Notion of Technological Unemployment', *International Labour Review*, Vol. 123, No. 2, 1984

Wanatabe, S., *Microelectronics and Employment in the Japanese Automobile Industry*, ILO, Geneva, 1984

Training

Alfthar, T., 'Developing Skills for Technical Change: Some Policy Issues', *International Labour Review*, Vol. 124, No. 5, 1985

Kanawaty, G., 'Training for a Changing World', *International Labour Review*, Vol. 124, No. 5, 1985

NEDO, *Competence and Competition: Training and Education in the Federal Republic of Germany, the United States and Japan*, London, 1984

OECD, *The Future of Vocational Education and Training*, Paris, 1983

OECD, *Education in Modern Society*, Paris, 1985

Watts, A., *Education, Unemployment and the Future of Work*, Open University Press, Milton Keynes, 1983

The Informal Economy

Gary, P., and Hatch, S., *Voluntary Work and Unemployment*, Manpower Services Commission, Research and Development series, No. 15, 1983

Gershuny, J., 'The Informal Economy: its Role in Post-industrial Society', *Futures*, February 1979

Gershuny, J., and Pahl, R., 'Britain in the Decade of the Three Economies', *New Society*, 3 January 1980

Heinze, R., and Olk, T., 'Developing the Informal Economy: a Strategy for Resolving the Crisis of the Welfare State', *Futures*, June 1982

Miles, I., and Irvine, J., 'Changing Ways of Life', *Futures*, February 1982

OECD, *The Hidden Economy*, Paris, 1982

OECD, *Clandestine Employment in the Industrialised Market Economies*, ILO, Geneva, 1984

Robertson, J., *Futurework*, Gower, Aldershot, 1985

Shankland, G., and Turner, R., *A Guide to the Informal Economy*, Department of Employment, 1984

Small Businesses

Amin, A., Johnson, S., and Storey, D., 'Small Firms and the Process of Economic Development: Explanations and Illustrations from Great Britain, Italy and the United States', Centre for Urban and Regional Development Studies, University of Newcastle, 1986

Dennis, W., *Cultural and Institutional Bases for the US Small Businesses Revolution*, National Foundation of Independent Businesses, Washington, DC, 1986

Johnson, S., and Storey, D., 'Employment and Occupational Structure in Smaller UK Businesses: Recent Trends and Projections to 1990', Centre for Urban and Regional Development Studies, University of Newcastle, 1986

OECD, *Innovation in Small and Medium-sized Firms*, Paris, 1982

OECD, 'Employment in Small and Large Firms: Where Have the Jobs Come From?' *Employment Outlook*, Paris, 1985

Schumacher, E., *Small Is Beautiful*, Blond and Briggs, London, 1973

Storey, D., and Johnson, S., 'Small Firms Policies in the UK', Centre for Urban and Regional Development Studies, University of Newcastle, 1986

Labour Markets and Structural Change

AFL–CIO, *The Changing Situation of Workers and Their Unions*, Washington, DC, 1985

Atkinson, J., and Meager, N., 'Flexibility in Firms', Institute for Manpower Studies, Report to National Economic Development Office, 1986

Brown, C., and Gary, P., 'Racial Discrimination 17 Years After the Act', Policy Studies Institute, 1985

Day, G. (ed.), *Diversity and Decomposition in the Labour Market*, Gower, Aldershot, 1982

Dore, R., *Structural Adjustment in Japan 1970–82*, ILO, Geneva, 1986

Freedman, D., 'Employment and Unemployment in the 1980s: Economic Dilemmas and Socio-political Challenges', *International Labour Review*, Vol. 123, No. 5, 1984

Gershuny, J., and Miles, I., *The New Service Economy: The Transformation of Employment in Industrialized Societies*, Frances Pinter, London, 1984

ILO, *Into the 21st Century: The Development of Social Security*, Geneva, 1984

Jahoda, M., *Employment and Unemployment: A Social Psychological Analysis*, Cambridge University Press, 1982

Joshi, H., Layard, R., Owen, S., 'Female Labour Supply in Post-war Britain: a Cohort Approach', Centre for Labour Economics, LSE, Discussion Paper No. 79, 1981

Meager, N., 'Temporary Work in Britain: its Growth and Rationale', Institute of Manpower Studies, Report No. 106, 1985

NEDO, New Jobs Programme, various reports

OECD, *The Challenge of Unemployment*, Paris, 1982

OECD, *Labour Supply, Growth Constraints and Work Sharing*, Paris, 1982

OECD, *High Unemployment: A Challenge for Income Support Policies*, Paris, 1984

OECD, *Inter-governmental Conference on Employment Growth in the Context of Structural Change*, Paris, 1984

OECD, *The Nature of Youth Unemployment*, Paris, 1984

OECD, *The Public Employment Service in a Changing Labour Market*, Paris, 1984

OECD, *Social Expenditure 1960–1990: Problems of Growth and Control*, Paris, 1985

Roberts, B., *et al.* (eds.), *New Approaches to Economic Life: Economic Restructuring, Unemployment and the Social Division of Labour*, Manchester University Press, 1985

Walsh, K., *Long-term Unemployment: An International Perspective*, Macmillan, Basingstoke, 1986

Walsh, K., and Pearson, R., 'The UK Labour Market Guide', Institute of Manpower Studies, No. 5, 1984

White, M., 'Long-term Unemployment and Labour Markets', Policy Studies Institute, 1983

INDEX

FOR THE BEST IN PAPERBACKS, LOOK FOR THE 🐧

In every corner of the world, on every subject under the sun, Penguin represents quality and variety – the very best in publishing today.

For complete information about books available from Penguin – including Pelicans, Puffins, Peregrines and Penguin Classics – and how to order them, write to us at the appropriate address below. Please note that for copyright reasons the selection of books varies from country to country.

In the United Kingdom: For a complete list of books available from Penguin in the U.K., please write to *Dept E.P., Penguin Books Ltd, Harmondsworth, Middlesex, UB7 0DA*

In the United States: For a complete list of books available from Penguin in the U.S., please write to *Dept BA, Penguin, 299 Murray Hill Parkway, East Rutherford, New Jersey 07073*

In Canada: For a complete list of books available from Penguin in Canada, please write to *Penguin Books Canada Ltd, 2801 John Street, Markham, Ontario L3R 1B4*

In Australia: For a complete list of books available from Penguin in Australia, please write to the *Marketing Department, Penguin Books Australia Ltd, P.O. Box 257, Ringwood, Victoria 3134*

In New Zealand: For a complete list of books available from Penguin in New Zealand, please write to the *Marketing Department, Penguin Books (NZ) Ltd, Private Bag, Takapuna, Auckland 9*

In India: For a complete list of books available from Penguin, please write to *Penguin Overseas Ltd, 706 Eros Apartments, 56 Nehru Place, New Delhi, 110019*

In Holland: For a complete list of books available from Penguin in Holland, please write to *Penguin Books Nederland B.V., Postbus 195, NL–1380AD Weesp, Netherlands*

In Germany: For a complete list of books available from Penguin, please write to *Penguin Books Ltd, Friedrichstrasse 10 – 12, D–6000 Frankfurt Main 1, Federal Republic of Germany*

In Spain: For a complete list of books available from Penguin in Spain, please write to *Longman Penguin España, Calle San Nicolas 15, E–28013 Madrid, Spain*

The Second World War (6 volumes) Winston S. Churchill

The definitive history of the cataclysm which swept the world for the second time in thirty years.

1917: The Russian Revolutions and the Origins of Present-Day Communism
Leonard Schapiro

A superb narrative history of one of the greatest episodes in modern history by one of our greatest historians.

Imperial Spain 1496–1716 J. H. Elliot

A brilliant modern study of the sudden rise of a barren and isolated country to be the greatest power on earth, and of its equally sudden decline. 'Outstandingly good' – *Daily Telegraph*

Joan of Arc: The Image of Female Heroism Marina Warner

'A profound book, about human history in general and the place of women in it' – Christopher Hill

Man and the Natural World: Changing Attitudes in England 1500–1800
Keith Thomas

'A delight to read and a pleasure to own' – Auberon Waugh in the *Sunday Telegraph*

The Making of the English Working Class E. P. Thompson

Probably the most imaginative – and the most famous – post-war work of English social history.

A CHOICE OF PENGUINS AND PELICANS

The French Revolution   Christopher Hibbert

'One of the best accounts of the Revolution that I know . . . Mr Hibbert is outstanding' – J. H. Plumb in the *Sunday Telegraph*

The Germans   Gordon A. Craig

An intimate study of a complex and fascinating nation by 'one of the ablest and most distinguished American historians of modern Germany' – Hugh Trevor-Roper

Ireland: A Positive Proposal   Kevin Boyle and Tom Hadden

A timely and realistic book on Northern Ireland which explains the historical context – and offers a practical and coherent set of proposals which could actually work.

A History of Venice   John Julius Norwich

'Lord Norwich has loved and understood Venice as well as any other Englishman has ever done' – Peter Levi in the *Sunday Times*

Montaillou: Cathars and Catholics in a French Village 1294–1324
Emmanuel Le Roy Ladurie

'A classic adventure in eavesdropping across time' – Michael Ratcliffe in *The Times*

Star Wars   E. P. Thompson and others

Is Star Wars a serious defence strategy or just a science fiction fantasy? This major book sets out all the arguments and makes an unanswerable case *against* Star Wars.

FOR THE BEST IN PAPERBACKS, LOOK FOR THE

A CHOICE OF PENGUINS AND PELICANS

The Apartheid Handbook   Roger Omond

This book provides the essential hard information about how apartheid actually works from day to day and fills in the details behind the headlines.

The World Turned Upside Down   Christopher Hill

This classic study of radical ideas during the English Revolution 'will stand as a notable monument to . . . one of the finest historians of the present age' – *The Times Literary Supplement*

Islam in the World   Malise Ruthven

'His exposition of "the Qurenic world view" is the most convincing, and the most appealing, that I have read' – Edward Mortimer in *The Times*

The Knight, the Lady and the Priest   Georges Duby

'A very fine book' (Philippe Aries) that traces back to its medieval origin one of our most important institutions, modern marriage.

A Social History of England   New Edition   Asa Briggs

'A treasure house of scholarly knowledge . . . beautifully written and full of the author's love of his country, its people and its landscape' – John Keegan in the *Sunday Times*, Books of the Year

The Second World War   A. J. P. Taylor

A brilliant and detailed illustrated history, enlivened by all Professor Taylor's customary iconoclasm and wit.

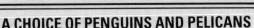

FOR THE BEST IN PAPERBACKS, LOOK FOR THE 🐧

A CHOICE OF PENGUINS AND PELICANS

Lateral Thinking for Management   Edward de Bono

Creativity and lateral thinking can work together for managers in developing new products or ideas; Edward de Bono shows how.

Understanding Organizations   Charles B. Handy

Of practical as well as theoretical interest, this book shows how general concepts can help solve specific organizational problems.

The Art of Japanese Management   Richard Tanner Pascale and Anthony G. Athos   With an Introduction by Sir Peter Parker

Japanese industrial success owes much to Japanese management techniques, which we in the West neglect at our peril. The lessons are set out in this important book.

My Years with General Motors   Alfred P. Sloan   With an Introduction by John Egan

A business classic by the man who took General Motors to the top – and kept them there for decades.

Introducing Management   Ken Elliott and Peter Lawrence (eds.)

An important and comprehensive collection of texts on modern management which draw some provocative conclusions.

English Culture and the Decline of the Industrial Spirit   Martin J. Wiener

A major analysis of why the 'world's first industrial nation has never been comfortable with industrialism'. 'Very persuasive' – Anthony Sampson in the *Observer*

Dinosaur and Co   Tom Lloyd

A lively and optimistic survey of a new breed of businessmen who are breaking away from huge companies to form dynamic enterprises in microelectronics, biotechnology and other developing areas.

The Money Machine: How the City Works   Philip Coggan

How are the big deals made? Which are the institutions that *really* matter? What causes the pound to rise or interest rates to fall? This book provides clear and concise answers to these and many other money-related questions.

Parkinson's Law   C. Northcote Parkinson

'Work expands so as to fill the time available for its completion': that law underlies this 'extraordinarily funny and witty book' (Stephen Potter in the *Sunday Times*) which also makes some painfully serious points for those in business or the Civil Service.

Debt and Danger   Harold Lever and Christopher Huhne

The international debt crisis was brought about by Western bankers in search of quick profit and is now one of our most pressing problems. This book looks at the background and shows what we must do to avoid disaster.

Lloyd's Bank Tax Guide 1986/7

Cut through the complexities! Work the system in *your* favour! Don't pay a penny more than you have to! Written for anyone who has to deal with personal tax, this up-to-date and concise new handbook includes all the important changes in this year's budget.

The Spirit of Enterprise   George Gilder

A lucidly written and excitingly argued defence of capitalism and the role of the entrepreneur within it.

A CHOICE OF PENGUINS AND PELICANS

Metamagical Themas Douglas R. Hofstadter

A new mind-bending bestseller by the author of *Gödel, Escher, Bach*.

The Body Anthony Smith

A completely updated edition of the well-known book by the author of *The Mind*. The clear and comprehensive text deals with everything from sex to the skeleton, sleep to the senses.

Why Big Fierce Animals are Rare Paul Colinvaux

'A vivid picture of how the natural world works' – *Nature*

How to Lie with Statistics Darrell Huff

A classic introduction to the ways statistics can be used to prove *anything*, the book is both informative and 'wildly funny' – *Evening News*

The Penguin Dictionary of Computers Anthony Chandor and others

An invaluable glossary of over 300 words, from 'aberration' to 'zoom' by way of 'crippled lead-frog tests' and 'output bus drivers'.

The Cosmic Code Heinz R. Pagels

Tracing the historical development of quantum physics, the author describes the baffling and seemingly lawless world of leptons, hadrons, gluons and quarks and provides a lucid and exciting guide for the layman to the world of infinitesimal particles.